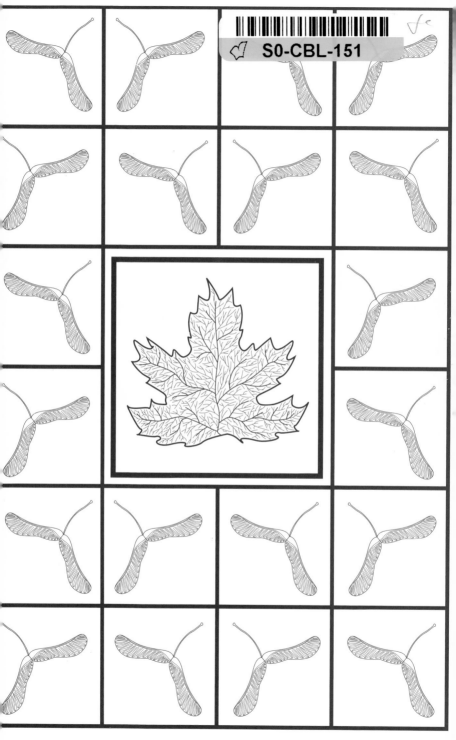

A VETERAN OF 1812

THE LIFE OF

JAMES FITZGIBBON.

BY

MARY AGNES FITZGIBBON.

PROSPERO

CANADIAN COLLECTION

TORONTO
2000

A Veteran of 1812:
The Life of James FitzGibbon

This edition first published by
Prospero Books in 2000
from the 1894 William Briggs edition

Canadian Cataloguing in Publication Data

FitzGibbon, Mary Agnes, 1851-1915
A veteran of 1812: the life of James FitzGibbon

(Prospero Canadian Collection)
Facsim. reprint.
Originally published: Toronto: W. Briggs, 1894.
ISBN 1-55267-137-2

1. FitzGibbon, James, 1780-1863.
2. Canada - History - War of 1812.*
3. Soldiers - Canada - Biography.
4. Canada - Officials and employees - Biography.
I. Title. II. Series.
FC443.F58F57 2000☐☐   971.03'4'092☐☐   C00-931934-4
F1032.F58F57 2000

Prospero Books
90 Ronson Drive, Toronto, Ontario, Canada
M9W 1C1

Printed on acid free paper
Printed and bound in Canada

Yours sincerely
James Fitz Gibbon

Incalculable is the value of a firm purpose, and a determination not to be defeated in one's pursuits. If there be one thing more than another cal=
=culated to ennoble the human soul it is the high faith in its own power. Where this living principle exists, a courageous impulse is generated which never calculates on difficulties. — And even when repulsed and defeated, it turns all things to its own advantage, and makes a virtue of necessity, so that its very failures redound to its present glory and ultimate success.

To the above I add — Cultivate this firmness incessantly until it becomes habitual.

J. F. S

TO

The Militia of Canada

AND TO

The Descendants of the Men of 1812=14,

THIS BOOK

IS RESPECTFULLY DEDICATED

BY THE AUTHOR.

PREFACE.

THE collection of notes for the life story of "A Veteran of 1812" was suggested to me some three years ago by the enquiries of Mr. Edwards, late editor of the *Dominion Illustrated*, who was then anxious to devote a portion of the columns of that paper to the record of men who had been more or less prominent in Canadian history.

I began with a handful of private letters, a brief epitome of his services, and the cherished recollections of my childhood—stories, told us in the nursery, of the soldier and his early life in Canada. After spending some months in Ireland, visiting what my friends called "the cradle of the race," I devoted long hours to patient research in the Archives at Ottawa, and with the kind help of friends who had valued FitzGibbon's correspondence sufficiently to preserve his letters, I have not only been enabled to verify these early traditions, but have accumulated sufficient material to put together a fairly consecutive biography of a man who lived through one of the most interesting periods of our history.

He was one whose personality was sufficiently pronounced, and whose courage, integrity and singleness of purpose were strong enough to leave an impression on his time. "One," to quote from a letter addressed to Lord Stanley, then Secretary for the Colonies (July 2nd, 1842), by Sir Augustus d'Este, "whose happy destiny it was to have the opportunity of rendering important services to his adopted country, which services will cause his name to be remembered with respect and admiration by the loyal inhabitants of Upper Canada as long as devotion to the parent state, manly valor and clear-sighted intelligence are admitted to be entitled to places in the catalogue of estimable qualities."

The fac-simile of FitzGibbon's handwriting given on the page facing the frontispiece is taken from a postscript to one of his many letters to his young nephew Gerald FitzGibbon.

Whether the sentiment it expresses is original or from one or other of his favorite authors, I have no means of ascertaining. It is, however, so indicative of his life and character, so evidently one of which he had proved the value, that it is worth preserving and reproducing as the text of his faith.

My thanks are due to the Right Honorable Gerald Fitz-Gibbon, Lord Justice of the Court of Appeal in Ireland; to D. B. Read, Esq., Q.C., author of the "Lives of the Judges," and other works; to Ernest Cruikshank, Esq., author of "Butler's Rangers," the "Battle of the Beech-woods," etc., etc.; to E. B. Biggar, Esq., whose graphic account of the battle of Stony Creek led to my applying to him; to Charles Lindsey, Esq., William Lyon Mac-kenzie's able biographer, and to J. H. Land, Esq., the secretary of the Wentworth Historical Society, for the kindly assistance they have given me, either personally or through their works, in accomplishing the "labor of love" I have undertaken.

I am indebted also to J. Ross Robertson, Esq., the enthusiastic Past Grand Master of the Freemasons of Ontario, for much of that portion of the book relating to FitzGibbon's life as a Mason; also to the kindness of Murray Jarvis, Esq., of Ottawa, for valuable extracts from unedited letters now in his possession, as well as to many friends and well-wishers for aid and encouragement in prosecuting the researches necessary in order to find what one of them aptly designated, "the hinges of my narrative."

If, owing to inferior workmanship, these "hinges" creak, may I hope that an indulgent public will, in their interest in the man, overlook the faults of his biographer.

For the rest, I may add that I have had the book published in Canada rather than in England, preferring it should first see the light in the city whose loyalty and homes he had guarded with so jealous an arm in life, and to which his last conscious thoughts turned in the hour of death.

M. A. F.G.

Toronto, *May 24th, 1894.*

TABLE OF CONTENTS.

CHAPTER I.

CHAPTER II.

CHAPTER III.

CHAPTER IV.

TABLE OF CONTENTS.

TABLE OF CONTENTS.

CHAPTER VII.

CHAPTER VIII.

CHAPTER IX.

TABLE OF CONTENTS.

A VETERAN OF 1812.

CHAPTER I.

ON the 16th of November, 1780, in the little village on the south bank of the Shannon immortalized by Gerald Griffin's graphic pen and the sad story of the Colleen Bawn,* was born the lad whose after life was destined to be more eventful than generally falls to a soldier's lot.

The square stone house, then forming three sides of a paved court-yard, is now a heap of ruins. Ivy drapes the roofless walls; the barred doorway through which the faithful Danny-man went in and out about his work attending to his master's horses, is gone; a pile of loose stones and weed-choked crevices alone mark the spot, but the little brook still winds its way in tiny leaps and bounds down the steep hillside— still ripples over its stony bed, widening as it reaches the foot of the old grey tower of the ruined castle of the Knights of Glin, and under the high-arched bridge

---

* Colleen Bawn, a dramatic adaptation of Gerald Griffin's novel, "The Collegians."

to the broad river below, as merrily at the end of the
nineteenth as during the latter years of the eighteenth
century.

In some of the family letters extant, James Fitz-
Gibbon's descent is spoken of as being in the direct
line from the White Knight, but I have no positive
knowledge of the family tree beyond the three preceding generations. At the time of his birth, the
property he d by his father was little more than the
small fre hold and the old stone farm-house at Glin.

His father and grandfather, both Geralds, were
good classical scholars, and though James' early
recollections of his childhood are of the village school
where Ned FitzGerald dispensed learning to the lads
of the village and neighboring district, his education
was not by any means entirely dependent upon that
pedagogue. James owed much to his maternal grand-
mother, who must have been a superior woman,
much looked up to, loved and honored by her sons.
His mother was a Wyndham, a name well known in
Jacobite annals in the '45. In after years, when a
member of the Highland Society, James often declared his claim to election should be derived from
his maternal grandfather's connection with the " true
men" of that day, he having only escaped attainder
and loss of property through arriving too late to take
part in the battle of Culloden.

James was the second son. Of his elder brother,
John, we hear little. He died unmarried at the age
of nineteen. The third son, Gerald, afterwards was

the well-known Irish Master in Chancery, and father of the present Lord Justice FitzGibbon. Thomas and Henry, the latter father of the present Judge and Recorder of Belfast, and three sisters. These made up the home-circle at Glin.

Gerald Griffin drew his character of Danny-man in "The Collegians" from the hunch-backed stable-boy at the stone house, and that of Lowry Looby from another of the family retainers, who followed their fortunes when they moved to Prospect Lodge, near Limerick.

"The earliest recollection of my childhood," writes James, "was that of a bird being brought me by one of the laboring men. The eagerness with which I grasped it, my delight in the bright eye and beautiful plumage, made a lasting impression, never forgotten in after life. Again, sometime later—one of those landmarks of childhood's memories, which stand out like mile-stones by the roadside—one of the men took me with him in his cart to a distant farm. The way lay over a neighboring hill. Turning to look behind me as we reached the summit, I was filled with surprise and awe at the vast extent of land and water spread so far below me. It was a mild, beautiful, but cloudy autumn day. The broad Shannon, the distant hills beyond, melting, as it were, into the soft grey sky, roused a hitherto unknown sensation. I felt as if my body and spirit were alike swelling into a vast magnitude. The delight of perception, the sense of the beautiful, the dawning knowledge of the greatness and grandeur of nature, and the dimly conscious, although unrealized, sense of the spirit to feel it, was a revelation to me.

"The first book I ever read, and which forms my only recollection of my first reading, was the 'History of Troy's Destruction.' I yet well remember the difficulty in understanding the first few pages. I read, or rather spelled, it over and over, until I believed I understood it. It was a small volume of not more than forty or fifty pages. I had no other book except my spelling book, and I read it again and again. It contained four prints, of Agamemnon, Achilles, Hector, and Penthesilea, to me objects of great wonder and admiration. I found incidents in it at the second perusal which, in my ignorance, I thought had, by some miracle, been inserted since my first reading. I kept my little book hidden away from others, and read it to pieces unaided by any explanations.

"In those days the only books sold in the village shops, beside the 'Primer Spelling Book' and the 'Child's New Plaything,' were such as 'The Seven Wise Masters of Greece,' 'The Seven Champions of Christendom,' 'The History of the White Knight,' 'Parismus and Parismenus,' 'The Arabian Nights' Entertainment,' and a few others of the like character. I soon gained the reputation of being the greatest reader in the school. I found a new world opening before me, and looked with avidity for a new book. The boys from the neighboring farms and mountains came to me to help them to select one whenever they had the money to purchase it, and I, with childish wisdom, invariably chose one hitherto unknown to me, that I might borrow and read it, too. Thus in time I read every book brought into the school or possessed by my companions, often incurring the schoolmaster's displeasure by absenting myself from school to lie under the hedge and read a tale so absorbing as to render me forgetful of all else.

"At eleven years of age, I was taken from school to help my father and elder brother on the farm and in carrying on a small branch of the linen manufacture. I read the 'History of Telemachus,' by candle light during the long winter evenings, my father pointing out to me the derivations of the words, and rousing an intense interest in the connection between the Latin and English languages and my first attempts at the construction of sentences. I used to save and hoard the candle ends that I might pursue my unaided studies when the household were asleep."

James was as fond of out-door life as other boys. He always retained an affection for the yellow wall-flower, as it reminded him of the bright blossoms he had climbed the old stone tower of Glin to gather when little more than a baby. He describes, with a keen sense of pleasure in the excitement, his delight in his first salmon.

"I was paddling barefoot in the brook which ran down through the meadows and round the foot of the castle, when I spied a fine salmon lurking under a big stone. To climb down round the boulder and make a grab at him was the work of a moment. I did not catch him, but the startled leap he gave cast him at the very edge of the brook; I flung myself bodily upon him and caught him by the gills. After a hard fight I dragged him up on the bank, gaffed him with a rusty old knife, and carried him home in triumph. I have no recollection of his weight, but remember his length was more than I could lift from the ground—although I was a tall boy for eight years —but trailed his shining body along the grass."

Of his early religious impressions the first mention among his papers shows, also, the dawning reasoning faculties and clear judgment which were afterwards his strongest characteristics.

"One day, while working in the field, my attention was drawn to the conversation between the hired laborers on the subject of the Protestants and Englishmen and their religion.

"I already knew that Protestants and Englishmen were disliked, nay, hated, as the Irish had but one word in their language to express either. I knew no Protestants (all in the village were Roman Catholics), and I knew that, could they do so with impunity, few among these men would hesitate to take the life of a Protestant.

"'Why do you hate the Protestants?' I asked.

"'Because they are heretics and go to hell.'

"To this reply I made no answer, but thought, 'Surely you ought rather to pity them—blame them

—for being such fools as to live in this world for seventy-five years as Protestants only to be sent to hell for seventy-five million.'

"My mind dwelt long on what I thought was the unaccountable insensibility of these Protestants. In those days, about the year 1790, the judges going to the circuit were escorted and guarded by a troop of mounted men bearing halberds and pikes. A trumpeter rode in advance, and upon approaching a village sounded his trumpet.

"This procession was to us boys a splendid spectacle, and looked for every half year with lively anticipation. When I learned that these judges were Protestants, my surprise was great. That men so wise as they must be could so disregard their future salvation for any present wealth or power seemed incredible, and the information that the king, who in my childish faith, must of necessity be the wisest man living, was also a Protestant, filled me with amazement. It was about this period that I read for the first time the parable of the good Samaritan, and, though ignorant that the Jews hated the Samaritans, the conviction was impressed upon me that the Catholics were wrong, and by hating their neighbors were not following the teaching of our Saviour. This was the first doubt raised in my mind of the infallibility of my teachers."

The boy's anxiety for new books had by chance put him in brief possession of a New Testament. He purchased it from a travelling pedlar, who probably was very glad to find a customer for such unsalable stock in that part of the world.

James crept under the hedge with his treasure, and was soon absorbed in the wonderful story.

Here he was discovered by the parish priest, who, spying the boy and curious to know what study he was so deeply immersed in, accosted him. Unfortunately I cannot find any detailed account of the discussion between them over the right of the parishioner as well as the priest to the privilege of reading the Bible for themselves, but I have heard those who had the story from FitzGibbon say, that " he got the best of the priest in the argument, but the priest got the better of the boy in size, for the Testament was forcibly confiscated, but what he had read was indelibly fixed in his memory."

Some years afterwards, about 1795 or 1796, the people of Ireland were called to arms and formed into yeomanry corps to defend the country against the threatened invasion of France.

" My father enrolled his own, his eldest son's and my name, although I was only fifteen. With the military bias already given to my mind by my early reading, this excited me very much. On entering the corps each had to take the oath of allegiance, part of which contained the following words: 'And I do further swear that I do not believe that any Pope, Priest or Bishop has power to forgive sins.'

" My father, my brother and I took the oath without hesitation, as did many others, but many refused.

"On the following Sunday the priest proclaimed from the altar that all might take the oath, as it was only upon condition of confession and repentance that the priest could absolve the sinner.

"Some time after the yeomanry corps were raised, the French fleet, with a large land force on board intended for the invasion of Ireland, anchored in Bantry Bay. Troops were sent, for the first time in the century, into that remote part of Ireland, and the first regiment that appeared in our village was the Devon and Cornwall Fencibles. We had thus an opportunity of encountering the 'hated Englishmen'—hated to the extent of a proverb, of which the literal translation is, 'An Englishman is not more hateful to me than thou art.'

"A sergeant and two privates presented their billet at my father's door and were admitted, not only rooms but meals also being provided for them. Their quiet behavior, their gratitude for my father's kindness and hospitality, astonished me. Could these be the dreaded Englishmen? My former fears were changed into admiration.

"The sergeant often spent an hour or two in the evening drilling us boys in the old stone-paved kitchen, and my military ambition and desire to be one day a soldier was fanned into a flame.

"A storm driving the French fleet to sea again, it was feared their coming to Bantry Bay was but a feint to draw off our troops from the north, where they meant to land without opposition.

"In the uncertainty the troops were marched and counter-marched from one place to another, and the Fencibles often again passed through or were quartered in our village. Our former hatred became friendship and liking; no one of our own militia regiments were greater favorites with us than these English soldiers.

"About this time the corporal who drilled the yeomanry corps to which I belonged, was ordered to join his regiment, and we were without a teacher. Our captain, the Knight of Glin, who had hitherto been in England, returned soon after the corporal's departure. The first time he inspected us in the field, he attempted to put us through our exercises. He gave orders of which we knew nothing. Not having learned the new system ordered for the instruction of the army in 1792, he was following the one acquired with the volunteers at the close of the American war. In striving to obey him, we fell into confusion and disorder. He flew into a violent passion and swore roundly at us, declaring, with an oath, that if he had the 'scoundrel' who had drilled us within reach, he would 'cleave his flesh from his bones with his sabre.'

"A good landlord, an excellent and just magistrate, to whose active exertions we were indebted for the peace of the surrounding country during the rebellion of 1798, the knight was yet a hot-tempered man, whose rage sometimes found expression in hard blows as well as in words. His language was so offensive on this occasion that, unable to endure it longer, I stepped out from the ranks and said: 'The men are not to blame, sir. You are giving us words of command we have never heard. . The man who drilled us was a good teacher, and were he here, he could make us appear to greater advantage.'

"For a moment I thought my bold words would bring the knight's wrath upon my head, but, reflecting that my father was a freeholder and no man's tenant, though inwardly quaking I stood my ground.

"After a pause, probably of astonishment at my daring, he asked if there was anyone there who could put the men through their exercises. Upon my replying that I did not know, he asked me to show him what they could do. I did the best I could, and the men did well. He then desired me to go on drilling them until he could procure another instructor from the army. A sergeant and twenty men were soon after added to the corps, and, on returning from my work some days later, I found a sergeant's pike, sword and sash sent to me with an order appointing me sergeant. Thus was I, at the age of seventeen, promoted over my father and elder brother. What wonder that my boyish enthusiasm was greatly increased by such unexpected honor."

In 1798, the first lieutenant of the corps obtained a company in the Tarbert Fencibles, then being raised by Sir Edward Leslie, and James was easily persuaded to join him; an additional inducement being offered in the promised appointment of pay-sergeant to the company.

The Tarbert Fencibles were soon afterwards sent to England to do garrison duty in the room of the regulars required in Holland.

Before leaving home reiterated promises were extorted, both from the boy and his captain, that he should not, on any account, be induced or permitted to enlist for active service abroad. His mother's fears, prompted by the boy's well-known bias, took this precaution to ensure his return before she would consent to his departure. Much, however, as the lad loved soldiering, there was a stronger deterrent to his taking the Queen's shilling than even his mother's fears or his captain's promise to bring him back in safety to his native village.

Corporal punishment was at that time inflicted in the army for the most trifling offences, and the reports of the sufferings of the men under it had so excited his indignation that FitzGibbon believed no persuasions could ever induce him to put himself voluntarily in a position to run the risk of incurring such degradation.

CHAPTER II.

ON the 9th of June, 1799, Major-General White-
lock arrived at Poole, in Dorsetshire, where
the Tarbert Fencibles were then quartered,
authorized to recruit non-commissioned officers and
men from its ranks for active service in the army
awaiting embarkation for the invasion of Holland.

Before leaving his quarters, FitzGibbon received a
hasty visit from Captain Creagh. He came to remind
him once more of the many promises he had made to
bring him back to Ireland, and added, "If you are
firm in your refusal to volunteer for active service,
I'll take you with me to Ireland, where I hear I'm to
be sent shortly on recruiting duty."

FitzGibbon assured him he had no intention or
desire to volunteer, so he might make his mind easy
on that score.

An hour afterwards the sergeants were paraded in
the barrack-yard to be addressed by the general.
He spoke at considerable length, saying, among other
things, that "as the enemy would not come to fight
us, it was determined by the Government that we
should go and fight them;" that he "was quite confident we would rather go and fight for our king and
country than remain at home walking the streets of
Poole with powdered heads;" and, in short, that he

"expected to see us in a few months' time up to our knees in French blood."

Little as he knew of the world, this speech sounded an extravagant one to FitzGibbon. His position placed him directly opposite to where the general stood. His evident interest attracted that officer's attention, and he repeatedly addressed him directly, asking if he understood what he said

The sergeants were then dismissed to join their companies.

After parade the regiment was formed into a hollow square, when the general addressed the men, much in the same strain as he had used with the sergeants, desiring those who wished to volunteer to step out of their ranks into the centre; and going from company to company he urged the men individually to do so. Upon reaching FitzGibbon's, he expressed surprise at seeing him still in the ranks.

" I thought you would be one of the first to volunteer."

" I am determined not to volunteer, sir," replied the soldier.

" And why should a young man of your appearance not seize so glorious an opportunity of pushing his fortunes in the service of his king and country ?"

" Because, sir, I am not willing to spend all my life as a private soldier, nor as a non-commissioned officer, and from the little I have seen of the army, I have no hope of obtaining a commission without money or friends."

"Can you write?" asked the general.

"Certainly he can, very well," answered Captain Creagh for him, and added some kindly expressions commending the lad's diligence and knowledge of his drill.

"Why, then," said the general, "I will be the first to recommend you."

"You will not, sir," replied the boy, with youthful conviction as well as priggishness, "venture to recommend me until you know if I be qualified to hold a commission, which I am now convinced I am not."

"All this," replied the general, "only tends to convince me that you are, or very soon will be."

But FitzGibbon was still determined. The general turned and went along the ranks, urging the men. At length, in answer to his representations of the many advantages to be derived from active service, a number replied that if FitzGibbon would volunteer they would.

"What was I to do?" FitzGibbon often asked when telling the story in after years. "I must either forget my promises, my fears, silence my doubts, or brand myself forever a coward, not only in the eyes of my comrades but in my own."

He assented, and carried forty men with him into the ranks of the English army.

The step was taken and could not be retraced, but with a mentally registered vow that if it should ever be his fate to incur a sentence to the infliction of the

lash, justly or unjustly, he would take his own life
rather than suffer such degradation.

FitzGibbon joined the army under Sir Ralph Abercrombie, then encamped on Bareham Downs, and on
August 6th, 1799, he was draughted into the 49th,
with the rank of sergeant. On the following morning
they were marched to the coast, and embarked at the
neighboring seaport.

The fleet with the transports put to sea on the
12th. Bad weather prevented the vessels approaching the coast of Holland until the 26th, when they
anchored near the Helder. The troops were landed
on the 27th, but here we may quote FitzGibbon's
own words :

" The flat boats in which we were sent from the
transports moved off for the shore in the grey light
of early day. Our mortar ships had been throwing
bombs to the shore for a short time before. The
distance, however, was so considerable that I did not
think they could do much execution. My early
studies in Greek and Roman history had given me
an exaggerated idea of heroism, bravery and battle,
and I fully expected to find the French battalions
drawn up in battle array upon the beach, ready to
greet us with a volley the moment we were within
range, and, as our boats touched the shore, to oppose
our landing in a fierce hand-to-hand conflict.

"As we approached, and the light increased, I could
see five dark lines to our right, moving down upon
us, as I expected, to oppose our landing, but upon

nearer approach I could distinguish their scarlet uniforms. They were in fact the five British regiments landed some distance to our right, and which as yet had met with no resistance. Were the French so deficient in courage, I wondered, as not to make the most of such evident advantages?

"The low line of sand-hills opposite our landing place was lined with troops. A volley was fired upon us as we jumped ashore. The regiments already landed charged up the hill and drove the enemy back at the point of the bayonet, while we landed without further molestation.

"After fifty years of life, and having had some experience of warfare, I am convinced my boyish opinion was the correct one. Had the enemy realized my expectation and opposed our landing in earnest, the boats must have been destroyed or captured. To know the value or force of fear upon the human mind is one of the most important qualifications for a commander to possess, second only to the power of banishing fear from his own ranks and driving it before him into the ranks of the enemy. The officer who has not this power will never be distinguished from the herd of ordinary men, and should never be entrusted with a separate command.

"The brigade to which I belonged, Sir John Moore's, was marched to the left, towards the Helder, where we found no enemy. All the fighting was on our right, where our men drove the enemy back into the country."

There is a gap here in FitzGibbon's narrative from August 27th to October 2nd. During that period the Duke of York had joined the army and assumed the command.

"Long before day on the morning of the 2nd of October, the Russian and British forces advanced to attack the French posted in the sand-hills on the coast near Egmont-op-Zee. The column to which the 49th belonged advanced along the beach, having the sand-hills to the right, the rolling sea in close proximity on our left. About eight o'clock the advance commenced skirmishing, and the column was halted. Several of the officers ran up a few paces on the sides of the hills to snatch a view of our troops on the level beach. I followed their example. Eighteen thousand men were on the plain before me. The long lines of cavalry and artillery deploying to their several positions, the life and stir of coming battle surprised and filled me with delight. I had dreamed of deeds of bravery, of fierce single combats, but now that the battle was imminent, I was surprised to find that I was not nearly so brave as I had imagined myself.

"The first man I saw killed was a fine handsome young ensign, a lieutenant of grenadiers, who had volunteered from the South Middlesex militia to the line, still wearing the uniform of his late regiment. He carried one of the regimental colors, and was one of the finest-looking men I had ever seen. I stood for a moment to look upon him as he fell, and thought sadly of the young wife he had left to mourn his untimely end. It was but a moment. I had to run on to keep pace with my company and find myself in the midst of a great battle. I was a supernumerary sergeant; I had no definite duties or position, nothing to do but look about me. My preconceived ideas of the discipline of the regular army were soon dissipated. The nature of the ground, the confusion and apparent hastiness of the officers served to cause disorder, and I thought, 'Surely the French must be better soldiers than we are.'"

FitzGibbon had evidently mentioned Colonel Brock in the missing leaf of his reminiscences, as the following paragraph indicates:

"After the deployment of the 49th on the sandhills, I saw no more of Lieut.-Colonel Brock, being separated from him with that part of the regiment detached under Lieut.-Colonel Sheaffe. Soon after we commenced firing upon the enemy, and at intervals rushing from one line of sand-hills to another —behind which the soldiers were made to shelter themselves and fire over their summits—I saw, at some distance to my right, Savery Brock, the paymaster, passing from the top of one sand-hill to another, directing and encouraging the men. He alone kept continually on the tops of the hills during the firing, and at every advance from one range to another he led the men, and again was seen above the others. Not doubting but that great numbers of the French soldiers would be continually firing at him—a

large man so exposed—I watched from moment to
moment to see him fall, but for about two hours
while in my view he remained untouched.

"After witnessing Savery Brock's conduct, I determined to be the first to advance every time at the
head of those around me, and I soon saw that of
those who were most prompt to follow me, fewer fell
by the enemy's fire than I witnessed falling of those
more in our rear.

"Still we advanced, and the French retreated from
one range of sand-hills to the next. About five
o'clock I was well on in advance, when, on the opposite side of a valley facing us, we saw dragoons in
green advancing toward us. Believing them to be
Russians who were moving against the enemy on the
other side of the hills, a cry was raised to 'cease
firing.' The moment the cry was obeyed, a body of
French infantry issued from a copse in the valley
and charged up the hill toward us. We opened fire
instantly, but instead of retreating they advanced,
their officers waving their hats and swords as if
desircus of holding a parley with us. Upon this
someone cried they were Dutch troops who wished
to join us as three battalions had done a few days
before. Again we ceased firing. Our officers advanced to meet theirs. While we waited I formed
the men, about a hundred in all. Presently one of
my men, without orders, presented his musket. I
tossed it up with my pike, and declared I 'would
shoot any man who dared to fire without orders;'

then, turning to learn the cause of the man's action,
I saw five of the enemy approaching. Believing they
meant to surrender, I went to meet them; I disarmed
two, throwing their muskets on the ground, but in a
moment my pike was wrenched from my hold and I
was seized by the collar. Struggling to free myself,
I found two bayonets at my back. My men fired.
The Frenchman at my right fell, but in an instant I
was dragged over the hill. There they halted and
searched me. One drew my sword and threw it far
from me with an oath. Another took my sash and
wound it around his own waist. Two contended for
my great coat and nearly dislocated my shoulders in
their struggle for it. Then my coat and waistcoat
were pulled off in order that they might get at my
shirts, a flannel and a linen one, for I never could
endure the flannel next my skin. They had the
flannel one when a dragoon galloped up, snatched
my waistcoat from the infantry and drove them off.
Possessing himself of what money was left in the
pocket, he flung it back to me and bade me dress
myself. He then gave me in charge of another dragoon, who seized my left wrist in his right hand and
trotted down the hill to where the dragoons were
drawn up.

"All this could not have occupied more than three
or four minutes. While my captor trotted down the
slope, we were met by another dragoon who, as he
passed me, brought up the hilt of his sword to his
ear and gave point at me. Fortunately I had learned

the sword exercise and was able to parry his thrust. He rode on as if indifferent whether he hit me or not. The man who held me swore roundly at him, and instead of ascending the hill turned sharply to the left, and followed the valley until we were quite in the rear of the French lines. He then released me from his hold.

"If I had had extravagant ideas of the glories to be won in battle, I had also of the fate of prisoners of war. I had recently read the memoirs of Baron Trenck, and expected nothing less than confinement in a dungeon with sixty pounds of iron about my neck and limbs.

"The approach of another prisoner, an old sergeant of the 49th, who had seen service in the West Indies, was a relief to my mind. We soon after entered a wood, where the dragoon ordered us to be searched. Alas, my fine linen shirt pleased him, and I was ordered to give it up. When I hesitated my fellow-prisoner advised me to obey, adding, "A soldier of the 92nd, who was taken with me, refused to give up his canteen and a murderous Frenchman shot him through the back."

"The dragoon gave me a shirt from his saddle-bag in exchange. It was coarse as a barrack sheet and nearly worn out. It was, however, clean from the wash, and had ruffles to the wristbands as well as the usual frill to the front. I remembered a song my grandfather used to sing for me of 'French ruffles and rags.' Now was I possessed of some to my no small discomfort and mortification.

"While the exchange of garments was being made, Lieutenant Philpott and some grenadiers of the 35th were brought in. He stopped and asked me why they stripped me. Before I could reply, a French soldier struck him a blow from behind with the butt of his musket that made him stagger forward several paces before he could recover himself.

"We were marched into Alkmaar and put into a church, where I slept on the flags from six till eight o'clock, when we were awakened, hurried out into the street and marched off under an escort.

"I supposed we were to be lodged in some prison in the town, but to my surprise we soon left it behind us. Exhausted from fatigue, I dreaded a long night march. The dragoons of the escort frequently pushed their horses upon us. One of them plunged in among us, his horse dashing the man walking beside me to the ground, and striking me a violent blow in the side with his foot. To escape this danger I pushed on to the front and strained every nerve to keep in the advance. We were marched without halting to Beverwick, a distance of eighteen miles.

"This was the most distressing night of my life. I had already suffered so much from fatigue during our marches and countermarches since our landing at the Helder, as to make my life a burden to me. Fifteen days later we reached Valenciennes, five officers and one hundred and seven men." (See Appendix I.)

During this and the few weeks that intervened before the exchange of prisoners was effected, Fitz-Gibbon was not idle. He seized every opportunity within his reach of conversing with his French captors and learning as much of their language as possible.

Among some odd scraps of letters and manuscripts, I find the following anecdote:

" The exchanged prisoners of war were landed at Ramsgate from Flushing, in January, 1800. On the march to Beccles and Bungaye, where the 49th were then stationed, I was sent forward to have the billets ready for delivery to the men at the end of each day's march. On entering the inn at Witham, near Colchester, a gentleman standing at the door asked me if I did not belong to the 49th ? Upon my replying that I did he said:

" ' Why then are you in such a ragged and stained dress ?'

" ' I am returning from French prison, sir,' I replied.

" ' Come in, come in here,' he said, and immediately ordered the waiter to bring breakfast and a glass of brandy for me. He was surprised when I declined the latter, as I never drank it.

" ' What, a soldier and not drink brandy? Well, well, I am very glad of it; and now, where were you taken prisoner ?'

" ' At Egmont-op-Zee,' I replied. Then to my surprise he asked a number of questions as to the behaviour of certain of the officers in that battle.

" Ignorant of who my questioner might be, I could only reply faithfully as to what I had seen and knew, and unconsciously was able to remove the odium of cowardice from at least one to whom it had been imputed. I learned later that my interrogator was the surgeon of the 49th. He shook hands with me, and bade me take care of myself and I would rise to be a general officer. I was not very sanguine of that, but they were kindly words to cheer on the hopes and ambition of a lad who loved his profession."

In the summer of 1800 the regiment was sent to Jersey. During the senior Lieut.-Colonel's absence on leave, the second assumed the command. Of this officer's ability, FitzGibbon speaks highly.

" He was the best teacher I ever knew, but he was also a martinet and a great scold. His offensive language often marred his best efforts. The latitude taken at drill in those days was very great and very injurious to the service. The late Duke of York saw this, and by appropriate regulations greatly abated the use of offensive language.

"To such a state of feeling was the regiment worked up by this man's scolding, that upon the return of the senior officer,* his first appearance on the parade was greeted by three hearty cheers from the men. This outbreak of welcome was promptly rebuked by the returned colonel and the men confined to barracks for a week."

FitzGibbon does not name either of these officers,

---

* Colonel (afterwards Sir Isaac) Brock.

adding only: "I might record the future career of the two men, but will only say that they were not on the same level. The history of the one officer who won the affection and respect of his men by kind though firm discipline bears the higher military reputation."

While the regiment was in Jersey, several recruiting parties were sent from it to England. With one of these FitzGibbon was ordered to Winchester. The party consisted of a captain, two sergeants, a corporal and drummer. The captain appointed, being on leave, was to join the party later from London.

Before embarking, and without FitzGibbon's knowledge, his fellow-sergeant drew the month's pay for the corporal and drummer, went out of barracks, and either gambled or, as he said, lost it, by having his pocket picked. For this he was tried and sentenced to be put under stoppages as a private until the amount was refunded. Notwithstanding, before going on board the Rowcliffe sloop for Portsmouth, the man again drew the month's pay, and soon after their arrival in Winchester, lost or spent the money. The captain had not yet joined them, and upon pay-day FitzGibbon's duty would be to report the case to the regimental headquarters. This would inevitably result in the reduction of the sergeant to the ranks, or possibly the infliction and degradation of the lash. The man was of respectable parentage, in education equal if not superior to FitzGibbon, and his pleasing, gentlemanly manner had won his fellow-soldiers' affection. Having full confidence in his truthfulness, FitzGibbon out of his own month's pay, as yet untouched, gave the corporal and drummer their week's pay. Another week passed without the captain having joined the party, and again he paid the men. This was repeated until he had not a penny remaining.

"Twenty-four hours had elapsed since I had tasted food. We were walking down the high street of Winchester, poor —— as hungry and miserable as myself, neither of us knowing what to do nor where to turn for help. To sell any part of our regimentals was impossible. It was a military offence, and its commission would inevitably have brought the disgrace I dreaded. Walking slowly and in silence, weary with thinking and the vain effort to puzzle a way out of the difficulty, I had almost given way to despair, when, the light of a street lamp falling across my path, my eye caught the gleam of a coin lying on the wet pavement at my feet. I picked it up, and carrying it to a neighboring shop-window, saw it was a half-guinea. I rang it on the sill to be sure my eyes had not deceived me. I did not stay to enquire who had dropped it. The street had many passersby; its owner might have passed long since, but the thought that it had ever been owned by anyone else never crossed my mind. I was hungry through no fault of my own, and this half-guinea was to me a direct gift from Providence, and as such I used it and was grateful."

CHAPTER III.

IN February, 1801, the 49th was ordered from Jersey to Horsham in Sussex, the recruiting parties receiving instructions to join it on the march from Portsmouth.

"Arrived at Horsham barracks, it was generally understood we were to be stationed there some months and much of the unpacking was done. An express, however, arrived the following morning from the Horse Guards, ordering our immediate return to Portsmouth. At Chichester an order met us to be on the south sea-beach at nine o'clock the following morning.

"During the two days' march conjectures were rife as to our ultimate destination. Some said we were intended for Ireland to quell a rebellion there; others for Manchester to put down a riot there, but it was soon ascertained that we were to be embarked at Spithead on board a man-of-war to serve as marines in the Baltic.

"The grenadier company to which I belonged, was taken on board the *St. George*, a three-decker of ninety-four guns, bearing the flag of Lord Nelson, and pleased and gratified was I at finding myself on the same ship with him. The ships at Spithead intended for the Baltic sailed to Yarmouth, and there,

greatly to my disappointment, we were transferred to
the *Monarch*, 74.

"The fleet sailed on the 12th of March, and anchored
below Elsinore on the 29th.

" On the 30th, the ships passed in single line before
the Castle, which opened a heavy fire upon them.
The *Monarch* led the van, and in passing fired 230
shot. Having passed beyond range the reports were
collected, and to everyone's surprise not a shot had
touched the ship, all having fallen short. Lord Nelson's ship followed, and he ordered that not a shot
should be fired from his guns, the others following
his example. Yet, a few days after the battle of the
2nd of April, a Danish account of the operations
stated that several men were killed and wounded and
some damage done to the walls by the shot from the
Monarch.

" This appeared to me unaccountable—that the constant fire from two or three hundred guns did no
damage to our fleet, while that from one ship should
in so short a time affect the castle walls and its
defenders.

" In 1806, at Quebec, when sent on board a mer-
chant ship to superintend the landing of some army
clothing, I entered into conversation with one of the
passengers, a Dane, who had served on board a
Danish vessel on April 2nd, 1801. He told me that
Governor Stricker, who was in command at the time
in the Castle, was brought before a court-martial of
enquiry, when he suggested that the powder he had

must have been damaged, it having been there during the long peace of seventy or eighty years, then just concluded, and asked leave to try the effect of newly purchased powder. Permission being granted, the shot told with considerable effect upon the Swedish shores at the opposite side of the Strait.

"On the 1st of April the fleet was divided into two divisions, one to anchor at each side of the shoal in front of the city of Copenhagen, that division in whose favor the wind was on the following morning to go in and fight the battle. The wind favored Lord Nelson's division, so it fell to his lot to achieve the victory. The *Monarch* was in Nelson's division, and had 53 men killed and 155 wounded—the greatest number ever killed or wounded on board any one British vessel.

"The battle lasted four hours and ten minutes. The shattered condition of the *Monarch* necessitating her being sent home; the survivors of the marines were transferred to the *Elephant*. In a few days the damaged ships were refitted and the fleet, with the exception of the *St. George* sailed up to Kiorge Bay.

"Sir Hyde Parker's ship, the *London* had her lower deck guns taken out in order to lighten her sufficiently to enable her to pass through the shallow entrance to the Baltic. There not being sufficient transports to take the guns of the *St. George* at the same time, she had to remain before Copenhagen until their return from the *London*.

"A hint, however, being given to Nelson that Sir

Hyde Parker intended to sail at once and attack the Swedes at Carlscrona, without waiting for him, lest he might again take the lion's share of the laurels to be won in a second engagement, he ordered his barge and started for Kiorge Bay.

"Coming on the poop the following morning at five o'clock," writes FitzGibbon, "I saw the admiral's flag flying at the fore, and asking the signal midshipman what it meant, was told that Lord Nelson had come on board at two o'clock, and was then asleep on the sofa in the cabin, Captain Foley not yet knowing he was there. Immediately I was all ears and eyes, the cabin being directly under the poop. Presently I heard Captain Foley's voice at the door, rebuking the servant for not letting him know that Lord Nelson had come on board, and in a sharp tone from within, I heard a thin, rather feeble voice call out, 'Foley, Foley, let the man alone; he obeyed my orders.'

"For many weeks while he was on board, I had an opportunity of seeing Nelson every day. He appeared the most mild and gentle being, and it was delightful to me to hear the way the sailors spoke of him. True, I was only at sea during the summer, but my greatest wish then was that I had been a sailor rather than a soldier."

While in the Baltic an incident occurred which might have interfered with FitzGibbon's career as a soldier.

The detachment of the 49th on the *Elephant* was commanded by Lieut.-Colonel Hutchinson, an impatient, hot-tempered man. One morning, very early, he sent for FitzGibbon to come on deck. While the ships were at anchor, both watches were in their hammocks at night. The hammocks being hung, all occupied, press closely together, and a man turning out singly must go down on his knees and there, with difficulty, put on his clothes. When FitzGibbon reached the deck, he found the colonel in a towering passion.

"How dare you not come quickly, sir, when I sent for you? You are an example of laziness to the men, and if the like of this occurs again, I will bring you to a court-martial and reduce you to the ranks."

Then giving him the order for which he had been called on deck, the colonel left the ship with Captain Foley to spend the day in another vessel.

Mortified by the publicity of the rebuke, administered as it was in the presence of not only the soldiers and sailors on deck, but of two of the midshipmen who had treated him with the kindly courtesy and tact of one gentleman to another, a consideration he was not entitled to by his rank as sergeant; hurt and indignant at its injustice, and naturally impulsive, FitzGibbon determined not to wait for his colonel to carry the threat into effect, but at once, voluntarily, to retire to the ranks.

Upon Colonel Hutchinson's return to the quarter-deck that evening, FitzGibbon met him, saluted, and said: "As I cannot discharge the duties of a sergeant, sir, without incurring such censure as I received this morning, I desire to retire into the ranks as a private."

The Colonel's face flushed with indignant surprise as he replied: "Very well, sir; from this moment you are no longer a sergeant. Go, sir, to your duty as a private, and remember I don't forget you. Take that with you."

A short turn on the deck brought him again in contact with the irrepressible soldier as he went below. Shaking his fist at him, he repeated his last words with greater vehemence, "*Remember, I don't forget you. Take that with you.*"

On the following morning the colonel again sent for FitzGibbon and asked if he remembered what had occurred the previous evening, and if he was still in the same mind?

FitzGibbon replied that nothing had since occurred to alter the opinion he had then expressed.

"Very well, then, join your company as a private." He then paraded the company on deck and informed the men that FitzGibbon, having found himself unequal to the performance of the duties of a sergeant, had resigned and retired into the ranks, closing his speech by advising those who might thereafter be promoted not to follow "the foolish example set them by FitzGibbon."

For three months FitzGibbon remained in the ranks. He was happy because answerable for no one's conduct but his own. Strict in enforcing obedience to duty when a sergeant, he was yet much beloved by his men, as many anecdotes told of him both then and in later years go to prove. He never allowed that any man could be wholly bad, but that there must be good in him somewhere, if one could but touch the right chord to reach it. Believing this, he looked for it, and though the result was often long delayed, the good was generally found.

In the battle of Copenhagen, where the loss was so severe, one of the most reprobate and unruly of the men in the regiment was terribly wounded in the lower part of the back. When carried into the cockpit, the surgeon bade FitzGibbon take him away —there was no use in dressing such a wound, it would only cause great pain. "Take him away," he said, "and tell him he will be in a better condition to be seen to to-morrow. Poor fellow, he will probably be dead by the morning."

The man lived for three days, and FitzGibbon's comforting prayers and trustful confidence in the mercy of God for the poor sinner soothed his pain, robbed death of its terrors, and won for himself a deeper affection in the hearts of his men.

Upon his reduction to the ranks, this love bore fruit. The companies were divided into messes of six men each, the duty of one of the six, each day, being to perform all the menial offices required, such as washing the dishes, etc. From all these the sergeants were exempt. On the first day upon which this duty fell to FitzGibbon, and he began to gather up the dishes, one of the men stopped him.

"I'll do that, sir."

"No," replied FitzGibbon, "it is my duty, and I did not become a soldier without making up my mind to do all the duties properly belonging to me, and, though greatly obliged to you, I am determined to do this."

"Then, begorra, sir, you'll fight me first."

It is needless to say that FitzGibbon declined such a combat, but during the time he remained in the ranks the menial duties that fell to his share were always done for him *nolens volens.*

The fleet had no more fighting. The death of the Emperor Paul altered the course of events, and after cruising about in the Baltic, putting occasionally into harbor at Dantzig and other ports, the fleet was ordered home in August.

The 49th was landed at different ports, the grenadier company being disembarked from the *Elephant,* at Portsmouth and marched to join the headquarters at Colchester. On approaching the town, Colonel Brock came out to meet them, and drawing his sword marched at their head into barracks.

At parade the following morning, Colonel Brock addressed the men. He thanked them for not only doing credit to the regiment and its officers by their bravery during battle, but for their general good conduct while separated on board the different vessels, the captains of which had written to him in the most favorable terms of the men while under their command.

" He (Colonel Brock) created by his judicious praise, his never-failing interest in his men, both individually as soldiers and collectively as a regiment, a noble spirit which bore fruit in many a well-won laurel in Canada, in China and the Crimea."

After the regiment was thrown back into column, FitzGibbon noticed his captain in conversation with Colonel Brock, and on the men being dismissed he received an order to present himself to the colonel. The following conversation is too characteristic of the two men to be omitted :

" Pray, young man," asked the colonel sternly, " Why did you resign your office as sergeant when on board the *Elephant?* "

" Because, sir, Colonel Hutchinson censured me publicly and in harsh language, when in reality I was not to blame."

" Now, was it not to insult him you did so ?"

" Positively, sir, such a thought did not occur to me. I felt mortified to be so publicly rebuked, and, as it happened, in the presence of two of the ship's officers who had from time to time treated me with more than the attention due from men in their position to one in mine. Then, during the whole of the day after I was so censured, and before Colonel Hutchinson returned to the ship, I felt that under such an angry officer I must be always liable to similar treatment, and this consideration, more than any other, determined me to resign."

" Have you any objection to tell Colonel Hutchinson so now ?"

"I have no objection, sir, to tell the truth at any time."

"Then I wish you to go at once to his quarters and tell him so. He thinks your object was to insult him by way of revenge."

FitzGibbon obeyed. Colonel Hutchinson accepted the explanation and went himself to request Colonel Brock to reinstate the self-reduced private to his rank as sergeant.

When sent for again, Colonel Brock told FitzGibbon that it was in consequence of "Colonel Hutchinson's request that he was reinstated, and that there having been no returns from the regiment sent in during their service in the Baltic, he had never been officially reduced, and would receive his pay as sergeant as though nothing had happened." Before leaving the colonel's room the young soldier had something to say. After thanking the colonel for his kindness he asked permission to make an observation without offence. The colonel nodded, "Go on."

"It is this, sir. I think that much harm is done to the discipline of the regiment by censuring the non-commissioned officers in the presence of the men. It lowers them in the estimation of the privates, and weakens their authority, besides the ill-feeling it creates towards the officer, which a private rebuke would most probably not create at all, but would rather leave the non-commissioned officer grateful for being spared in public."

CHAPTER IV.

IN the autumn of 1801, the regiment was moved from Colchester to Chelmsford, and passed the winter in peace and comfort.

FitzGibbon was pay-sergeant of the grenadier company. He was not a good accountant, and when making out his pay sheet for February, found himself deficient to the amount of nearly £2. He was horror-stricken at this discovery, knowing he had not expended it upon himself, yet dreading the consequences. A recent occurrence in the regiment, of a squad sergeant being tried and reduced to the ranks for the deficiency of one shilling, roused his fears lest the greater deficit should be punished with the lash, and " he would take his own life rather than endure the degradation of stripping in the front of the regiment to be flogged."

Under the pressure of this fear, FitzGibbon did what in after years he said was "no doubt due to my early reading of such romances as the 'History of the White Knight,' of 'Parismus and Parismenus,' 'The Seven Champions of Christendom,' etc., I decided upon applying to the Commander-in-Chief for protection.

" I asked for and obtained a pass for three days to go to London on pretended business. I walked up to town, and found my way to the Anchor and Vines tavern, close to the Horse Guards, and though tired, at once wrote a letter to the Duke of York, stating the case to him and praying of him to enable me to replace the money so that my colonel might not know of the deficiency; for, as I looked upon him as the father of the regiment, I dreaded the forfeiture of his good opinion more than any other consequence which might follow.

" On the following morning, I gave my letter in at the door to the orderly on duty. With an anxiety I cannot describe, I walked before that door till night fell, then in despair returned to my tavern. In the course of my romantic reading, I had learned how many were the evil influences surrounding courts and princes, and supposed my letter had been withheld— that probably such letters from people in humble circumstances were never presented to great men. I therefore wrote another letter, adverting to the one delivered at the office door, and again stating my case as before.

" The second morning I took my stand at the door before the hour of opening, and asked the sentry to point out the Duke of York to me.

" The Duke soon approached. He was in plain clothes and walking. I stepped up to him, saluted him, and held out the letter. He took it, looked at me from head to foot, and passed in without speaking.

" After the lapse of a few, to me most anxious, minutes, I was called, shown into a waiting-room upstairs and told that Colonel Brownrigg would see me. He came in presently with my two letters in his hand. He asked if I had written them. I answered, 'Yes.' Upon which he said, 'The Duke can do nothing in this matter before referring to your colonel.'

" 'But it is to avoid that I have made this application.'

" 'In all cases of this kind,' he replied, 'nothing can be done before referring to the Commanding Officer.' Then seeing my agitation, he added, 'The Duke is not displeased with you. Return to your regiment and you will not be treated harshly.' I retired, and it being too late in the day to return to Chelmsford, I went back to my tavern.

"Never having been in a theatre, and learning that I might go into the gallery at Drury Lane at half price, I went, and saw John Kemble and Mrs. Siddons in the characters of Jaffier and Belvidera. On leaving the heated atmosphere of the theatre I found it raining, and was pretty well drenched before I reached my room. This, following the excitement of the two previous days, brought on a bad feverish cold, and I was unable to rise in the morning.

"As my leave expired that day I wrote a note to the agents of the regiment, Messrs. Ross and Ogilvy, to report my illness, and begged of them to forward it to the regiment at Chelmsford. In the course of the afternoon the servant came to my room and told me that two gentlemen were below desiring to see me.

"Startled at this announcement I desired them to

be shown up, when to my dismay in walked the colonel and another officer of my regiment.

"'Well, young man, what's the matter with you?'

"I told him, 'a cold.'

"'Well,' he said, 'take care of yourself this night and return to the regiment to morrow.' Adding, 'Perhaps your money is all spent,' he laid a half guinea on the table beside me with the words, 'there is enough to take you home.'

"This kindness so affected me that I could hardly say, 'If you knew what brought me here, you would not be so kind to me.'

"'I know all about it. Get well and go back to the regiment.'

"It so happened that the colonel had come up to town that morning, and was at the agents' when my note was received. He then went to the Commander-in-Chief's where my letters were put into his hands, when he came on to my room. Later in the evening the colonel's servant came to see me. He was a private servant, not a soldier, and a very intelligent man.

"'What's this that you've been doing at the Horse Guards,' he began.

"'What I would gladly conceal from the world,' I replied.

"'Well, I know something about it, for while attending at table at the colonel's brother's house to-day, I overheard a good deal of what the colonel said of you to the company. It seems you have been writing letters to the Duke of York about some difficulty you have got yourself into, and mentioned the colonel in a way that pleased him and his brother. He said that when the Duke gave him your letters he recommended you to him, saying that he (the Duke) would not forget you. Then the colonel added, 'If the Duke forgets him I will not.'"

Upon his return to the regiment, FitzGibbon's accounts were examined and an error of £1 15s. erroneously entered against himself, discovered—his limited knowledge of arithmetic and book-keeping being accountable for the supposed deficiency.

The 49th, as indeed all the regiments of the line, were at that time in a very inferior state of discipline in regard to drill and field exercises. Sir John Moore's new code of drill was being generally introduced, and FitzGibbon's training under the drill-sergeant in Ireland, as well as his practical knowledge gained in the yeomanry corps, was of great value to him and his company.

In April, he was at Uxbridge recruiting from the militia just then disbanded.

In June, the 49th was sent to Quebec. FitzGibbon, in order to take advantage of the long voyage and comparative release from duty, to study, provided himself with books upon military tactics and field exercises. Lying in the boat which hung over the stern of the vessel, he made himself master of every detail contained in the "Rules and Regulations for the Field Exercises of His Majesty's Forces."

Such unusual application was not unnoticed by the colonel, whose attention had been already so favorably drawn to the young sergeant, and upon arrival in Quebec the sergeant-major was promoted to be quartermaster-sergeant, and the sergeant-major's sash given to FitzGibbon, over the heads of the forty older sergeants in the regiment.

In September, 1803, Lieutenant Lewis resigned the adjutancy but not the lieutenancy, and though Colonel Brock recommended FitzGibbon for the vacant adjutancy, there was no available lieutenancy for over two years, and he could only act as adjutant until 1806, when Colonel Brock obtained an ensign's commission for his "favorite sergeant-major," as FitzGibbon was known in the regiment, from the Duke of York, who had not forgotten the lad and his romantic application for his protection, and in December of the same year he succeeded to the adjutancy.

In September, 1802, his company was sent to Montreal, and in the following summer moved on to York.

During these first years in Canada, there are many stories told of the sergeant-major. Desertions from the regiments stationed in Canada to the United States were frequent, but it is recorded of Colonel Brock that he only lost one man during the three years of his personal command. He owed this to his popularity and personal influence with his men, and to the vigilance of his sergeant-major.

FitzGibbon always protested against the use of the "cat" for trifling offences, arguing that it degraded a man not only in the eyes of his comrades but in his own; that the sense of shame such punishment left in a man's consciousness pointed invisible fingers of contempt at him and robbed him of the courage necessary to face an enemy, as well as of the love for his officers which would carry him to the cannon's mouth with unflinching devotion.

The invariable kindness with which Lieut.-Colonel Brock, although a strict officer in enforcing duty, treated his men, was repaid by their devotion to him. In several of his letters he speaks of the ingenuity of the inducements held out by the Americans to the privates in the regiments at the frontier to desert, and of the necessity of great watchfulness on the part of his officers to defeat them.

Soon after their arrival at York, the sergeant of the guard informed the sergeant-major that three of his men were missing, and that a boat had been taken from a shed in charge of one of his sentries, who had also disappeared. Although at midnight, FitzGibbon reported the circumstance to the colonel, who ordered him to man a bateau with a sergeant and twelve privates.

The roll was called in the barrack-rooms, when three .other men, as well as a corporal of the 41st, who had been left at York as an artificer, were found to be missing.

At half-past twelve the colonel embarked, taking

FitzGibbon with him. They steered direct for Niagara, thirty miles across the lake, and arrived soon after daylight. The night was dark, but there was little wind, and though the passage had been made before in an open boat, it was considered a venturesome undertaking. Lieut.-General Hunter, who commanded the troops in both provinces, is said to have expressed his displeasure at the colonel for so rashly risking his life. The deserters were overtaken and induced to return to their duty.

A short time after this adventure a very serious mutiny was discovered at Fort George, then garrisoned by a detachment of the 49th, under the command of Lieut.-Colonel Sheaffe, which, had it succeeded, had certainly ended in the murder of that officer.

Although the day has long passed when such tyrannical rule in an officer's hands would be tolerated, yet one cannot read the account of the treatment the men suffered at the hands of this junior colonel without a feeling of just indignation.

The four black holes in the fort were constantly full. Flogging was the sentence awarded for even trifling offences. The passing of a sentence so heavy that it required to be inflicted at two, three, and even four different periods, when the victim was incapable of bearing the whole number at once, was not uncommon. The "cat" was steeped in brine, before as well as during the infliction of punishment, and the sufferings of the men and their hatred of the tyrant may be imagined. (See Appendix II.)

Upon the discovery of the intended mutiny, the officers in the garrison held a private meeting and decided to send a secret message to Colonel Brock before taking any public action.

Although not distinctly stated, the impression given is that Colonel Sheaffe was not one of the officers holding this meeting, nor was he cognizant of the message sent to Colonel Brock. The feeling against him was so strong in the Upper Province that, later, it was considered advisable to remove him to Lower Canada.

A schooner then in the river was despatched at once to York. Colonel Brock hurried back in the same schooner, taking his devoted sergeant-major with him. Upon arrival, the colonel requested that the boat should be anchored below the town, where he landed alone, leaving FitzGibbon behind, with orders not to appear until sent for.

Colonel Brock's prompt action in personally arresting the principal mutineer, and by the force of his commanding presence and influence over the men making each one of them in turn arrest his fellow-conspirator, is one of the most dramatic instances of a military command anywhere recorded.

From Brock's letters we know how terribly he must have regretted that any of his regiment had been under another's command, when at the trial and conviction of the ring-leaders in this unfortunate mutiny, they reiterated their assertion that "had they continued under the command of Colonel Brock they would have escaped their melancholy end."

Lieut.-General Hunter, then in Quebec, ordered that the delinquents should be tried in that garrison, and thither they were sent in September.

FitzGibbon was sent with them. In a letter from Colonel Brock (now in the Canadian Archives), in reference to this court-martial, he says:

"After what I have stated, the general may think proper to give directions to Colonel Mann to keep Sergeant Fern and Private Gagnes and the rest of the witnesses at Quebec during the winter, but I entreat His Excellency's permission for Sergeant-Major Fitz-Gibbon and Sergeant Steans being permitted to join me without delay, which I imagine they will be able to accomplish if allowed to depart the instant it is found their presence is of no further use. Being by themselves they will be able to travel infinitely more expeditiously."

Colonel Brock had been ordered to assume the command at Fort George, and the desertions ceased. He allowed the men greater latitude, permitting them to fish in their fatigue dresses, and in proper uniform to visit the town of Niagara freely, and even to use their muskets to shoot the countless wild fowl, on condition that they provided their own powder and shot.

In June, 1804, Lieut.-Colonel Brock, with a detachment of the 49th, removed to Kingston, and in the September following, to Amherstburg.

Colonel Brock was appointed to the command at Quebec in October, 1804, and it is probable that Fitz-Gibbon went to Quebec with him, but we have no letters or positive mention of him or where he was stationed until the summer of 1806, when he was in Quebec.

In the autumn of 1805, Colonel Brock returned to England on leave, and before his return to Canada in the summer of 1806, he laid before the Commander-in-Chief a scheme for the formation of a veteran battalion for service in the Canadas, in which Fitz-Gibbon was much interested; and as his ensign's commission was given him at this date, it is not unlikely, nor out of accordance with Colonel Brock's well-known character for generosity, that he gave his favorite full credit for all the information he had gathered for him of the feeling among the soldiers and the inducements offered to them to desert, both by the Americans across the international boundary line and the settlers in Canada who had taken advantage of the free grants of land and were now prosperous farmers.

FitzGibbon always said he owed everything to Colonel Brock. He lent him books, had him with him at every opportunity, encouraged him in the effort to improve and educate himself, not only in every branch of his profession, but in all that was either of worth or likely to be of practical use to him as a gentleman or in any position he was ever likely to fill, at home or in the colony. FitzGibbon called the orderly room of the 49th his grammar school, and the mess-room his university, Lieutenants Stratton, Brackenbury and Loring his tutors.

When in Quebec he often wrote to Colonel Brock's dictation, learning much of the correct pronunciation of words hitherto unknown to him, through the colonel's corrections.

Upon one occasion, at Quebec, in 1805, Colonel Brock asked the sergeant-major why he had not done something he had ordered. FitzGibbon replied that he had found it impossible to do it.

"By the Lord Harry, sir, do not tell me it is impossible," cried the colonel; "nothing should be impossible to a soldier. The word impossible should not be found in a soldier's dictionary."

Two years afterwards, in October, 1807, when Fitz-Gibbon was an ensign, Colonel Brock ordered him to take a fatigue party to the bateau guard, and bring round to the lower town twenty bateaux, in which to embark troops suddenly for Montreal, fears being entertained that the Americans were about to invade the province in consequence of the affair between the *Leopard* and the *Chesapeake.*

On reaching the bateaux the party discovered that the tide had left them, and about two hundred yards of deep, tenacious mud intervened between them and the water. It appeared to FitzGibbon impossible to drag the large, heavy flat-boats through such mud, and he had given the word, "To the right face," when it occurred to him that in answer to such a report the colonel would ask, "Did you try it, sir?" He therefore gave the word, "Front," and said to his men, "I think it impossible for us to put these bateaux afloat, but you know it will not do to tell the colonel so, unless we try it. Let us try—there are the boats. I am sure if it is possible for men to put them afloat, you will do it; go at them."

In half an hour the boats were in the water. The troops were thus enabled to embark a day earlier than if the order had not been carried out.

It was in this year, 1807, that the first suggestion was made by Lieut.-Colonel John McDonell, late of the Royal Canadian Volunteers, for raising a corps among the Scotch settlers of Glengarry, Upper Canada, but it was not accepted by the Horse Guards or any steps taken to carry it out until it was revived by Colonel Gore in 1811.

In a letter of this latter date from Colonel Baynes to Major-General Brock, a Captain George McDonell is spoken of as being appointed to attempt the formation of a corps from among the settlers of Glengarry. In a postscript endorsed "private," Sir George Prevost's intention of filling up the new corps with as many officers of the line as he could, and with permanent rank, is announced.*

It is interesting to note this, as we shall hear a great deal more of these Glengarry Fencibles before the close of our biography.

The year 1807 was spent in Quebec. The following spring the regiment was moved to Montreal. In September, the colonel, now Brigadier Brock, was

---

* Tupper's "Life and Correspondence of Sir Isaac Brock."

given the command at Quebec, from whence writing to his brothers, he regrets being separated from the 49th.

" Were the 49th ordered hence, the rank would not be a sufficient inducement to keep me in this country. In such a case I would throw it up willingly."[*]

He was succeeded in the command at Montreal by Major-General Drummond.

Owing to the unfortunate destruction of the books of the 49th, at the evacuation of Fort George, in May, 1813, it is very difficult to ascertain where the various companies were stationed, and, to the ever to be regretted destruction of a quantity of private letters and papers formerly belonging to FitzGibbon, by an ignorant autograph collector, we are deprived of much valuable and interesting information of this period.

Several companies of the 49th, under Major Plenderleath, were stationed at Three Rivers, on the St. Lawrence above Quebec, from 1809 to 1811. FitzGibbon was probably with their detachment, as from incidents in his later life it appears that this officer must have been closely connected with him in the regiment.

Major Plenderleath certainly valued FitzGibbon's friendship highly, and showed his affection for him and his in a substantial manner. Among the papers met with in my researches I found a deed of gift for 100 acres of land given to FitzGibbon's only daughter by his old brother officer and friend. I am not aware who now holds this property, or whether this deed has been sought to complete the validity of the title.

---

[*] Tupper's " Life and Correspondence of Sir Isaac Brock."

In September, 1811, the 49th was again in Montreal. Recruiting for the Glengarry Fencibles was in active operation in April, 1812. Lieut. Shaw, the acting pay-master of the 49th, was ordered upon that duty.

FitzGibbon wrote to Colonel Brock in July, 1812, with reference to a company being given to him in the new regiment, and received the following auto-graph reply:

"York, *July* 29th.

"Dear Sir,—I lament that you should so long have been impressed with the idea that I possessed the means of being serviceable to you. I had scarcely heard of Mr. Johnson's having declined a company in the Glengarry (which would have given me the nomination), but I received an account of his being reinstated. I consequently thought no more of the business, thinking that officer was enjoying the fruits of his good fortune. I know not positively whether Mr. Johnson is reinstated, but being under obligations to promote his views, I cannot possibly interfere to his prejudice. I rather wonder you did not know that Lieut. Lamont had long ago my promise of nomi-nating him to the company, provided it became vacant, which, of course, would have precluded my applica-tion in your behalf. Although you must be sensible of the impossibility of my taking any steps to for-ward your views in the present case, yet, be assured, I shall always feel happy in any opportunity that may offer to do you service.

"To a person unaccustomed to my writing I scarcely would hazard sending this scrawl.

"I am, dear sir,

"Yours faithfully,

"Isaac Brock.

"I should like to be among the 49th at this moment. I am satisfied they will support and even add to their former fame. They have my very best wishes. The 41st are behaving nobly at Amherstburg."

In the fac-simile of this letter from General Brock it will be noticed that the year is omitted in the date, but from the context and from reference to other correspondence now in the Canadian Archives at Ottawa, relative to Lieut. Johnson (a gentleman who apparently could not decide in which regiment he preferred to hold a commission, the Glengarry or the Canadian Fencibles), there is no doubt that the letter was written in 1812.

Owing to the fact that there are very few letters from Brock extant, and those in the keeping of the Archives, the original of this one is a valuable relic. Written on both sides of a single sheet, the paper yellow from age, and many of the characters indistinct, it was difficult to reproduce it faithfully.

The following letter bears an earlier date than General Brock's, and needs no explanation :

"MONTREAL, *May* 16th, 1812.

"SIR,—I beg you will be pleased to obtain for me His Majesty's permission to resign my commission of adjutant only, in the 49th regiment.

"It is incumbent upon me to state my reasons for wishing to resign the adjutancy, I therefore detail them. Before I entered the army the circumstances of my parents prevented my obtaining such an education as to qualify me to discharge the duties of an officer in His Majesty's service. Whatever know-

ledge I possess, I have acquired since I entered it.
I trust that I have so far succeeded as to have
rendered myself, at least as a regimental officer, respectable.   At this point I do not wish to stop; to
personal exertions I look principally for further success in the army, and by qualifying myself to hold
the higher and more important stations, I shall have
the best prospect of arriving at them, and of becoming most useful to my king and country, in whose
service I have been already so liberally rewarded.

"The duties attached to my present station employ
me so as to leave no spare time.   I am anxious to
study and become proficient in the languages, mathe-
matics, military drawing, etc., so as to qualify myself
to discharge, with honor to myself, the duties of any
situation to which I may hereafter have the good
fortune to be called.

"I have the honor to be, sir,
"Your most obedient, humble servant,
"(Signed)   JAMES FITZGIBBON,
"*Lieut. and Adjt. 49th Regiment.*
"*To* COLONEL VINCENT,
"*Commanding 49th Regiment.*
"A true copy.
"NOAH FREER,
"*Military Secretary.*"

This letter was forwarded to the Commander of the
Forces in Canada, with a letter from Colonel Vincent
soliciting approbation of its petition, and requesting
permission to recommend Sergeant-Major Stean for
the adjutancy if FitzGibbon's resignation is accepted.

We can, however, find no further record or entry
of any reply to either letter.

CHAPTER V.

IN July, 1812, immediately after the declaration of war by the United States against Great Britain and her colonies, we find FitzGibbon again addressing his colonel and applying for leave to resign the adjutancy, in order that he may be given the command of one of the companies of the 49th, whose captain was absent on leave. This request was granted at once. A week later FitzGibbon was placed in the desired command by Sir George Prevost and sent with his company to escort the first brigade of bateaux from Montreal to Kingston.

In these days of steamboats and canals, when heavily laden barges are towed in safety up our great water highway, passing the rapids by the canals, the difficulties of conveying the clumsily built, heavy bateaux and their freight up the south bank of the river, avoiding the rapids on the one hand and the enemy on the other, can scarcely be realized. From St. Regis upwards they were obliged to keep close to the shore, and were exposed to an enemy's attack at any moment.

Why they hugged the south shore instead of following the northern bank of the river does not appear. FitzGibbon says distinctly that for more than a hundred miles the American shore was close on their left.

Possibly the north channel was not so well known to
the boatmen as the south, or it might be that Fitz-
Gibbon, adhering to the very original idea formed on
the sand-hills of Holland, that the safest place was
close to the enemy, took that route in preference to
the other. If so, the result proved its value.

FitzGibbon's enthusiasm, his readiness of resource,
his willingness to take his share of work with his
men, while at the same time preserving his authority
over them, was long remembered.

A white-haired old man (the late M. Le Lievre,
of Three Rivers), when speaking of this expedition
to the writer in 1873, recalled the particulars with
vivid interest: "I can remember that journey well,
although I was only a very young lad at the time.
FitzGibbon was a fine man, and a splendid soldier.
The men adored him, although he was strict. His
word was law, and they had such faith in him that I
believe if he had told any one of them to jump into
the river, he would have been obeyed. He always
knew what he was about, and his men knew it, and
had full confidence in him."

The Americans, learning that the bateaux were
coming up the St. Lawrence, fitted out an expedition
at Ogdensburg to intercept them. They landed on
Toussaint's Island, but through the timely warning
given by a man who escaped from the island and
roused the militia on the Canadian shore, the boats
were prepared to receive them. When the Americans
made the attack they met with such a warm reception

that they were obliged to abandon one of their boats,
and in spite of the fact that they brought the fire
from their gunboat to bear upon the bateaux, and
obliged them to move out of range, their own loss
was so severe that they were forced to retreat. (Appendix IV.)

The bateaux reached Kingston without further
molestation. Owing to the loss of the papers already
referred to, it is impossible to ascertain with accuracy
where FitzGibbon was stationed during the next four
months. Whether with that portion of the regiment
stationed at York, or at Fort Erie, or with the four
companies left at Kingston, or whether he was with
Brock at Queenston Heights, we have no documentary evidence, no written record, to guide us.

In January, 1813, FitzGibbon was sent from Kingston in charge of forty-five sleighs containing military
stores for Niagara. This was an extremely arduous
undertaking, the difficulties of overcoming bad roads,
snowstorms, and the bitter cold of a Canadian winter,
being scarcely less than those which beset the river
highway from Montreal. Avoiding the trackless
forest and the softer snow beneath the trees, the
sleighs were obliged to follow the shores of the Bay
of Quinte, and after crossing the narrow stretch of
land between Prince Edward county and the mainland, known as the "Carrying Place," and along the
low shores of Brighton Bay, to face the wide sweep
of wind over Lake Ontario to York.

Upon his arrival at Niagara, he was detached with

his company and sent to the shores of Lake Erie, to
the most distant post on the right of the army on the
Niagara frontier.　The lake was frozen completely
over from shore to shore, and thus formed a firm
bridge upon which it was expected the enemy would
cross.　FitzGibbon was set to watch and prevent this.

When the ice broke up in April, he was withdrawn
to the Niagara River, and posted at Frenchman's
Creek.　It was from this post that FitzGibbon made
one of the daring raids for which he was afterwards
so well known.　Seeing a party of the enemy on one
of the islands in the river at sunset on the 6th of
April, he crossed in a bateau with twelve men,
succeeded in reaching the island unobserved, and surprising the party, took them prisoners and brought
them back with their own boat.

That FitzGibbon was frequently employed in conveying despatches from the frontier to headquarters
at Kingston, we know, but we have no detailed record
of each occasion upon which this duty was entrusted
to him.　His intimate knowledge of the roads, his
expeditious promptitude and rapid movements, as
well as the fact of his having been at so many different places, while that part of the 49th to which
he of right belonged remained at one post, makes
this more probable.

He was with his regiment on the Niagara frontier
on April the 6th, when the raid on Strawberry Island
was perpetrated.　He was at York when that post
was attacked by the Americans under Chauncey and

Dearborn, and back again at Fort George when it was taken by them on May 27th.

There is no official record extant of the strength of the force that, after the gallant defence of Fort George, retreated to Burlington Heights.

The situation was critical. The recent bombard-ment of York and its evacuation by its chief magis-trates and officials; the presence of the American fleet under Chauncey, a fleet capable of commanding every port on the lakes and in actual possession of the Niagara frontier shores; Fort George taken and occupied by the enemy; the British force, harassed and wearied by previous patrol duties, followed by defeat, and further weakened by the permission which almost amounted to an order given to the militia to return to their own homes.

The American force, 3,550 strong, flushed with victory, following up the retreat of the defeated and well-nigh disheartened British army, made the prospect appear gloomy indeed. Nothing but the entire evacuation of the western peninsula seemed possible. Against less odds York had been deserted. There seemed nothing for it but to destroy all the stores that could not be carried away, evacuate the Heights, and escape to Kingston, leaving the land to the enemy. Fortunately for Canada there were a few dauntless spirits to whom the words "defeat" and "retreat" required many letters to spell—enough of the ignorance of "when they were beaten" left in the British ranks to sustain them.

Collecting all the women and children in the fort on the Heights, and levelling all the fences on the deserted farms on the plains below, the British prepared to make a last stand against the enemy.

Tidings being brought to the camp of the approach of the American army, Lieut. Crowther, with a small party, was sent out to reconnoitre, and if possible, check the advance.

Upon reaching Red Hill, a scout brought him word that the enemy were close on the other side of the Big Creek. This information prompted the idea of attempting to surprise and capture the whole force. Concealing his party in the bush, the lieutenant watched the enemy approach in evident ignorance of the proximity of any ambushed foe.

All seemed to favor the successful issue of his stratagem, when the excitable Irish temperament defeated it. The Americans were scarcely within range when one of the 49th, forgetful of orders, fired. The enemy started, broke for shelter, and the lieutenant seeing all was up, fired a full volley to hurry them before withdrawing his party.*

Ascertaining that the main body of the enemy were preparing to encamp at Stony Creek, he returned to the Heights, and reported to General Vincent.

It was now FitzGibbon's turn. From his knowledge of the ground and the enemy's behaviour under sudden attack, of how the unsteadiness of the few

---

* The Battle of Stony Creek. E. B. Biggar, *Canadian Magazine*, July, 1893.

affected the steadiness of the many, FitzGibbon felt confident that a night attack might be made with success. Colonel Harvey was in favor of attempting it, and FitzGibbon volunteered to learn the exact position and disposition of the enemy's forces, and personally obtain all the knowledge necessary.

Disguising himself as a settler, he took a basket of butter on his arm, and went boldly into the American camp.

There is no doubt whatever that he made himself very entertaining to the soldiers, to whom he sold all his butter, getting the best price for it; or that the purchasers believed they were obtaining much valuable information of the position, panic and numerical inferiority of the British troops now fleeing before their victorious arms. The disguise was so complete, the vendor of butter so simple, that he was allowed to traverse the entire camp, and gain considerably more information than he appeared to give.

FitzGibbon returned more than ever convinced that if General Vincent would consent to a night attack it would be successful.

He reported the enemy camped on Mr. James Gage's farm, on the easterly bank of a rivulet just west of the Stony Creek, which ran through a shallow valley some two hundred yards wide, with steep banks twelve or fifteen feet high, their guns planted on the edge of the bank as on a parapet overlooking the flat. The infantry were encamped behind them in an orchard on the north and in the fields on the south of the road, while Generals Winder and Chandler had possession of Mr. Gage's house as their headquarters. The luckless advance guard was posted in the meeting-house on the west side of the flat, a quarter of a mile from the camp."*

Upon FitzGibbon's report being received, an anxious council of war was held, and Colonel Harvey proposed a night attack being made. It was the only chance, the forlorn hope. The men had but ninety rounds of ammunition remaining. Sail had been seen on the lake. If time were allowed them to effect a junction with the land force, disastrous, precipitate retreat or annihilation was inevitable. The proposal was accepted, and Colonel Harvey given the command.

Five companies of the 8th under Major Ogilvy, and five of the 49th under Major Plenderleath, with an unrecorded number of militia and other corps then in the camp—in all, a handful of seven hundred and four rank and file—set out in the silent summer night to strike what every soldier thought might be a last blow for the British flag on that fair Canadian frontier.

Ascertaining that every musket was empty, even the flints removed, that no excitable Irishman might again betray their proximity, Harvey gave the order to march.

Three hours passed. No sound broke the silence, no report of cannon carried tidings to the anxious hearts

---

* J. H. Land in Report of the Wentworth Historical Society.

GAGE'S HOUSE, HEADQUARTERS OF THE AMERICAN OFFICERS, STONY CREEK.

upon the Heights. Meanwhile, the troops had crept across the plains. Upon reaching the scene of Lieut. Crowther's ambuscade the men were halted, and the various posts of attack or vigilance assigned to the different officers.

Stealing from the cover, the enemy's advance pickets were bayoneted in silence ere the challenge had well passed their lips, and deploying into line the attacking force marched up the steep bank of the valley to the very mouth of the cannon, every man knowing that any moment they might roar forth wholesale destruction down the ranks.

FitzGibbon was one of the first men to reach the summit of the bank, at the moment that the first volley of the American musketry roused the sleeping gunners, who, springing to their feet, fired the guns just where they stood.

Heedless of the death-dealing shot, the 49th charged, and carrying the guns at the point of the bayonet, turned them upon the now flying enemy. The camp was taken; whole regiments fired but once and fled, leaving their dead to be buried by their enemies. The two American generals, Chandler and Winder, were captured by the British, together with seven other officers and 116 rank and file. The retreat of the front ranks carried panic with it to the rear; the ships, instead of supporting the land force, served only as a means of escape to the flying soldiers, and one of the most brilliant victories of the campaign was won by the British—a victory that more than compensated their arms for the loss of York and Fort George.

FitzGibbon always said in reference to this battle, that if the victory had been followed by immediate pursuit of the retreating Americans, Fort George might have been recovered without much, if any, loss. The advance, however, only reached Forty Mile Creek two days later.

This suggested to FitzGibbon the idea that he might do good work if he had a few men under his immediate command, detached for skirmishing duty in advance.

To decide upon a line of conduct and to act was one with the soldier. He lost no time in applying to Lieut.-Colonel Harvey, then Deputy Adjutant-General.

To his intense satisfaction his request was received by Lieut.-Colonel Harvey with the words, " Most cheerfully. I have been looking for an officer I could send in the advance, and did not think of you. Come to me in an hour with written details of your projected plan of operations, and I will propose you to the general."

The general's consent obtained, the next difficulty was to select men. Had all who volunteered and wished to go with him been accepted, he would have had nearly the whole regiment. But the number was limited to fifty.

" We all wanted to go," writes an old 49th man, in 1862. " We knew there would be good work, fighting and success wherever FitzGibbon led, for though

BATTLE-GROUND OF STONY CREEK.

From Gage's House.

impulsive he was prompt, and as brave as a lion. Though apparently foolhardy, every man in the regiment knew that he knew what he was about, and forgot nothing."

During the day, FitzGibbon made up the company's accounts and transferred them to another officer; selected his men from the several companies himself; purchased a sufficient quantity of fustian to make shell-jackets, in order that he might be able to show fifty red-coats at one point and fifty grey-coats at another, and three cow-bells to be used as signals in the woods, where the bugle, whistle or even words of command might serve only to betray their whereabouts to the enemy.

The 49th had long ere this date won for themselves the sobriquet of the " Green Tigers " from the enemy, the name being suggested by the color of the facing of their tunics and the fierceness of their fighting. Detachments of this regiment were generally sent to the front of every engagement. Batteries and guns, whose fire was proving disastrous to the advance or retreat of the British, had been stormed and carried by small handfuls of men from the regiment, and their appearance was now almost sufficient to ensure victory, and certainly carried fear into the ranks of the enemy.

FitzGibbon's little band well sustained the character of the regiment. He knew each one of the men and of what they were capable; knew that his faith in them was returned fourfold in their devotion to him, and in that *esprit de corps* so essential to the successful career of soldier or regiment.

With Ensign Winder and forty-eight rank and file, he successfully interrupted the communication between Fort Erie and Fort George, then in the hands of the enemy, and pursued and well-nigh captured a marauding troop of licensed freebooters under a Captain Chapin, whose warfare had been principally directed against defenceless farms, his men burning and destroying barns and farm produce, terrifying the women and children, and making prisoners of the few laborers they found in charge.

By dividing his company into three parties, and sending them by different pathways and tracks through the woods and ravines, FitzGibbon was able to cover a larger area and give the impression that he had a greater number of men under his command than had he kept them all together. A code of signals was arranged by which they could communicate with each other, and, though separated, be able to act in concert.

Each band must have had many tales to tell of narrow escape and adventure during those days of successful hunting of the enemy. Once when Fitz-Gibbon and two of his men were crossing from one rendezvous to another, they were nearly captured by a party of ten or twelve Americans. It being impossible to retreat unseen, they concealed themselves under an overhanging bank of earth, from which a luxuriant growth of wild vines formed a screen, and

waited. Listening intently, FitzGibbon made signs
to his men not to move, and, turning, crept cautiously
along close to the bank to where he knew there was
a deep hole or cave. A great tree had fallen and
partially barred the entrance; resting his hands on
the trunk, he raised himself and dropped lightly on
the other side, not, however, without having caught
a momentary glimpse of the enemy. The path they
had followed had come to an abrupt end on the top
of the rise; they were evidently uncertain of their
locality and had halted to consider, undecided whether
to return by the way they had come or to break a
fresh track and advance. FitzGibbon crawled along
until he was within a few yards of below where they
stood. Pausing a moment to recover his breath, he
uttered a succession of Irish yells and Indian war
cries, which, reverberating from side to side of the
cave, startled and struck terror to the hearts of the
enemy above. Believing themselves surrounded by
ambushed Indians, they decided that there was but
one path and took it, not stopping to look behind
them. FitzGibbon returned to his men, and they
went their way without further encounter with the
enemy that day.

On the 21st, FitzGibbon, by a judicious disposal of
his men through the woods and destroying the bridge
over the Chippewa by removing the planks, had
Chapin's whole troop in a corner, and would have
captured them had not 150 infantry coming from
Fort Erie been entrapped at the same time. The

combined force so far outnumbered FitzGibbon's that he deemed it advisable to draw off his men and let the United States infantry escort their own cavalry back to Fort George.

Later on the same day, when entering a village through which the enemy had just passed, FitzGibbon saw a dragoon's horse at the door of a tavern, and, hoping to surprise and capture the rider in order that he might obtain information of the enemy's movements and intentions, he advanced.

When within a few paces of the door, an infantry man came out and presented his musket. FitzGibbon, having his grey fustian jacket on over his uniform, still advanced, saying quietly, "Stop, my friend, don't fire." The musket dropped to the charge, while Fitz-Gibbon went on, "I advise you to go away quickly as there are British soldiers in the barn over there." Then, being within reach, he sprang forward, seized the man's musket and ordered him to surrender. Instead of obeying, the man held on firmly. The sound of voices attracted the dragoon, who, issuing from the door, pointed his piece at FitzGibbon's shoulder. Lithe as a cat and of great muscular strength, Fitz-Gibbon turned, and still retaining his hold upon the infantry man's musket with his right hand, he caught the one pointed at his shoulder with his left, and brought it to the front beside the other. The man pulled but FitzGibbon held fast. Finding he was too strong for them, the dragoon drew FitzGibbon's own sword with his left hand, and attempted to cut him over the head with it, but failed. He then grasped it as a dagger and tried to stab him. But there was help near. As he raised his arm to strike, FitzGibbon saw two small hands seize it from behind, grasp the wrist, and the sword was wrenched from his hold by a woman. An old man coming up at the moment, the two Americans were made prisoners, and carried off from within hearing of their own detachment, had it occurred to them to call out.

It may be interesting to add that at the close of the war, in 1816, FitzGibbon obtained from the Government a grant of 400 acres of land for the woman's husband, as a reward for her assistance, and in 1837 when her son, who had joined the rebels, was taken prisoner, and tried, and would have suffered the penalty of death, FitzGibbon, in consideration of certain circumstances which came out in the investigation, obtained a full pardon for the lad from Sir George Arthur.*

On the 24th of June occurred an incident which has been more or less correctly described, both in poetry and prose, at various times, more than once being spoken of as " the most brilliant episode of the war," that known as the "affair" or battle of Beaver Dam. We have two accounts of it, one written at the time by a correspondent of the Montreal *Gazette*, and published in the columns of the issue of that paper of July 6th, 1813, and one written by FitzGibbon in

---

* An account of his case was published in the *London Times*, in August, 1839.

later years for the information of his grandchildren.
(The former will be found in Appendix V.)

Tupper also publishes an account in his " Life and
Correspondence of Sir Isaac Brock," which, in a foot-
note, he says is abridged from *The Soldier's Companion or Recorder.* It has also been ably dramatized
by Mrs. Curzon, a well-known Canadian authoress of
the present day.

To tell the story fairly, I must, although reluctant
to load this biography with details belonging more
exclusively to the history of the campaign and the
country, endeavor to sketch briefly the condition of
affairs upon the frontier at that time.

We must recall the evacuation of Fort George by
the British—or its capture by the Americans, to put it
either way—followed by the battle of Stony Creek,
the pursuit of the retreating Americans, and the
desultory warfare carried on between the rival armies
along the frontier. This sort of guerilla warfare
between, not only the regulars, but the volunteer
companies and straggling bands of Indians as well,
had resulted in nothing decisive.

After their defeat at Stony Creek, and their precipitate retreat from the Forty Mile Creek, the American army were unable to undertake any offensive
measures. Their communication between Forts Erie,
Niagara and George were cut off by FitzGibbon and
his handful of the 49th men, now more dreaded than
ever as " FitzGibbon's Green 'uns."

FitzGibbon had chosen De Cou's house as his head-

BATTLE OF BEAVER DAM.

Diagram showing relative positions, distances, etc., in the field of operations, attached by the Court to the proceedings in the case of Col. Boerstler. (Copied, through the kindness of Capt. Cruikshank, from the *New Weekly Register*, Vol. X., p. 121.)

quarters, a choice which evinced an intimate knowedge of the locality as well as considerable strategic ability. The position gave him the command of four roads—to Queenston *via* St. David's, to St. Catharines and the lake, to Colonel Bisshopp's station, and to that most important post, Burlington Heights. The accompanying map does not give the last mentioned road, but as FitzGibbon speaks of it as the chief object of the American attack, and the later local maps place the road to Burlington at right angles from that to St. Catharines, it is reasonable to suppose it was there.

Personal terror of the Indians was excited in the minds and imagination of the American soldiers by the wild tales of their cruelties to prisoners told by the settlers on whose lands they were quartered. The hatred of the latter for these intruders was increased by the brutalities perpetrated by Chapin and his men, and their love and admiration for Fitz-Gibbon was raised almost to hero-worship by his daring and success in checking the progress and interrupting the communication between the enemy's posts.

This check was not satisfactory to the Americans. Complaints being made by the authorities at Washington of the sluggishness of the generals in command, orders were issued at headquarters that, at all hazard, an effort must be made to dislodge or capture this irrepressible soldier, batter down De Cou's house, and, by securing the road to Burlington Heights, open the way to a successful attack upon that key to the position.

The plan mentioned in the following letter to Fitz-Gibbon from William Kerr, the Chief of the Indians at Beaver Dam, and Brant's son-in-law, has, I regret to say, been lost, and though every effort has been made, both by myself and others interested in the records of our country, we have not been successful in recovering it:

"WELLINGTON SQUARE, *June* 4th, 1842.

"MY DEAR FITZ,—This is the birthday of our good old King George IV., which is still celebrated by the militia of the country in Canada West.

"I wish you to get some good hand to sketch the accompanying little plan of the country about the Beaver Dam—that is, to copy it, and at the same time point out any inaccuracies you may meet with, both in the plan and account of the morning's work. The plan of the country I did a few days after the battle—and the account of that morning's work you can add to, or make alterations. But you must keep, or send to me, the original plan and account of the battle, as, you observe, it may be pleasing some thirty or forty years hence to look or talk over the same, when we ride to Owen Sound on the railroad. Mrs. Kerr is quite well.

"Thine,

"WILLIAM J. KERR.

"JAS. FITZGIBBON, ESQ."

Burlington Heights in the possession of the Americans meant the probable occupation and possible subjugation of the entire peninsula. (See map, p. 79.)

LAURA SECORD.

The duty of striking a preparatory blow, this surprise and capture of FitzGibbon, was entrusted to Lieut.-Colonel Bœrstler and a force of upwards of five hundred men.

The natural confidence of success which the comparative strength of the two forces gave the Americans was eventually the cause of their defeat. At the Beaver Dam, some of the junior officers with Lieut.-Colonel Bœrstler were overheard discussing his plans, and a woman undertook the difficult task of attempting to reach and warn FitzGibbon.

The story of Laura Secord, her loyalty, bravery, and perseverance under great difficulties, has been told more than once, yet I must repeat it once again. James Secord, formerly an officer in the Lincoln militia, had been wounded at Queenston Heights. Too crippled for further service, he had settled on a grant of land in the Niagara district, in that part of the peninsula at the time in the hands of the Americans. A couple of their officers coming into Secord's house to demand food, had stayed long enough, and talked loud enough, to allow his young wife to learn the danger threatening FitzGibbon and his handful of brave men. Her husband was incapable by reason of his lameness, but she could be fleet of foot and strong in purpose. From the moment she obtained her husband's consent to go, until she reached Fitz-Gibbon, her courage never failed.

Putting everything in order, even setting the breakfast table ready, that the appearance of her

presence might deceive any chance visitor to the
house, and learning the particulars of the best route
to follow, so as to avoid the enemy's pickets as much
as possible, she set out at the earliest peep of dawn.
Clad only in a short flannel skirt and cotton jacket,
without shoes or stockings, her milking stool in one
hand, her pail in the other, she drove one of the cows
close to the American lines. While ostensibly making
every effort to stay the animal's progress, she at
the same time gave it a sly prod to keep it moving.
Accosted by the picket, who questioned her anxiety
to milk the cow so early, and chaffed her for her
apparent inability to overtake it, laughing at her
fruitless efforts to bring the creature to a stand, Laura
merely grumbled at it for being "contrary." The
scantiness of the woman's clothing, and her well-
simulated wrath at the animal's antics, quite deceived
the man, who let her pass without further protest.

The moment she was out of his sight, Laura Secord
drove the cow on more quickly, following the course
of a small ravine which concealed her from both
sight and hearing. A mile away, she hid the pail
and stool under the bushes, first milking the cow
sufficiently to prevent her returning too soon to the
clearing. She then set out on her long tramp through
the woods.

The 23rd of June, the morning was hot and close,
and through the lower lands the flies were plentiful.
The underbrush in the forest was tangled and dense,
making the tree-clad slopes more difficult to climb

The fear of encountering outlying pickets, or wandering bands of marauding Americans, who would stay or question her, led her to avoid even the slightly marked tracks, and took her a long way round. Her first stopping place was the mill on the little stream not far from St. David's. Her friends there, a widow and a lad, endeavored to dissuade her from attempting to reach FitzGibbon, and added much to the terrors of the way by exaggerated descriptions of the fierceness and cruelties of the Indians, who then infested the woods. But Laura had set out with a definite object, and she meant to accomplish it at all risks. She knew the enemy was to march the next day, and she must reach De Cou's, where FitzGibbon was, before them. The last half of her journey was even more trying than the first. She knew nothing of the way ; there were so many paths and "blazed" tracks through the woods, that she several times took a wrong one. When almost despairing of reaching her destination, she came to an opening in the forest and at the same time encountered a party of the dreaded Indians.

One, who appeared to be their chief, sprang to his feet and accosted her. Terrified, she was at first unable to speak, but reassured by the obedience of the others to a sign from their chief, she soon recovered sufficiently to try and explain by signs that she wished to be taken to FitzGibbon. Reiterating the name and pointing to the knife in the chief's belt, she at last made him understand that many "Big

Knives" * were coming. With an expressive "Ugh" of satisfaction and intelligence, the Indian turned, and led the way through the beaver meadows to De Cou's.

"Thus," wrote FitzGibbon, "did a young, delicate woman brave the terrors of the forest in a time of such desultory warfare that the dangers were increased tenfold, to do her duty to her country, and by timely warning save much bloodshed and disaster." †

---

* Michigans, "Big Knives," the Indian name for Americans.

† The following paper was signed by FitzGibbon :

"I do hereby certify that Mrs. Secord, wife of James Secord, of Chippewa, Esq., did, in the month of June, 1813, walk from her house, near the village of St. David's, to De Cou's house in Thorold by a circuitous route of about twenty miles, partly through the woods, to acquaint me that the enemy intended to attempt, by surprise, to capture a detachment of the 49th Regiment, then under my command, she having obtained such knowledge from good authority, as the event proved. Mrs. Secord was a person of slight and delicate frame, and made the effort in weather excessively warm, and I dreaded at the time that she must suffer in health in consequence of fatigue and anxiety, she having been exposed to danger from the enemy, through whose lines of communication she had to pass. The attempt was made on my detachment by the enemy ; and his detachment, consisting of upwards of 500 men and a field-piece and 50 dragoons, were captured in consequence.

"I write this certificate in a moment of much hurry and from memory, and it is therefore thus brief.

"(Signed) JAMES FITZGIBBON,
"*Formerly Lieutenant 49th Regiment.*"

[Given by Auchinlech, page 175, but Mrs. Secord possesses the original, December 1863.—"War of 1812," Coffin, page 146.]

DE COU'S HOUSE, NEAR BEAVER DAM.

Sending her to a farm beyond De Cou's to be cared for, where, as she graphically expressed it, she "slept right off," FitzGibbon repeated her tidings to the chief, and remained on guard himself all night.

In the meantime the American detachment had lain over at Queenston, and in the early morning of the 24th continued their march to Beaver Dam.

They had not gone far before they came upon Kerr and his Indians, in number between two and three hundred, chiefly Mohawks and Caughnawagas from the Grand River and the St. Lawrence. Kerr and young Brant saw at once that their force was too small to oppose the American advance, so resorted to Indian tactics to retard and harass the enemy. They threw themselves upon the rear and flank of the enemy, and opened a desultory fire. The Americans, throwing out sharpshooters in reply, still advanced.

The track was narrow and rough, the forest on either side forming a safe shelter for the Indians, who were neither to be shaken off nor repulsed. Their yells, echoing their rifles, rang on the national conscience, and the many sensational stories told of their savage treatment of prisoners had the usual effect on nerve and brain.

About 7 o'clock, FitzGibbon heard firing in the direction of Queenston. Taking a cornet of dragoons, who happened to be at De Cou's, with him, he sallied out to reconnoitre, and soon discovered the enemy. They had retired from the road and taken up a position on a rising ground in the centre of a field of wheat. The firing had nearly ceased, the Indians having to creep through the standing corn to get within range, and the guns of the Americans replying only to the spot where the smoke was seen to rise from the concealed rifle.

The Americans being about fourteen miles from Fort George and several of their men lying killed on the road before him, FitzGibbon suspected that they probably believed themselves in desperate circumstances. He sent the cornet back to bring up his men. Addressing a few animated words to them, he then led them at the double across the open in front of the American position, about 150 yards distant, to the wood between it and Fort George, as if to cut off their retreat, so disposing his men as to give the appearance of greater numbers.

A discharge of grape from the enemy's guns passed through his ranks and cut up the turf, but did no further damage. The desired ground was occupied without losing a man.

Upon discovery of the enemy, FitzGibbon had sent a despatch to Colonel De Haren, who was in command of a detachment of about two hundred men, as he believed about a mile from his own post, but who he afterwards learned had retreated to a distance of seven miles. While anxiously expecting the arrival of De Haren, FitzGibbon heard that the enemy were expecting reinforcements. The Indians were dropping off, and fearing to lose such a prize, he determined to "come the old soldier over them and demand their instant surrender." Tying a white handkerchief to his sword he advanced. His bugler sounded the "Cease firing," which to his surprise and satisfaction the Indians obeyed.

An American officer advanced to meet him, also bearing a flag.

FitzGibbon informed him that it was principally from a desire to avoid unnecessary bloodshed that he demanded the surrender of the American force to the British now opposing their advance, and wished the officer to recommend the necessity of such action strongly to the general in command. Colonel Bœrstler's reply to this was, "That he was not accustomed to surrender to any army he had not even seen."

Upon this, FitzGibbon represented that "if such was his (Colonel Bœrstler's) determination, he would request his (FitzGibbon's) superior officer to grant permission for any officer Colonel Bœrstler might depute for the duty, to inspect the British force, and see for himself the advisability of not risking a battle or the rancor of the Indians."

FitzGibbon then retired, ostensibly to obtain this permission. Upon reaching his men he found that Captain Hall, of Chippewa, with about twenty dragoons, had joined them, he having been attracted by the firing. Requesting Captain Hall to represent the mythical "superior officer," "receive the request and refuse it," FitzGibbon returned to the American officer who awaited the reply. Colonel Bœrstler then requested to be given until sundown to consider and decide. To this FitzGibbon replied promptly in the negative, "I cannot possibly grant such a request. I could not control the Indians for such a length of time," and taking out his watch, he added, "I cannot give your general more than five minutes in which to decide whether to surrender or not."

During the negotiations which followed concerning the conditions of surrender, FitzGibbon heard the name of Colonel Chapin constantly repeated. While delighted at the success of his stratagem, FitzGibbon endeavored to keep all appearance of satisfaction out of his manner. When the condition that "the volunteers and militiamen should be allowed to return to the United States on parole," was advanced by Capt. McDowell, the officer who acted for Colonel Bœrstler, FitzGibbon asked if the volunteers mentioned were not Chapin and his mounted men. Upon receiving an answer in the affirmative, he said: "The conduct of that person and his troop has been so bad among our country people, plundering their houses and otherwise behaving ill, that I do not think him deserving of the honors of war." Pausing a moment as if to consider, he added: "But as I am aware that the Americans accuse us of stimulating the Indians to destroy you, whereas we have ever used our best endeavor, and almost always successfully, to protect you, therefore, rather than give you cause to think so upon this occasion, I agree to that condition as well as the others."

"Then, sir," replied Captain McDowell, "if you will send an officer to superintend the details of the surrender, we will be ready to receive you, and we shall depend upon you as a British officer to protect our men from the Indians."

"I can only give you this assurance," he replied; "the Indians must take my life before they shall attack you."

FitzGibbon went at once to the chiefs, and repeating his promise made to the American officer to them in French, begged of them to do nothing to interfere with its fulfilment. They agreed at once, shaking hands with FitzGibbon in token of their faith. At this moment, most unexpectedly, Major De Haren appeared, galloping into the open and accompanied by a colonel of militia.

"I would have given all I ever possessed," says FitzGibbon, "that they had been twenty miles distant, fearing that they would rob me of at least some of the credit of the capture. It became important to let Major De Haren know what had been already done, and I requested him to stop and hear it from me, but he most cavalierly replied, 'You need not be alarmed, Mr. FitzGibbon, you shall have all the credit for this affair which you deserve.'

"'I desire merely, sir, to make known to you what has been done, that you may proceed accordingly;' but he would not stop his horse, and Colonel Bœrstler, seeing us approach, rode forward to meet us. I introduced them to each other, and then Major De

Haren began offering certain conditions to Colonel Bœrstler, upon which he would accept his surrender.

"In an instant I saw myself on the point of being robbed of my prize, and stepping quickly to the head of Major De Haren's horse, on the near side, and laying my left arm and elbow on its neck and my head upon my arm, my face towards Major De Haren so that my voice might reach his ear only, I said in a low but most imperative tone, ' Not another word, sir ; not another word ; these men are my prisoners.' Then stepping back, I asked in a loud, firm voice, ' Shall I proceed to disarm the American troops ? ' And he could not help answering, ' You may.'

"The American troops fell in at once in answer to my command, and Major Taylor, Colonel Bœrstler's second in command, asked me how I would have the men formed, in file or in column.

"'In file, if you please,' I replied, for I wished to keep their ranks broken as much as possible, and dreaded every moment that Major De Haren, in conversation with Colonel Bœrstler, would, by some blunder, ruin all. The moment, therefore, that I saw eight or ten files formed, I gave the order, 'American troops, Right face—Quick march,' that I might drive Colonel Bœrstler and Major De Haren before me, and prevent their conversing together further during the crisis.

"As we approached near where our men were formed, I stepped up to Major De Haren and asked, ' Shall the American troops ground their arms here ?'

' No,' he answered in a harsh tone, ' let them march through between our men and ground their arms on the other side.'

" Filled with indignation at this great folly, I thought, almost audibly, ' What, sir, and when they see our handful of men, will they ground their arms at your bidding?' but said, in an impressive tone, ' Do you think it prudent to march them through with arms in their hands in the presence of the Indians?'

" Before he could reply, Colonel Bœrstler, holding out his hand, exclaimed, ' For God's sake, sir, do what this officer bids you!' ' Do so,' said De Haren.

" ' Americans, Halt!—Front!—Ground your arms!'

" The order was obeyed promptly. Then the Indians sprang forward from their hiding-places and ran towards the prisoners, who in terror began to seize their arms again. The moment was critical. I sprang upon a stump of a tree and shouted, 'Americans, don't touch your arms! Not a hair of your head shall be hurt,' adding, 'Remember, I am here'—a bombastic speech, but I knew I could rely on the promise given me by the chiefs. The Americans stood still, and the Indians went among them, taking possession of such articles of arms and accoutrements as pleased them, especially the pistols of the dragoons, but in all other respects with perfect forbearance and propriety.

" After the arms were grounded, and the prisoners saw that the Indians were so orderly, I ordered, ' Right face—Quick march!' and marched them away

from their arms.   All being now safe, I mounted my
horse and rode forward to Major De Haren, and asked
him if he had any special order for me.   For the first
time that day he spoke civilly to me, and requested
me to ride on and join Colonel Bœrstler and his
friend, Dr. Young, and conduct them to De Cou's
house."

The kindly intercourse between FitzGibbon and the
men he had so recently captured, during this memorable ride, and until they were sent on to Quebec, has
been attributed to the fact that he revealed himself to
them as a Mason.   There is, however, no mention of
this among FitzGibbon's papers, and, knowing the
man from his life and the nobility of his nature, I am
much more inclined to believe it due to the natural
courtesy with which a true soldier and gentleman
would treat a fallen foe.   FitzGibbon made them feel
that they were more the victims of circumstance than
responsible for defeat.

The following are the articles of capitulation made
between Captain McDowell, on the part of Lieut.-
Colonel Bœrstler of the United States Army, and
Lieutenant FitzGibbon, although signed by Major De
Haren, of His Britannic Majesty's Canadian Regiment,
on the part of Lieut.-Colonel Bisshopp, commanding
the advance of the British, respecting the surrender
of the force under the command of Lieut.-Colonel
Bœrstler.   It is taken from the original document,
now in the Canadian Archives.

"First. That Lieut.-Colonel Bœrstler and the force under his command shall surrender prisoners of war.

"Second. That the officers shall retain their horses, arms and baggage.

"Third. That the non-commissioned officers and soldiers shall lay down their arms at the head of the British column and become prisoners of war.

"Fourth. That the militia and the volunteers with Lieut.-Colonel Bœrstler shall be permitted to return to the United States on parole.

"ANDW. McDOWELL,
"*Captain of the U. S. Light Artillery.*

"Acceded to.

"C. G. BŒRSTLER,
"*Lieut.-Colonel comd'g detach't U.S. Army.*
"B. W. DE HAREN,
"*Major Canadian Regiment.*"

The number captured were 25 officers and 519 non-commissioned officers and men, of whom 50 were dragoons, including 30 mounted militiamen; also one 12-pounder, one 6-pounder, two ammunition cars, and the colors of the 14th Regiment United States army.

The Indians killed and wounded 56 men. Colonel Bœrstler was also wounded.

FitzGibbon's force consisted of 46 muskets, a cornet of dragoons, and his own cool effrontery, his reinforcement a captain of the dragoons (Provincial), a sergeant, corporal and 12 dragoons—"the first of our dragoons ever seen in that quarter, and their arrival had an excellent effect upon the negotiations." (Account sent at his request to the late Sir Augustus d'Este.)

"His Royal Highness the Prince Regent was graciously pleased to bestow a company upon me for this service, and the commander of the forces, Sir George Prevost, wrote with his own hand a letter of thanks to me for it." (*Ibid.*)

Lest we should be accused of too highly coloring the account, which undoubtedly reads more like a chapter in a novel than sober history, we give an account taken from an American writer, who made the best of it from a national point of view :

"After the disaster of Winder and Chandler at Forty Mile Creek, Colonel Bœrstler was pushed forward with six hundred men of all arms, dragoons, artillery and infantry, to dislodge a strong picket posted in a stone house about two miles beyond a hilly pass, called the Beaver Dam, seventeen miles from Fort George.

"Arriving at the Beaver Dam, Colonel Bœrstler was surprised by a large body of Indians under the conduct of young Brant and Captain William J. Kerr, numbering about 450 warriors. The battle was maintained for about three hours, the Indians, of course, fighting after their own fashion, in concealment, having apparently surrounded Colonel Bœrstler in the woods.

"Indeed the enemy must have conducted the battle with considerable adroitness, for Colonel Bœrstler, galled on all sides, dared neither advance nor retreat, while the result of every observation was a conviction that he was surrounded by far superior numbers.

" At length, Lieut. FitzGibbon of the 49th (enemy's) Regiment arriving on the ground with forty-six rank and file, sent a flag of truce to Colonel Bœrstler demanding a surrender. After some parleying, the British lieutenant magnifying the number of their troops and pretending to conduct the negotiations in the name of Major De Haren, not forgetting a few occasional suggestions touching the horrors of the Indian massacre, Colonel Bœrstler, having neither reserve to sustain him nor demonstration to favor him, surrendered his detachment as prisoners of war. This battle occurred on the 24th of June, and was a brilliant affair for young Brant, since it was fought by Indians alone, not a single cartridge being expended by the regular troops of the enemy."*

In a private letter from William Kerr (who was Brant's brother-in-law) to Lieutenant FitzGibbon, he gives the number of "the Indians as 250, who were actually retreating when Colonel Bœrstler surrendered to your handful of men."

The following are the official despatches in which the notice of the event was conveyed to headquarters :

"TOWNSHIP OF LOUTH, *June* 24th, 1813.

"SIR,—At De Cou's this morning, about seven o'clock, I received information that about 1,000 of the enemy with two guns were advancing towards me from St. David's. I soon after heard firing of cannon and musketry, and in consequence rode in advance

---

* "Life of Brant," by William I. Thom, 1838. Dearborn & Co.

two miles on the St. David's road. I discovered by the firing that the enemy was moving for the road on the mountain. I sent off Cornet McKenzie to order out my detachment of the 49th, consisting of a subaltern and forty-six rank and file, and closed upon the enemy to reconnoitre.

"I discovered him on the mountain road and took up a position on an eminence to the right of it. My men arrived and pushed on in his front to cut off his retreat, under a fire from his guns, which, however, did no execution. After examining his position, I found it difficult to approach him, there being no wood in front or on the flanks to cover the Indians, and his force (apparently 600) I could not approach. I was here informed that he expected reinforcements. I therefore decided upon summoning him to surrender.

"After the exchange of several propositions between Colonel Bœrstler and myself in the name of Lieut.-Colonel De Haren, Lieut.-Colonel Bœrstler agreed to surrender on the terms stated in the articles of capitulation. On my return to my men to send an officer to superintend the details of the surrender—you arrived.

"I have the honor to be, etc.,
"(Signed)   J. FITZGIBBON,
"*Lieutenant 49th Regiment.*"

The soldier left his brother soldier to continue the account, knowing well that if fairly told the credit due would be given to him. Whether the misstatement in Lieut.-Colonel Bisshopp's despatch to Brigadier-General Vincent was due to him or to Major De Haren, we cannot now ascertain. All that we can find in reference to it in FitzGibbon's papers is the following :

" And here I will state what I believe caused Major De Haren to conduct himself so strangely towards me as he did, namely, his having retreated from the scene of action instead of advancing as I had done; and, afterwards witnessing my success, he felt how the two proceedings might be contrasted, and he hoped thus to give a turn to the passing circumstances which might change their appearance more in his favor than the real facts would do. Other proceedings were afterwards resorted to to rob me entirely of what was due to me on this occasion; but I decline to state them from tenderness to the memory of the officers concerned, who are long since dead. I was, however, afforded an opportunity soon after to plead my cause before Major-General Vincent, Sir James Yeo and Lieut.-Colonel Harvey, and justice was in part done to me in a private letter to Sir George Prevost, for the letter of Lieut.-Colonel Bisshopp to Major-General Vincent, afterwards published, wholly wronged me."

Lieut.-Colonel Bisshopp's letter to Brigadier-General Vincent, now in the Canadian Archives, is as follows :

"BEAVER DAM, *June* 24th, 1813.

"SIR,—I have the honor to inform you that the troops you have done me the honor to place under my command, have succeeded this day in taking prisoners a detachment of the United States army under the command of Lieut.-Colonel Bœrstler. In this affair the Indian warriors, under the command of Captain Kerr, were the only force actually engaged. To them great merit is due, and to them I feel particularly obliged for their gallant conduct on this occasion.

"On the appearance of the detachment of the 49th Regiment under Lieut. FitzGibbon, the Light Company of the 8th King's Regiment, the two flank companies of the 104th under Major De Haren, and the Provincial Cavalry under Captain Hall, the whole surrendered to His Majesty's troops. To the conduct of Lieut. FitzGibbon of the 49th Regiment, through whose address the capitulation was entered into, may be attributed the surrender of the American army.

"To Major De Haren, for his speedy movement to the point of attack and execution of the arrangements I had previously made with him, I am very much obliged.

"I have the honor to enclose the capitulation entered into between Colonel Bœrstler and myself, and a return of prisoners taken, inclusive of wounded, not yet ascertained. I lose no time in forwarding my Staff-Adjutant, Lieut. Barnard, to communicate to you this intelligence. He has been particularly active and useful to me on all occasions. I take this opportunity of mentioning him to you, and beg· the favor of you to recommend him to His Excellency Sir George Prevost, as an active and promising young officer.

" I have the honor to be, Sir,

"Your most obedient servant,

" CECIL BISSHOPP,

" *Lieut.-Colonel Commanding Troops in Advance.*

" BRIGADIER-GENERAL VINCENT,

" *Commanding Centre Division.*"

Tennyson's lines,

> " A lie that is all a lie can be met and fought with
>   outright,
> But a lie that is half a truth is a harder matter
>   to fight,"

might be applied here. The fact of including the
forces under De Haren with the small detachment
under FitzGibbon's immediate command in his report
to the General, leaves (and certainly did make on that
officer's mind) the impression that the combined forces
were present when the negotiations between Colonel
Bœrstler and the British were entered into—not, as
was actually the case, that they arrived *after* the
American general had surrendered at discretion to
FitzGibbon. It will also be remembered that De Haren
reached the scene accompanied only by a colonel of
militia, having in his anxiety outridden his detachment. In fact, FitzGibbon's fear lest his captives
should discover the smallness of his force, is but
another proof that De Haren's had not yet come up.
The situation was aptly described by the late Judge
Jarvis, of Brockville, who was with FitzGibbon at
Beaver Dam: " And when the Yankees *did* surrender,
we all wondered what the mischief he (FitzGibbon)
would do with them." That the " active and promising young officer " must, however, have let something
of the truth out, General Vincent's letter with which
he forwarded Lieut.-Colonel Bisshopp's, suggests :

"FORTY MILE CREEK, *June* 25th, 1813.

"SIR,—I have the honor of transmitting to Your Excellency a report I received from Lieut.-Colonel Bisshopp, commanding the troops in advance, of the success of a skirmish with a strong detachment of cavalry and infantry, advancing with two field-pieces.

"In the vigilance of Lieut.-Colonel Bisshopp, I feel much indebted, and beg leave to refer Your Excellency to his report of the conduct of the officers and men under his command, which is deserving every commendation. I cannot but particularize that of Lieut. FitzGibbon, 49th Regiment, commanding a small reconnoitring party co-operating with the Indians, through whose address in entering into the capitulation, Your Excellency will perceive by Lieut.-Colonel Bisshopp's report, that the surrender of the American detachment is to be attributed. I beg leave to recommend this officer to Your Excellency's protection.

"I have the honor to be, Sir,
"Your obedient, humble servant,
"JOHN VINCENT,
"*Brigadier-General.*"

RETURN OF AMERICAN PRISONERS TAKEN NEAR FORT GEORGE, JUNE 24TH, 1813.

CORPS.	Lieut.-Colonels.	Majors.	Captains.	Lieutenants.	Cornets.	Surgeons.	Sergeants.	Drummers.	R. and F.
Light Dragoons	..	..	..	..	1	..	1	..	19
Light Artillery	..	..	1	1	..	..	2	..	31
6th Regiment Infantry	..	..	1	1	..	..	3	..	54
14th " "	1	..	3	11	..	1	15	..	301
20th " "	..	1	..	..	..	..	..	..	..
23rd " "	..	..	1	..	..	..	4	2	57
Total	1	1	6	13	1	1	25	2	462

OFFICERS' NAMES AND RANK.

Lt.-Col. Bœrstler, 14th Regt.	Lieut. Kerney, 14th Regt.
Major Taylor, 20th Regt.	,, Marshall, ,,
Capt. McDowell, Lt. Artillery.	,, Waring, ,,
,, Macharnie, 6th Regt.	,, Mudd, ,,
,, McKenzie, 14th ,,	,, Murdock, ,,
,, Cummins, ,, ,,	,, Goodwin, ,,
,, Fleming, ,, ,,	,, Clarke, ,,
,, Reach, 23rd Regt.	,, Robinson, ,,
Lieut. Norris, Lt. Artillery.	,, Randall, ,,
,, Shell, 6th Regt.	Cornet Bird, Dragoons.
,, Saunders, 14th Regt.	Surgeon Young, 14th Regt.
,, Arnell, ,,	

(Copy.)   J. HARVEY,
Deputy Adjutant-General.

The history is not complete without a copy of Lieut.-Colonel Bœrstler's letter to General Dearborn, the original of which is in the Canadian Archives:

"TWENTY MILE CREEK, *June* 25th, 1813.

"SIR,—I am permitted to state the misfortune which has befallen myself and detachment entrusted to my care. We proceeded yesterday until near the Beaver Dam, when we were attacked by a large force of Indians, who were reinforced by regulars under Colonel De Haren, while other reinforcements marched in the direction of our rear. The action lasted three hours and ten minutes, during which time we drove them some distance into the wood, but finding our men not equal to that mode of fighting, I changed my position twice during the engagement to get more open ground; but such was the position that the enemy's balls reached us from every direction, while he was concealed. Our ammunition being nearly expended, surrounded on all sides, seventeen miles to retreat, where my force would have constantly diminished, especially after spending our ammunition while the enemy was gathering in from various out-posts; myself, Captain Macharnie, Lieut. Randall, and Lieut. Marshall wounded, I saw that in the ex-hausted state the men were in, that far the greater part, if any, could never reach Fort George, therefore was compelle¹ to capitulate. The officers under my command will state what may be requisite as to my conduct.

[Then follows the same detail of prisoners abridged from the one given above.]

"You will find enclosed articles of capitulation. I have the honor to be

       "Your distressed humble servant,

              "C. G. BŒRSTLER,

                 Lieut.-Colonel 14th.

"MAJOR-GEN. DEARBORN.

"I presume my destination will be Quebec. I beg I may be exchanged as soon as possible."

In the following extract from a letter dated June 28th, 1813, and signed, James J. Fulton, A.D.C., the effect of the capture is mentioned. After reverting to information and maps already sent to him (Sir George Prevost), relative to the position of the forces on the frontier, he adds: "When the western Indians arrive, which we hope will be this evening, the whole, amounting to about five hundred, will be sent to the Four Mile Creek. This movement will totally cut off any supplies that the enemy might receive from this side of the water. Indeed, from anything we learn since Colonel Bœrstler's disaster, they have not dared to send a patrol more than one mile from Fort George in any direction."

General De Rottenburg, who had recently been appointed to the command of the Niagara frontier, also speaks of the effect upon the enemy of the capture of the American general. After lamenting the failure of Sir James Yeo's expedition on the lake, and the consequent impossibility of his attempting to attack Fort George, which, in consequence of the panic the Americans were thrown into by the capture of Bœrstler, and the cutting off of all communication between the garrison and their supplies, or from reinforcements from the land and riverside, had been an easy prey, he adds :

"I have secured the position at Burlington Bay against a *coup-de-main*. That glory hold I must retire to ultimately and maintain myself there until the navy will be enabled to meet the fleet on Lake Ontario. Had Sir James had time to spare to co-operate with the army, Fort George would have fallen, but I do not now possess the means of attacking them on both sides of the river. Lieut. FitzGibbon is a deserving and enterprising officer, and I shall forward your letter to him."

Unfortunately the private letter to FitzGibbon from Sir George Prevost was among the papers the loss of which has given us so much to regret.

CHAPTER VI.

ALTHOUGH FitzGibbon speaks gratefully of the reward for his services at Beaver Dam, reference to Colonel Brock's letter, given in a previous chapter, as well as to the extract below, from the Canadian Archives, betrays the fact that the company "so graciously bestowed upon him" was not unsolicited on his part. In after years he regretted his removal into a colonial regiment. It took him from under the notice of the Commander-in-Chief, and interfered with his success and advancement in the army and as a soldier.

At the time, however, his ambition was satisfied by obtaining a company in a regiment which he knew to have been a favorite, and, to a certain extent, a creation of Sir Isaac Brock's.

"HEADQUARTERS, KINGSTON, *July* 1, 1813.

"SIR,—I have the honor to submit to your Excellency's consideration the copy of a letter from Lieut. Johnson, of the Canadian Fencible Infantry, soliciting to be permitted to resign all pretensions to promotion in the Glengarry Light Infantry, to return to his lieutenancy in the Canadian Fencibles.

"I beg leave to inform your Excellency that Lieut. Johnson, at an early period, resigned his recruiting orders, which were transferred to Lieut. FitzGibbon of

the 49th Regiment, but were afterwards recalled and
restored to Lieut. Johnson at the earnest solicitation
of his father, to the great disappointment and prejudice of Lieut. FitzGibbon, who, in consequence of
this prospect of promotion in the levy, resigned the
adjutancy of the 49th Regiment . . . . ;

"I beg strongly to recommend to your Excellency's
notice the pretensions of Lieut. FitzGibbon of the
49th, from the circumstances above stated, but most
particularly from his ability as an officer of a light
corps, in which line of service he has recently so
eminently distinguished himself." *

It would also appear from this letter that the gift
of such promotion had to be earned by the recipient
in the arduous and often expensive duty of recruiting a certain complement of the men to form the
company over which he was granted the command.

FitzGibbon's pretensions were favorably considered,
and the step in regimental rank given him, but he
did not join the new regiment until January, 1814.
He still retained command of the gallant little band
of the 49th.

On July 3rd, he sent Ensign Winder with a note
from Fort Erie, where he then was, to Chippewa,
bidding him give it to any militia officer he could
find who would assist him in carrying out the plan
it contained.

The following report gives the result:

---

* Letter from Colonel Baynes to Sir George Prevost, Canadian
Archives, 797, page 131.

"CHIPPEWA, *July* 5th, 1813.

"SIR,—For the information of General De Rottenburg, please say that I last evening received a note from Lieut. FitzGibbon, requesting me to assist Ensign Winder of the 49th Regiment, with what militia I could muster, to make a descent about daybreak of this morning upon Fort Schlosser, and bring off what public boats and stores we could find there. I accordingly, in the course of the night, assembled 34, including officers, who, together with Ensign Winder, volunteer Thompson and 6 privates of the 49th, crossed over in three boats and arrived at Schlosser a little after daybreak, and were so fortunate as to surprise the guard, consisting of 2 lieutenants, 1 sergeant, 8 privates, 3 civilians, and 3 of our own subjects, in the public storehouse at and upon the wharf. We found one brass 6-pounder, 57 stand of arms, 2½ kegs of musket ball-cartridges, 6 bulwarks (or musket-proof curtains for boats), 1 gunboat, 2 bateaux, 2 anchors, 20 barrels of salt, 17 casks of tobacco, 8 barrels of pork, 1 barrel whiskey, with some spades, bars and axes—all of which we brought to this place. We left at Schlosser 6 scows, 6 boats (some of them very large), and about 16 tons weight of cannon shot and shells. The scows and boats, from their being immersed in water, we could not bring off nor completely disable. We remained at Schlosser about one hour, during which time no person appeared to oppose us; however, we had scarcely embarked in the last boat, when from 12 to 15 men came to the beach, supposed to be militia or workmen from Patey Mills. They fired about twenty shots of musketry at us, which were returned by our last two boats. No damage was done to any person in the boats, and I believe little hurt was done to the people on shore.

"I have the honor to be, Sir,
"Your most obedient servant,
"THOMAS CLARKE,
"*Lieut.-Colonel 2nd Lincoln Militia.*
"To LIEUT.-COLONEL HARVEY,
"*Deputy Adjutant-General.*"

FitzGibbon had judged correctly in estimating that the celebration of their national festival, the anniversary of the Declaration of Independence, would occupy the enemy and render them less on the alert. When sending Ensign Winder upon this enterprise, he had a twofold object in view. He wished to give his subaltern a chance of distinguishing himself in a separate service, and so draw the attention of the officer in command to him, and obtain his recommendation for promotion. He also intended with the remainder of his party to make a simultaneous raid or attack upon Black Rock, a more important and strongly garrisoned post on the enemy's shores. To his great disappointment, he could not obtain sufficient boats in which to convey his men across the river, and was reluctantly obliged to postpone the intended descent.

Sir George Prevost thought the success at Schlosser of sufficient importance to issue a general order upon it.

Two days later, Lieut.-Colonel Bisshopp informed FitzGibbon that he desired to attack Black Rock, and had asked General De Rottenburg for three hundred men, but could obtain only two hundred.

"Do you think this number sufficient?"

FitzGibbon smilingly replied, "I hope, sir, you will not be offended when I tell you that I am only waiting for boats to make the attack with less than fifty men."

"Then you think two hundred will do," returned the colonel; adding, "You must not attack, but wait until I return with the men, and you shall accompany me."

Colonel Bisshopp came back the following morning. He allowed FitzGibbon to arrange the plan of attack, to lead the advance, and to undertake to cover the retreat should the main attack be frustrated.

At two o'clock on the morning of the 11th, the men embarked. A thick mist lay over the water, making the morning very dark. FitzGibbon's men were in the first four boats. Owing to the darkness and the strength of the current, they were carried farther down than their intended point of landing, and had to pull up about a quarter of a mile on the enemy's side.

Although it was broad daylight, the mist still hung over the river and its shores. Advancing at once, their approach was soon discovered by the one hundred and fifty militiamen occupying one of the barracks, who were under arms to receive them. Rightly judging that Colonel Bisshopp with the main body had been carried farther down the stream, FitzGibbon had recourse to his old tactics to gain time, in order that they might join him.

Leaving his handful of men in the background, trusting that the nature of the mist would magnify their number in the eyes of the enemy, he advanced with his bugler and a flag of truce. He was met by the American commander, Major Hall, with his militiamen close at his back. Speaking in a voice loud enough to be heard by all, FitzGibbon summoned them to surrender. "I see you are all militia, and I do not wish to be killing the husbands, fathers and brothers of your innocent families. You shall all be allowed to retire on parole."

He had scarcely finished, when the men broke their ranks and made off down the hill towards Buffalo as fast as they could run.

"Stop your men, Major Hall," called out Fitz-Gibbon, though secretly delighted at the success of his speech, "this is quite irregular while negotiating under a flag of truce."

"I know it, sir," replied the indignant officer, "but I cannot stop them."

"Then I must detain you as my prisoner," answered FitzGibbon; but upon Major Hall reiterating his inability to "stop his men," he added, "I see it, sir, therefore I will not detain you; you may retire."

Colonel Bisshopp now came up. Eight large boats belonging to the enemy were seized, loaded with two 12-pounders, one 6-pounder, a large quantity of provisions and military stores, and sent over to the

Canadian side in charge of about half his men. The barracks and block-house, sufficient to accommodate five thousand men, were burned, and a schooner also set on fire.

Had Colonel Bisshopp been content with such measure of success, the enterprise had ended without loss, but excited by the unexpected result he refused to listen to FitzGibbon. He wished to carry off four hundred barrels of salt that were piled on the beach.

FitzGibbon knew that the panic caused by his bold words among the American militia would be only temporary—the light of the burning buildings would discover the small number of the attacking party, and unless they put the river speedily between them and the enemy the result would be fatal.

FitzGibbon never liked to speak of this, and in all his brief accounts of the affair I can find only the following statement regarding this part of it:

"The details of what followed I am unwilling to give, because it would be imputing blame to others and taking credit to myself. I will only add that we remained longer than was needed, and were attacked by a body of militia and Indians. About half of our own force having been already sent back to our own shore with the captured boats, the other half were driven to their boats, leaving behind a captain and fifteen men killed and wounded, and having twenty-seven killed and wounded in our boats. Colonel Bisshopp himself was wounded on shore and carried to a boat. He received two wounds more in the boat, of which he died five days after.

"For no man fallen in battle did I grieve so much as for him. He was a man of most gentle and generous nature, and was more beloved by the militia, over whom he was an inspecting field officer, than any other who served in the province during the war. But he wanted either experience or judgment, and fell in consequence in the prime of life, in the twenty-eighth year of his age."

From other sources, recollections of hearing the story as told by some who shared the enterprise, I have been able to piece together what the soldier could not tell himself.*

The blazing buildings attracted the Indians. The militiamen, ashamed of their panic, when reinforced by Major Parker and the force at Buffalo, returned and attacked the British with irresistible spirit. Fitz-Gibbon, true to his command, endeavored to rally his men and cover the retreat, but the disorder was too great. In the confusion the wounded colonel narrowly escaped being left in the enemy's hands. Some of the boats had already been pushed off, when the cry arose that the colonel was wounded and down. FitzGibbon shouted, "To the rescue!" Then as the men still scrambled for the boats, he called out, "Come, my lads, we'll try for him anyway," and followed by a handful of the devoted "Green 'uns," made a rush and succeeded in rescuing and carrying the wounded

---

* Losing refers to this in his "Pictorial History of the War"—in a note—where he says: "He (Bisshopp) was taken care of by the gallant FitzGibbon and carried to the boats," etc.

officer to the boat. Alas, that the few strokes willing arms plied could not evade the shot which carried death with it.

In reading the few private letters extant, and the scanty allusions to the condition of the army employed on the frontier of Upper Canada during the summer and autumn campaigns of 1813-14, one learns something of the hardships and suffering patiently endured by the men. The breaking down of the commissariat here, as in the other quarters both before and since, was the cause of much unnecessary privation and anxiety on the part of those in command, who, for want of the material and adequate supplies, were unable to take advantage of either their own military success or the blunders of their adversaries. The often heavy loss of life, the cruel carnage, the heap of slain which marked the taking of the enemy's guns, the loss of the hastily erected battery, or a determined stand against the onslaught of the enemy, appear much more terrible under the reflection that had the duty of those at headquarters to furnish the machinery of war been more faithfully performed, much of it might have been saved. When one reads, too, of battles fought and won, of daring deeds done in the face of the foe, victories won against great odds, one scarcely realizes that the report of killed and wounded is more than mere statistics, and is apt to dwell upon the comparison of a small numerical loss with the greater as the chief item of congratulation.

On the contrary, the weary record of men dying singly of fever, exposure, or deprivation of the absolute necessaries of life, due to an inefficient commissariat, acquires an importance out of all proportion to the actual loss. A soldier will understand this. Would he not rather die a hundred deaths in the moment of victory, than one on the lingering, weariful bed of fever in camp?

A touch is given here and there in a private letter, a bitter word of censure levelled against the Commissariat department, of indignation at the apparently wilful ignorance of the situation displayed by the Home Government, or even as near the scene of action as the headquarters at Kingston; a bare fact stated in official despatches, or a sympathetic regret expressed by an officer for the useless sufferings of his men; these are all we have to enable us to judge of the daily life of the soldier watching and waiting on the Niagara frontier.

"On my arrival here I found the troops in great distress for necessaries; shirts, shoes and stockings. Most of the 49th are *literally naked*," writes James J. Fulton, A.D.C. to Sir George Prevost, on June 18th. The italics are his. (Canadian Archives.)

Speaking of the 41st on July 14th, General De Rottenburg says: "That regiment is in rags, and without shoes." (*Ibid.*)

The letters of that date reveal a history of wearisome marches and counter-marches, unceasing vigilance, long watches, miserable worn-out camping necessaries, where there were any at all, and scarcity of provisions and medicine.

The anxiety of the poor settlers, who were also soldiers, to harvest their crops and save the produce of their farms for their own use, their reluctance to sell at any price, necessitated the placing of districts in the immediate vicinity of the headquarters under martial law.

The inefficiency of the officials, who omitted to take stock of the quantity of stores of either food or ammunition; the harassing character of the warfare in the forest; the heat, drenching rains, sickness, and the anxiety of each scattered handful of troops for the safety or success of the others, knowing that the defeat of one added tenfold to the dangers to be incurred by the other; and the mystery and uncertainty in which the intentions of the Commander-in-Chief were shrouded, even to the officers immediately under his command, added to the great distance from their homes and all that life held dear to them, rendered the situation a most trying one for both officers and men to endure with patience.

"For many months past the prospect has appeared so clouded to my imagination, and men and measures so different to those which you and others have so repeatedly expatiated on with sensations of pleasure and confidence, that I have been for months a silent spectator of events which I durst not trust my pen to dwell on. A veil of mystery and seclusion has, alas, but too long been the prevalent feature in this part of the world."*

Sickness decimated the ranks, and the great heat increased the dangers.

"The weather is intensely hot," writes General De Rottenburg from St. David's, 30th of August, in a private letter to Sir George Prevost, "and everybody is more or less affected by it. Colonels Stewart, Plenderleath, May, Williams, FitzGibbon, and a great number of others are laid up with the lake fever. We are in great want of medicine and wine for the sick."

Colonel Plenderleath had been obliged to retire from the outposts at Long Point on July 31st, owing to the great heat, drenching rains, and the sickness among his men.

In the list of the troops to be employed on the south side of the river in the projected attack on Forts Niagara and George, on August 24th, are 350 of the 49th under Major Plenderleath, including the party of Lieut. FitzGibbon.

In the plan of attack, the Light Corps under General Vincent are detailed "to rendezvous at the headquarters at St. David's; a sufficiency of boats and craft to be previously at a convenient place for crossing the river between Lewiston and the Fort. The Voltigeurs, Lieut. FitzGibbon's party and the Indians to cross in the leading boats, and to possess themselves

---

* Extract from a letter written by Major Glegg, 49th Regiment, from camp at Cross, to the Hon. William Dummer Powell, Oct. 8th, 1813.

of the woody, close country near the fort. Major
Plenderleath to attack and possess himself of the
guns and batteries on the bank of the river facing
Fort George."*

There is no record of this carefully planned attack
upon Fort Niagara having been carried out, except
that portion of it under Major Plenderleath, including
Lieut. FitzGibbon's party. The enemy were driven
in to their inner works, and fourteen prisoners taken.
The 49th had two officers and three rank and file
wounded.

The tidings of the defeat of General Proctor at
Moraviantown on the 5th of October, and the probable fate of the remnant of his small but brave force,
made instant retreat imperative.

"My friend General V—— has only one decision
to make, and, if I do not greatly err, his time is very
short. Our sick and baggage are hastening to the
rear, and I hope to God we may follow them to-
morrow," writes one of the bravest and best officers of
the 49th, from camp at Cross, Oct. 8th. "I shall not
consider our retreat safe until we reach Burlington,
and little advantage can arise from remaining there.
I have this instant received a private note from Fort
George, from a source to be depended on, which men-
tions that the Indians have been crossing all morning
to this side, and an attack has been promised by
Major Chapin this night or to-morrow."†

---

* Canadian Archives, 1812, p. 480.

† Major Glegg to the Hon. William Dummer Powell, from camp
at Cross, October 8th, 1813.

That this promise was not kept, the miserable condition of the retreating British force discovered, and a hot pursuit, of more than possible success, made by the American army, was due entirely to the bold front, the vigilance and bravery of the light troops covering the retreat.

On the 14th, Major Glegg again writes to Mr. Powell, from headquarters, Bensley's:

"I am obliged to send you hasty but very important details of our proceedings. Your consideration must make the necessary allowance. We arrived here (Bensley's) on the 12th, after undergoing a very harassing march for our poor fellows, particularly the numerous sick, whose pallid countenances cut me to the quick. The elements were most unkind during our retreat, but anything was pleasing after quitting that sink of disease on the Twelve Mile Creek, where an inactive residence had nearly annihilated as fine a body of men as were ever led against an enemy. Our men are comparatively comfortable in this position. They are all under cover, but of course barns will not last much longer. Considering all things, the casualties of our retreat have been very trifling. Fortunately the enemy did not pursue us. Colonel Murray brought up the rear with the 100th and Light Company of the King's, and he is still at the Forty Mile, merely waiting until the bateaux with the sick have passed it. He will then fall back upon Stony Creek, watching the two roads on the right and left of that place.

"Of our further movements I can give you no certain information at present. A plain statement of our situation has been transmitted to Kingston and

Montreal, and the wisdom of others must decide the ultimate fate of this once efficient army. At all events nothing will be done, unless compelled by the enemy, before our sick are sent off."

According to the records of the 49th, that regiment marched for the Forty Mile Creek on October 2nd, embarked in bateaux for York on October 4th, and re-embarked for Kingston on the 5th, reaching that place on the 11th; yet Major Glegg writes on the 14th, without making any reference to the departure of his own regiment, or of its having been separated from the main body before their retreat from the frontier.

The rest in barracks in the more comfortable quarters afforded them in Kingston was of short duration. When the American army, under the command of General Wilkinson, crossed the St. Lawrence below Kingston early in November, the 49th was brigaded with the 89th and detachments of the Canadian Fencibles and Voltigeurs, the whole under the command of Colonel Plenderleath, and sent to watch the movements of the enemy.

On the 11th, the battle of Chrysler's Farm was fought, but of it FitzGibbon gives no detail. He was still with his old regiment, as he distinctly says that he did not join the Glengarry Fencibles, in which his promotion had given him a company, until January, 1814. He remained with the 49th until that regiment reached Montreal on December 16th, and joined the Fencibles at Kingston, where they were quartered in January, 1814.

CHAPTER VII.

THE campaign of 1814 was begun soon after the opening of navigation. The first important engagement was the attack upon Oswego on May 6th, in which the light companies of the Glengarry Regiment were attached to De Watteville's regiment.

The landing in the face of a shower of grape and round shot, followed by the storming of the hill and capture of the batteries, was a brilliant affair. The Glengarries, who covered the left flank of the troops in the advance, added a share in the honors of one more victory to their former reputation.

The regiment remained stationed in Kingston until early in June, when they were again ordered to York, and in July were sent forward to the Niagara frontier, there to take part in the "most active and severe campaigns of any during the war. But it afforded no opportunity of doing anything individually," writes FitzGibbon. "I was almost constantly employed in the advance, and the Glengarry Regiment forming part of the small brigade under Colonel (now Sir Thomas) Pearson, he was best acquainted with me that summer, and to him I would gladly refer for his opinion of me." *

---

* Letter to Sir Augustus d'Este, May, 1841.

On the 5th of July the enemy, three thousand strong, were repulsed with spirit by a small British force from Fort Mississauga, and Major-General Riall urged the advance of troops from York to enable him to act upon the offensive, "while the militia and Indians are flushed with their success, and their enthusiasm against the enemy is still burning with indignation at the wanton destruction of houses and property at St. David's, every house between Queenston and the Falls having been burned by them."*

Information was obtained from deserters (one of whom candidly acknowledges "a fear of hard fighting" as his reason for deserting) of the advance of the enemy upon Fort George,† seven or eight thousand strong, with heavy guns and mortars; of the building of the batteries at Youngstown and other points to bear upon the forts and prevent the advance of gunboats to their assistance; of the confidence of success which animated the enemy's ranks owing to their superior numbers. This information is conveyed in detail to Major-General Drummond in Major Riall's despatches of this date.

It is not my intention to enter into the details of

---

* Canadian Archives.

† Fort George had been occupied by General Murray when evacuated by McClure on December 12th, 1813, who, on the 9th, had committed the dastardly outrage of burning the town of Newark (Niagara) in order to prevent the British being able to winter in Fort George. Fort Niagara had been taken by assault on December 18th, and a bitter revenge wreaked on the American frontier in retaliation for the burning of Niagara.

the defending force, the weakness of the British, the small garrisons, the sort of make-shifts of guns mounted in Fort George, the anxiety caused by the short-sighted policy of one of our officers in permitting the American Indians to attend a council meeting held by those allied to the British, "thereby arousing much dissatisfaction amongst our Indians and western people."

The delay in the arrival of the much-needed reinforcements created fear lest the ardor of the militia for revenge should cool, or their numbers be decreased by the necessity of returning to their farms to cut the hay receiving damage already from neglect.

Major-General Riall does not exaggerate the situation when he speaks of himself as "being in a very unpleasant predicament." He had not sufficient men or guns at his command to relieve Fort George without endangering the safety of the whole province. He could not proceed against the enemy in one direction without the risk of being outflanked and surrounded on the one hand, or of losing the forts on the other.

Lieut.-Colonel Tucker, who was in command at Fort George, had watched with intense interest and apprehension the great preparations being made by the enemy to attack it. The report of the engineers who had been sent some time previously to inspect the condition of the defences of that important post, was unfavorable. Fort George was not in a condition to withstand a cannonade. The necessity for reinforcements and concerted measures, to enable the

British to attack the enemy before their offensive works were completed, was imminent. The enemy had crossed the River Niagara, had erected and were still erecting further batteries, from which they might attack the fort, or cover their retreat if they were repulsed. Major-General Drummond had pushed on all the force at his command, and was hastening himself to support Generals Riall and Tucker. He had sent on the Glengarry Regiment in advance, and on the 22nd of July we find General Riall again reiterating the necessity of haste and of all available support.

All the details may be gleaned from letters now in the Canadian Archives, but I must endeavor to confine myself as much as is possible to those only in which FitzGibbon is mentioned.

"TWELVE MILE CREEK, *July* 22nd, 1814.

"SIR,—I had the honor to write to you this morning by Captain Jarvis, and enclosed you a letter I had from Lieut.-Colonel Tucker, stating his apprehensions for the safety of Fort George, from the vast preparations the enemy seemed to be employed in making for its reduction, and urging me to advance immediately to its relief. About 3 o'clock p.m., I received a report from Captain FitzGibbon of the Glengarry Regiment, whom I had sent out with a party for the purpose of reconnoitring and gaining information of the enemy's intentions, that he had withdrawn from his position before Fort George, and was again falling back upon Queenston. From the top of the hill over that place, where Captain FitzGibbon was, he was enabled to see his whole force, which was in column extending from near the village to De Puisaye's house.

The waggons and baggage seemed to be halted at Brown's. When Captain FitzGibbon left the hill, which he was obliged to do by the advance of a body of cavalry and riflemen, the column was moving towards St. David's, and when about a thousand centred into that direction, it was halted. Captain FitzGibbon was obliged to retire with his party through St. David's, and was pursued about a mile upon the road leading from thence to this place. I understand some riflemen have advanced to within a mile of the Ten Mile Creek, which is the rendezvous for Lieut.-Colonel Parry's brigade of militia. That officer has been indefatigable in his exertions, and has acquired great influence with the militia. I have directed Lieut.-Colonel Pearson to detach two companies of the Glengarry Regiment to his support, and he has beside a considerable number of Indians with him."—(General Riall to Major-General Drummond, Canadian Archives.)

The battle of Lundy's Lane was one of the hardest fought and most important engagements of the war. Waged at night, in darkness and against a superior force, augmented by relays of fresh troops, it was a hand-to-hand conflict, and nobly did the British hold their ground. The particulars of the struggle have so often been recounted, that I need not dwell upon them here. The Glengarry Regiment had been sent in advance to reconnoitre the American camp at Chippewa, and watch the movements of the enemy. They occupied the high ground near Lundy's Lane, and were given the post they had occupied before—the right wing of the army. At first the principal attack was sustained by the left and centre, but before the close of the engagement the right had their share of the fighting. On the defeat and retreat of the enemy, who were in such haste to return to Fort Erie that they threw the greater part of their camping equipage and provisions into the rapids, the light troops were detached in pursuit.

In General Drummond's report of the battle, he speaks of the Glengarry Regiment as displaying "most valuable qualities as light troops." (Despatches, July 26th, 1814.)

A sharp affair of outposts took place between the pickets of the rival camps before Fort Erie on the 8th of August.

The enemy threw out the whole of his riflemen into the woods for the purpose of driving out the British Indians. At first they appeared to be successful. The Indians retired rapidly on the advance pickets, carrying them with them. The retreat was, however, only temporary. The Glengarry Regiment advanced with promptitude and great spirit, and, being supported by the reserve, the Americans were driven back and the advance post re-established. In this engagement the regiment had two men killed, seven wounded, one taken prisoner and two reported as missing.*

"I cannot forbear," writes Lieut.-General Drummond, from his headquarters camp before Fort Erie, on August the 12th, "taking this occasion of express-

---

*Canadian Archives, 685, page 47.

ing to your Excellency my most marked approbation of the uniform exemplary good conduct of the Glengarry Light Infantry and Incorporated Militia—the former under the command of Lieut.-Colonel Battersby, and the latter under Major Kirby. These two corps have constantly been in close contact with the enemy's outposts and riflemen during the severe service of the last fortnight. Their steadiness and gallantry, as well as their superiority as light troops, have on every occasion been conspicuous." Yet it was just at this time that one of the officers of the Glengarry Regiment asked for leave.

The story of FitzGibbon's marriage has been told so often as a romantic incident of a soldier's life by those who heard it at second or third hand from his fellow-soldiers, that it is difficult to ascertain the correct details of time and distance with sufficient accuracy to put the story into print. I can find no record of it among his papers, yet my readers will readily recognize that a man of FitzGibbon's character would be of all men the most unlikely to tell it on paper, although by a friendly fireside it might be frequently alluded to among those who were his companions in arms at the front.

FitzGibbon was certainly with his regiment during the whole campaign, with the exception of the few days for which, to the astonishment of his colonel, he asked leave, asking without giving any reason for such an apparently unreasonable request. It is safe, perhaps, to say that no other officer but Fitz-

Gibbon would have had such a request granted. His reputation as a capable officer and for great personal bravery stood his friend.*

His word that the need of leave was important to him, that he would return before any decisive battle was fought and his presence required, was sufficient. Permission was given, and the soldier set off to meet his bride.

Despatches were sent to the Commander-in-Chief at Kingston on the 8th of August, and again on the 10th. Whether FitzGibbon was the bearer of either we have no means of ascertaining, but he certainly found some means of sending a private despatch by one or either of them to the girl he was engaged to marry.

---

* Lieut.-Colonel Bullock in his "Operations of the Army under General Wolfe," published in the columns of the *Canadian Loyalist and Spirit of 1812*, Kingston, June 13th, 1844, tells the following anecdote of FitzGibbon apropos of the bursting of shells from the enemy's guns:

"Those shells are very dangerous customers, and yet they sometimes afford amusement, for I remember in August, 1814, Colonel FitzGibbon and myself were on picket together near our batteries before Fort Erie, he with his company of the Glengarry Light Infantry, and I with my Grenadiers of the 41st. The batteries and Fort Erie were exchanging fire. It was a fine summer day, and we were seated on the ground amidst some young second-growth oak trees. FitzGibbon was quoting with great volubility some parts of the 'Rejected Addresses,' when suddenly a shell burst in the air close to us, and my brave friend's tongue received an immediate check, and no wonder, for the fragments of shell made an awful clatter among the trees; we were fortunate enough to remain uninjured, and away went my friend again at the 'Rejected Addresses,' as rapidly as ever. Such is courage."

He bade her meet him in Adolphustown, then an important little town on the road between Kingston and York.*

Landing at the Carrying-place, he rode sixty miles to the church door. On Sunday, the 14th of August, he was married to Mary Haley, by the Rev. George O'Kill Stewart, the Church of England minister at Kingston, by license, in the presence of Gavin H. Hamilton and R. MacKay.

The knot tied, the soldier said farewell to his wife on the church steps, and rode back to keep his word to his colonel.

The condition of affairs on the frontier, hard fighting, privation and sickness being the inevitable order

---

In an editorial column of the same paper from which the above is taken is the following paragraph :

"Under the head of 'Operations of Wolfe's army before Quebec,' the conclusion of which will be found in the first page, there is an anecdote given by the gallant author (C. J. Bullock) which fully bears out the character for resoluteness and *sang-froid* ever attributed to the old Forty-ninther. Those only, however, will feel an interest in the anecdote who have ever seen a shell forced from an enemy into the heart of his own position. They, on the contrary, whose knowledge of the effect of shells is confined to a few field days when men play at soldiers, cannot be expected to understand either the danger to which Colonel FitzGibbon was exposed, or the piquancy of the composure he manifested on this occasion."

* Adolphustown was settled almost entirely by the U. E. Loyalists, who came over from the opposite shore of the lake upon the Declaration of Independence. It boasted of a court house and registrar, and still possesses one of the oldest churches, if not indeed the oldest, in the Province.

of the day; his regiment being always sent to the
front, and the officers exposed to constant danger; the
possibility, indeed, the probability, of an American
bullet finding a billet in his breast, and the girl he
loved being thus left unprovided for, seemed to Fitz-
Gibbon ample justification for such an extraordinary
and romantic step. If he fell, as his widow she would
be entitled to a pension and thus be provided for.

The notes and letters from which I have taken the
principal incidents of FitzGibbon's life were written
after his wife's death; there is no particular mention
of her in them. Always delicate, the tragic death of
one of their sons in 1834 was a blow from which she
never recovered. She died in Toronto, on March 22nd,
1841, and was laid beside her brother-in-law, Simon
Washburn, in St. James' churchyard. His tomb-
stone is still to be seen close under the walls of the
east aisle.

There are two or three fragments of loving letters
extant, written during their rare separations from
each other, but none of any interest to the public.

From several books in my possession, such as the
"Beauties of Hervey," on the fly-leaf of which is
written her name and the words, "From a friend in
the 49th, Quebec," and in ink of a later date, the
initials, "J. F. G.," Mrs. FitzGibbon must have been
a woman of some taste and education. She was not
a society woman, and is only remembered among the
few remaining friends as one whose health kept her
a close prisoner to the house. FitzGibbon always

spoke of her with sadness and loving pity; her eldest
son with the devotion of one to whom she had been
a good mother and a tender dependent charge.

The privations suffered by the troops, the want
of provisions, ammunition and clothing, had begun
to assume alarming proportions by the 18th of
August, 1814.

Constant skirmishes with the enemy, the wanton
destruction of the crops, the harrying of the settlers'
cattle and burning of their barns, stores and mills,
roused the strongest feeling against the Americans,
and kept the force camped before Fort Erie constantly on the alert. The erection of batteries to be
directed against Fort Erie or reinforcements from
the American shore occupied every available man and
moment. The light troops were employed constantly
in the advance to protect the men at work. Early
in September the rain set in with such violence that
the discomfort of the men was much increased. The
roads were rendered almost impassable for artillery.
The enemy had been largely reinforced from the
opposite shores and had an ample supply of ammunition, while the weakened British force were reduced
to counting their rounds and were in hourly anticipation of attack. This was indeed ardently desired
by men and officers alike. Too weak to assume the
offensive, they yet felt themselves equal to resisting
an attack and proving to the enemy that they still
had British soldiers and British pluck against them.

General Drummond speaks about this period of the

campaign, as one "which has been marked by a
series of unlucky circumstances, as well as, of late,
by severe hardships and privations on the part of the
troops, who, I am most happy in reporting, have borne
them with the utmost cheerfulness and have evinced
a degree of steadiness and spirit highly honorable
to them"

FitzGibbon was sent to Kingston in September
with despatches from the camp before Fort Erie,
which resulted in Major-General Stovin being ordered
to Lieut.-General Drummond's support. In a letter
now among the papers buried in the Militia Department at Ottawa, FitzGibbon is spoken of as being in
charge of a convoy with stores and necessaries for the
front. In another and later letter he is addressed
as "in command of the incorporated militia now on
the frontier at Niagara."

There are probably other letters among these buried
records in which FitzGibbon's name occurs, but the
bundles being as yet unsorted, I was not allowed
further access to them.

FitzGibbon accompanied Major-General Stovin
when he joined Drummond on September 17th. On
the 19th, the Americans attacked the batteries so
recently erected by the British, " the fire from which
annoyed them much." (Despatch to Washington.)

The attack was made under cover of a heavy fire
from their artillery, and with their whole force,
amounting to about five thousand men. The state of
the roads and the torrents of rain falling at the time

enabled them to succeed in turning the right of the line of pickets without being perceived. A simultaneous attack being made on the batteries, they penetrated as far as No. 4 picket.

" I myself," writes Drummond, " witnessed the good order and spirit with which the Glengarry Light Infantry under Lieut.-Colonel Battersby pushed into the wood, and by their superior fire drove back the enemy's light troops." (Canadian Archives.)

Lieut.-Colonel Pearson, with the Glengarry Light Infantry under Lieut.-Colonel Battersby, pushed· forward by the centre road, attacked and carried with great gallantry the new entrenchment then in full possession of the enemy. (*Ibid.*) The British line of pickets was again established as it had been before the attack.

The American general, writing from Fort Erie, speaks of this sortie as one " which, as respects hard fighting, is not excelled by any one since the war." The American loss was much greater than the British, the loss of officers being exceptionally great. The situation on the Niagara frontier was critical. The enemy were increasing their force at every point, and had even induced their militia to cross to Fort Erie to the number of three thousand.

Fort Niagara had been so damaged by the incessant rain as to render it unfit to resist an attack. The difficulty of obtaining provisions was increasing. Ammunition was short; the men in need of clothing, many of them in rags, and entire companies without shoes; the roads so bad that the heavy ordnance could not be moved without great difficulty; their camps pitched literally in the water on a swampy ground; the nights growing cold, the early mornings frosty, and sickness increasing; constant vigilance, frequent roll calls, and skirmishes with the enemy harassing the men. The sickness among the troops increased to an alarming extent, while an incessant downpour of thirteen consecutive days rendered the camp a lake in the midst of a thick wood.

The extreme wretchedness caused by these circumstances determined Lieut.-General Drummond to order a retreat towards Chippewa, to about a mile from their present camping-ground, where, "if attacked, better conditions would enable the brave handful of troops which I command to at least have the advantage of fighting on ground somewhat open." (Gen. Drummond's despatch, Sept. 21st.)

The retreat was well executed, disturbed merely by the advance of the enemy's pickets, who were driven back by the British, and the new camp occupied on the 22nd. Here, too, we find the Glengarry Regiment forming part of the advance, in case the enemy "should attempt to penetrate towards Chippewa in force," to "guard and prevent the enemy crossing Black Creek." (Archives, page 268.)

Reports of the enemy having received large reinforcements of regular troops reaching him, General Drummond decided to further concentrate his force behind Chippewa, and with the advance composed of the Light Companies of the 6th, 82nd, and 97th regiments under Major Stewart, the Glengarry Light Infantry, a squadron of the 9th Dragoons, and one gun, the whole under the command of Lieut.-Colonel Battersby, be prepared "to withstand any attack he (the enemy) might make upon the position."

The movements of the enemy and the rumored extent of his reinforcements rendered it prudent to withdraw the defending force yet nearer to Chippewa, although advance posts were still left a little in front of Black Creek. These advance posts were "fifty men of the Glengarry Light Infantry." The remainder of the regiment were stationed at Street's Grove. (Canadian Archives, C. 686.)

"On the evening of the 13th, the enemy advanced to Black Creek, and having effected the passage of that creek during the night, he continued his advance as far as Street's Grove on the following morning, the Glengarry Light Infantry retiring before him with the utmost regularity. A line of pickets was taken up at a short distance in front of the *tête de pont,* and occupied until the morning, when they were obliged to retire into the works before the whole of the enemy's army." (*Ibid.* p. 31.)

The fire from his guns continued the whole day, but at night he retired to his camp at Street's Grove. During the 16th, he continued to deploy columns of infantry in front of the British position at the mouth of the Chippewa, without, however, venturing within the range of the guns. About one o'clock on the 17th, his troops disappeared. Pickets were immediately thrown out, and both cavalry and infantry pushed in different directions to reconnoitre. The enemy had abandoned Street's Grove and retired to Black Creek. The steadiness of the retreat of the Glengarry Regiment, and the position of the British being stronger than they had anticipated, as well as the rumored approach of the British fleet on the lake, were the probable causes of this sudden retreat on the part of the Americans.

On the 18th, a large body moved up Black Creek in the direction of Cook's Mills, on Lyon's Creek. The Glengarry Light Infantry are here again to the front. They, with seven companies of the 82nd, were immediately sent in that direction. Upon the receipt of further tidings of the enemy's force and probable intentions, the 100th Regiment, and the three remaining companies of the 82nd, with one gun, were ordered to join them. With this force, in all about 750, Colonel Meyers was ordered to "feel the enemy very closely."

Colonel Meyers carried out his instructions, and, in his letter to Major-General Drummond, speaks very highly of the conduct of the Glengarry Infantry. "I found the enemy's advance," he writes, "with a strong support, posted on the right bank of a ravine which runs to Lyon's Creek, a small distance from the mills. A part of the Glengarry Regiment turned down a small wood, which covered the front of the enemy, and crossed the head of the ravine, whilst the remainder passed through the wood.   By this movement the enemy's light troops were driven back in admirable style, whilst a part of his force crossed Lyon's Creek for the purpose of annoying our left.   Having chiefly the recognizance in view, and finding that object not to be attainable by a forward movement, from the thickness of the woods, I retired the Glengarry Regiment, and fell back a small distance in the hope of drawing the enemy forth to the open ground, and, if circumstances would justify it, to bring him to a more general action."   (Canadian Archives.)

The force thus coaxed into action or skirmish, from which they suffered greatly, amounted to from 1,500 to 2,000.   "The conduct of the Glengarry Regiment during the campaign has been so conspicuous, that Lieut.-Colonel Battersby and the officers and men of the corps can receive little further praise from any report of mine, but on this occasion I cannot refrain from adding my humble tribute of applause to their earned fame."   (Colonel Meyers' letter.)

This was replied to by a letter to the troops from the Lieut.-General, thanking them for their gallant behaviour.

In the General Orders of October 22nd, the regiment is brigaded with Major-General De Watteville's, and formed at Street's.

The success of Colonel Meyers' reconnaissance resulted in the retreat of the American army.

The American commander, General Brown, had detached two of his regiments to cover his retreat

from Cook's Mills, and so well had the Glengarry
Regiment "felt them" that they retreated in haste to
the shelter of the guns the state of the roads had
prevented their bringing with them, without stopping
to burn the mills, or pausing to hazard the engagement their pursuers were so anxious to provoke.

Falling back over the heights opposite Black Rock,
they crossed over to their own shores, leaving only a
few hundred in Fort Erie. Although General Drummond was able to report all the positions held by the
British troops in good order, he was too well aware
of the critical state of affairs, the want of provisions,
the state of the roads, and the uncertainty of Sir James
Yeo's movements on the lake, to heed the letters from
headquarters urging him "not to let the season pass
without striking some decisive blow."

The retreat of the American army might well have
been construed as a feint to draw the British on, that
by turning their position and outflanking them, they
might obtain by strategy what they had failed to
accomplish by force. The British, however, were too
well aware of the numerical superiority of their enemy
to either imagine such a course necessary or doubt
the reality of their retreat.

General Drummond had faith in his advance pickets,
in the vigilance of his officers, and in the impression
the valor of his light troops had made upon the
enemy.

A rumor reaching the commanding officer that the
enemy were about to evacuate Fort Erie, FitzGibbon

was detached with a small party to reconnoitre at closer quarters.

True to his usual custom of going himself to the front when there was any risk of capture, or the information acted upon being incorrect, FitzGibbon posted his party in the wood, and rode forward alone to within a few yards of the fort. There appearing to be none of the usual signs of activity or life within its walls, he ventured nearer, and entering the fort rode through every part of it.

The enemy had evacuated it only a few hours before, having blown up the works and in every other respect completely dismantled and destroyed it, leaving nothing but ten or twelve kegs of damaged musket ball and cartridge. (Canadian Archives.)

The Glengarry Regiment was destined for York, to be quartered there during the winter, but the movements of the enemy made it necessary to retain a force on the frontier. FitzGibbon's company was stationed at Turkey Point.

Although the war was practically over, the country along the frontier and throughout the Niagara peninsula had been so desolated, and was still in such a defenceless condition, a prey to bands of marauding freebooters, that the Glengarry Regiment had still some exercise for its abilities as light troops, in pursuing these wretches and protecting the inhabitants.

Upon the official declaration of the peace in March, the Glengarry Regiment was stationed at York.

The knowledge of woodland warfare acquired during these two campaigns on the frontier of Canada, bore fruit in after years in a paper written for the advice of his second son, when in 1840 he obtained for him a commission in the 24th Regiment (see Appendix VI.), then serving in Canada.

The "Hints," as he calls the letter, were printed for private circulation among his soldier friends. The following letter from Sir John Harvey, at that time Lieut.-Governor of New Brunswick, is an acknowledgment of one of these sheets:

"GOVERNMENT HOUSE,
"NEW BRUNSWICK, *October* 29th, 1840.

"MY DEAR SIR,—It will always afford me, as it has ever done, very sincere satisfaction to hear of your welfare and of the high degree of esteem and respect which your public and private worth appears to have obtained for you, on the part not only of the authorities under which you have acted, but of the community in which you have lived.

"I have not forgotten, nor am I capable of forgetting, how admirably you justified my selection of you for a difficult and hazardous service—one from the able and successful accomplishment of which both the country and yourself reaped honor and advantage.

"I thank you for the paper you have sent, but more for the warm expression of your friendly goodwishes, and accept mine for yourself and all your family, and believe me very faithfully yours,

"J. HARVEY.

"COL. FITZGIBBON,
"*Toronto.*"

CHAPTER VIII.

BEFORE the disbanding of the Glengarry Fencibles, then stationed at York, in 1816, the Adjutant-General of Militia in Upper Canada offered FitzGibbon a position in his office at £125 per annum.

Although the salary was small, FitzGibbon gladly accepted it. Having no private means to draw upon when extra expenditure was required, the purchase of his uniform and horse, when first appointed to the adjutancy of the 49th, formed the nucleus of debt from which he was not entirely free until within a few years of his death.

Generous, impulsive, and sanguine to a fault, FitzGibbon could take no thought for the needs of the morrow when those possible contingencies were likely to fall upon himself. He could close neither his door, his purse, nor his kindly helpful sympathy to anyone; he would give away his last penny, share his last crust, rather than turn a deaf ear to one in need of either. He used his influence to further the interests of others, without considering for a moment that he was thereby jeopardizing his own. His sanguine temperament always brightened the distant horizon, although the clouds overhead might be black and lowering. Simple in his living, of great physical strength and sound health, his creed was comprised in the brief maxim, "Trust in God and do good to your neighbor." Full of gratitude himself, he had faith in the gratitude of others. Knowing that the country owed him much, he never doubted that sooner or later the debt would be paid. How this confidence was misplaced and the reward of his work denied him, is the saddest part of his biography. Disappointment embittered for a time his warm-hearted, enthusiastic nature. The gradually increasing requirements of a growing family, the accumulation of debt, the petty annoyances of the office, springing from the incapacity or ignorance of those above him, and the absence of generosity on the part of some whom he had served in spite of themselves, fretted his excitable nature almost to the verge of insanity. His self-unconsciousness and frequent disregard of appearances gained him the reputation at one time of being "just a little cracked" in the eyes of the dullards among his contemporaries.

This, however, belongs to a later period of his biography. At present all was hopeful, happy with his wife and young children. Conscious of the value and capabilities of the new country, and of the field it might be made for the exercise of the talents, energies or loyalty of its population; finding plenty to do to occupy his time, and being among the men and friends with whom he had fought for the country of his enforced adoption, FitzGibbon was then fairly content with his position and prospects.

THE OFFICERS' QUARTERS, OLD FORT, TORONTO.

From Photograph by E. Henry.

He lived at this time in a white house within the precincts of the fort, a house which I believe at one time formed part of the barracks. It has often been pointed out to me, as a child, as the house in which his eldest son was born. It is still standing.

In 1819, finding the small salary from the office he held insufficient to support a family, he resigned it and devoted himself to the business of a land agent, which brought in larger returns. He also held the office of Administrator of the Oath of Allegiance.

In 1820, he was appointed one of the Justices of the Peace in the Home District. His name appears frequently in the records of the Quarter Sessions during the succeeding years.

In 1821, he was again offered an appointment in the Adjutant-General's office, but refused to accept it unless the salary was increased to ten shillings a day, that being the sum received by the senior clerks in the other departments.

The. Adjutant-General applied to Sir Peregrine Maitland, and an order-in-council was passed to grant the sum. FitzGibbon then accepted the post, retaining the privilege of administering the oath of allegiance with its attendant fees.

In the following year, 1822, a readjustment of salaries was made in the department. FitzGibbon was raised to the position of Assistant Adjutant-General, but, to his intense indignation, his salary was reduced instead of being raised. The revenue at the disposal of the Provincial Government was small, and in order to increase the salary of the Adjutant-General, a decrease in those of the officials below him was necessary. FitzGibbon was unfortunate enough to be the principal sufferer. Although justly incensed at such treatment, and at the injustice of putting him in a position requiring greater expenditure, while lessening the means of defraying it, FitzGibbon, believing it must be remedied, retained the post.

I have hitherto said nothing of FitzGibbon as a Freemason, although his name is intimately associated with the work of Masonry in Upper Canada. He had been made a Mason in and a member of the military lodge in Quebec, in 1803, when stationed there with Colonel Brock and the 49th. In the minutes of this Lodge No. 40, A. Y. M., held on August 12th, 1813, at Petrie's Hotel, Quebec, is the following congratulatory notice of FitzGibbon's success at Beaver Dam :

" The recent events that bear testimony of the professional abilities of Lieut. FitzGibbon of the 49th Regiment, will be duly appreciated by his country, and the soldier receive a recompense worthy of the laurels he has earned.

" All that concerns the reputation or interest of a brother Mason merits the attention of the fraternity in general, and becomes more immediately interesting to that Masonic Lodge to which he may have belonged. The members of Lodge No. 40 feel that they are called upon to express their admiration of the judgment and bravery of Lieut. FitzGibbon, who they have had the satisfaction of taking by the hand as a member of their society, and they unanimously desire he will accept their fervent wishes that fortune may continue to afford him opportunities which his professional talents and manly character can improve to the advantage of his country and his own reputation.

"Resolved unanimously, that a copy of the foregoing minute, signed by the officers of the lodge, be transmitted to Lieut. FitzGibbon of the 49th Regiment.

"(Signed) THOMAS STOTT, W.W.,
Lodge No. 40.
WM. MCCABE, S.W., *No.* 40.
PIERRE DOUCET, J.W.
WILL. GIBSON, *Secy. No.* 40."

In 1822, when Simon McGillivray, the special craft envoy of the Duke of Sussex, the Grand Master of England, came to Canada to reorganize the craft, which had fallen into a somewhat shattered condition after the death of R.W. Bro. Jarvis, the Provincial Grand Master, he selected FitzGibbon as the Deputy Provincial Grand Master. It was a position of great honor, and his conduct of the affairs of the craft, particularly exemplified in his courteous bearing, his attention to the work and the excellent address which he prepared and gave to the craft, will forever keep his name bright in the annals of the fraternity in this country.

As an instance of his thoughtfulness for his brethren

in the hour of trouble, the story is told, and though, as I have said in a former page, there is no written record of it among his papers, it is one that is generally believed among the fraternity, who possibly have traditional data for it, and there is no reason why it should not be true. It is to the effect that on the day of the surrender at Beaver Dam, FitzGibbon discovered that two of the American officers, Lieut.-Colonel Bœrstler and Dr. Young, were members of a Masonic Lodge in New York city, and for the sake of the brotherhood, which they mutually loved, he displayed towards them after the surrender many kindly courtesies which made that dark day for our American friends less unhappy than it would otherwise have been.

From the advance sheets of " Freemasonry in Ontario," by Mr. J. Ross Robertson, Past Grand Master of the Order, I have been permitted to make the following extracts which refer to the work of Fitz-Gibbon as a craftsman. His letter was written after his acceptance of the office, and the testimonial which accompanied it was one of which he might well be proud. Both the Lieutenant-Governor and his Secretary, Captain Hillier, were members of the craft. They knew the purpose for which the certificate was required, and were satisfied that the fraternity was being placed in good hands under the charge of Fitz-Gibbon.

The labors of years were nearing completion in

the latter days of 1821. With a due sense of the responsibility involved, and an evident appreciation of the honor conferred, Bro. James FitzGibbon, of York, acceded to the request and accepted the nomination of Provincial Grand Master. His letter of acceptance, couched in courteous and fraternal words, was addressed to the Grand Secretary of England. Bro. FitzGibbon writes:

" YORK, UPPER CANADA,
"*December* 8th, 1821.

" *Right Worshipful Sir and Brother*

" Having accepted the offer of a recommendation to the very honorable and responsible situation of Provincial Grand Master in this Province, I do myself the honor of addressing you upon the occasion.

" Although I am not devoid of ambition, I beg to assure you that I am not influenced by that feeling in acquiescing in the wishes of my brethren. I have given their request my best consideration, and have complied with it from a sense of duty and from a feeling of gratitude.

" I am not insensible to the many and important duties which I would assume, and I know that at present I am not well qualified to discharge those duties. But having had some experience of what zeal and perseverance can do, I am emboldened to hope that, with the assistance and kind indulgence of the brethren, my humble efforts in their service may not be altogether unprofitable ; and that by our united efforts the characteristic harmony of the craft will be restored, and the reputation of Freemasonry in this province become not only irreproachable but honorable.

> " I have the honor to be,
>> " Right worshipful sir,
>>> " Your faithful and obedient
>>>> " Servant and brother,
>>>>> " JAMES FITZGIBBON.

" *To* R.W. BRO. EDWARD HARPER, ESQ.,
> " *Grand Secretary, etc., etc., United Grand*
> " *Lodge of England, London.*

" Since writing the foregoing letter it has been suggested to me that some testimonial of my rank and character should be transmitted, to be produced should a question arise on these points. I have in consequence obtained of Sir Peregrine Maitland, our Lieut.-Governor, a certificate which His Excellency has been pleased to grant to me, and which I have the honor to transmit to you herewith.

> " JAMES FITZGIBBON."

That Bro. FitzGibbon stood in high esteem with the official head of the Province of Upper Canada, is attested by the following letter of recommendation :

{ Official Seal
  At Arms. }

" By Sir Peregrine Maitland, K.C.B., Lieut.-Governor of the Province of Upper Canada, Major-General commanding His Majesty's forces therein, etc., etc.

" *To all whom it may concern.*

" GREETING : I do hereby certify that James Fitz-Gibbon, Esq., a captain on half pay, a magistrate in this province and a lieut.-colonel of militia, is a

faithful servant of His Majesty, and of irreproachable character.

"Given under my hand and official seal at York, in
Upper Canada, this twelfth day of December, in the
year of grace one thousand eight hundred and twenty-
one, and of His Majesty's reign the second.

"By His Excellency's command,

"G. HILLIER.

P. MAITLAND."

On April 23rd, 1822 (St. George's Day), FitzGibbon
was in command of the forces representing the militia
of Canada, and assembled before the Government
House to receive the colors ordered to be presented
by His Majesty, in token of his appreciation of, and
gratitude to, the militia for their services in the war
of 1812-14.

Immigration and the necessity of encouraging the
influx of population was then, in 1821, '22 and '23,
as important a question for Upper Canada as it is
to-day for Manitoba and the still unsettled districts
of our wide Dominion.

A number of Irish families from the poorest districts in their own land—well-nigh "wild Irish"—the
majority ignorant of any language but their own
native Celtic, had been sent out under the auspices
of the Roman Catholic Bishop of Upper Canada, and
had been settled on land in the county of Lanark,
where many of them were employed in the construction of the Rideau Canal, not far from the town of
Perth.

Unused to the ways of the country, and coming out, as many do still, with extravagant expectations of fortunes to be made, without the trouble of earning them, and with exaggerated ideas of the privileges and freedom of the New World and absence of the controlling arm of the law,—this with the national animosity of Roman Catholics and Protestants among them, resulted in disturbances and threatened riot.

Alarmed at the aspect of affairs, the magistrates of Perth applied to Sir Peregrine Maitland for a detachment of troops to be sent thither. Before complying with this request the Governor sent for FitzGibbon, with the result that he begged to be allowed to go alone to the district, report upon the condition of affairs, and endeavor to settle the difficulty before calling out the military.

Confident in his knowledge of and influence over his countrymen, FitzGibbon repaired to the scene. He made enquiries and investigated the causes of the disturbance, and reiterated his determination not to resort to arms until all other means had failed. He assured the magistrates that the mere appearance of the military would but serve as a match to kindle the flame, and insisted that not a shot should be fired until he had at least spoken to the belligerents.

Arriving at the spot he jumped down into a cutting, where gangs of these " wild Irish " had struck work and were assembled, one faction headed by a big, broad-shouldered giant, ready for a free fight and broken heads.

Facing them boldly, FitzGibbon poured forth a volley in their own language, the native Irish, and before the magistrates realized what he was attempting, the mob had paused to listen, and when he ceased, both sides cheered him to the echo. He then went among them, made friends of them, explained away misunderstandings, which their ignorance of the country and of English had originated; expostulated with them upon the folly of thinking that any country could be governed, or order, peace or safety to themselves or their property ensured, without the law being enforced and magistrates obeyed, and ended by standing sponsor for them with the authorities for their future good behavior.

The result of his efforts was so satisfactory that such a report was sent to the Colonial Office as obtained him the personal thanks of Bishop Mac-Donell upon the return of the latter to Canada. This was the more satisfactory owing to the fact that before FitzGibbon's visit to the Irish settlement, the report of their riotous behavior had been communicated to the Colonial Office, and Lord Bathurst had written to Bishop MacDonell, then in Rome, on the subject. The settlers having been sent out by his advice, he was to a certain extent held responsible for the result.

Fifteen years afterwards FitzGibbon had also the gratification of receiving from one of the magistrates, who had been the most anxious for the aid of the military, the information that, wonderful as it might appear, not a single instance of riotous behaviour had occurred in that district since his visit in 1823.

In 1826, riots broke out in the township of Peterborough, among the Irish settlements there, and FitzGibbon was sent to keep the peace and restore order. Again was the service accomplished without other force than his personal influence and individual efforts.

An incident occurred in 1866, in Toronto, which illustrates his wonderful knowledge of and power over his countrymen's childlike nature, and the lasting impression his efforts made upon their mind and memory. FitzGibbon's daughter-in-law, a widow, then living in a little cottage on Dundas Road, almost opposite the gates of Rusholme, and one of the very few houses at the time in that neighborhood, was sitting up with a sick child. Probably attracted by the light in the window, a tipsy Irishman forced his way into the house. Throwing himself into an armchair, he noisily demanded something to eat. Having no one in the house with her but the children, and unable to eject him forcibly, Mrs. FitzGibbon thought the best means of ridding herself of the intruder was to comply with his demands. The noise made in opening the door of the chiffonniere attracted the unwelcome visitor's attention. He turned his eyes full upon a large half-length portrait of Colonel FitzGibbon in his uniform. Staggering to his feet, the man stared, raised his hand to his cap in military salute, and stammered out:

"Lord Almighty, save us, but it is the Kurnel him-

self. An' is it in any house belonging to himself I'd
be doin' mischief? God bless him, but he saved me
from a bad scrape wanst, an' was a kind frind to me
afther."

Waiving the proffered food aside, the man staggered
out, reiterating alternate apologies for his intrusion
and anathemas against himself for " doin' the loike
furninst the Kurnel's very face, God bless him," until
his uncertain steps and muttering accents died away
in the distance, and the grateful old reprobate, who
thus justified his benefactor's faith in the good in
every human heart, went away into the night.

In 1826, FitzGibbon was gazetted Colonel of the
West York Militia Regiment of Canada. His com-
mission is dated the 2nd January. In the same year
he resigned both his position as Assistant Adjutant-
General and the Provincial Grand Mastership of the
Freemasons of Upper Canada.

Among his papers I find the following address to
the Orangemen of Perth and Cavan, showing that he
took a lively interest in the men over whom his
influence had been so beneficially exercised. It is
printed, but signed in autograph, and dated York,
June 18th, 1826:

"*To the Orangemen of Cavan and Perth:*

" FELLOW-COUNTRYMEN,—I have recently been informed that the Orange Lodges of Cavan and Perth
intend to march in procession on the 12th of July
next. Having for some years past observed with
increasing anxiety the conduct of the two classes of

our countrymen who have come to reside in this province, I cannot withhold from you an earnest expression of the feelings which have been raised in my mind by this information.

" When the Irish emigrants began to arrive in Canada, the old inhabitants often expressed their fears that the evils so unhappily rooted in Ireland would be transplanted into these hitherto peaceful provinces, and I could not help participating in their fears. I was also afraid that even if party strife were not revived, individual Irishmen would be found more prone to irregular habits than the other immigrants, and such was also the general opinion in this province. I cannot express how great my satisfaction has been to see that my countrymen, individually, are as orderly and well behaved as I could, under all the circumstances, have expected of them, nor have I any fear for the future, except of the evil which may possibly grow out of the proceedings of the Orange lodges.

" The organization of the Protestants into societies for self-defence was in former times, it appears, deemed necessary for their mutual safety; but those times are happily fast passing away, and the wise and good of all parties and of all countries, now recommend to our countrymen to practise forbearance and to cultivate peace and good-will towards each other.

" Without the practice of this forbearance, and the cultivation of this peace and good-will, shall we venture to call ourselves Christians? No, my friends, let us not deceive ourselves, but rather let us humble ourselves before God and pray—fervently pray—for His good grace to guide us in these times of increasing knowledge, and of peace and security. Who will now pretend that your religion, your persons, or your property are in danger? Not one; no, not one, can say so with even a shadow of truth. I cannot now, in this province, see one justifiable reason for your continuing to go abroad in processions, which have ever been considered by your Catholic fellow-subjects as offensive and insulting to them in the highest degree, and which have been regarded by many good and enlightened men as actually unlawful.

"The law, it is true, might suppress these processions; but how much more honorable to yourselves, and pleasing to your friends, would it be for you to follow the example of the lodges in Ireland, who, from a love of peace and a desire to conciliate their neighbors, have generously resolved to give no more offence to them?

"I can assure you that the great body of the Catholics wish you to take this step towards a good understanding with them, rather than to have the law enforced against you, and which, sooner or later, must be enforced, if it should continue to be called for.

"I have copied from a London paper of 30th of March last, several extracts from the speeches of some of your best friends and others in the House of Commons, that you may be made acquainted with their sentiments relative to your processions; and I hope and trust that the reading of these extracts will have upon your minds a similar effect to what they had on mine, namely, to satisfy you that these processions are no longer necessary; that they are insulting to the Roman Catholics, offensive to all your other fellow-subjects, and contrary to the laws of your country and to the laws of your religion, the second (commandment) of which is, that you love your neighbor as yourself. And that you may well understand who your neighbor is, I request you to read the words of our Saviour himself, as written in the tenth chapter of St. Luke, beginning with the twenty-fifth verse and ending with the thirty-seventh, and having done this, kneel and pray to Him to incline all your hearts 'to go and do likewise.' This also is my fervent prayer for you, and not for you only, but for every misguided fellow-being who thinks that he can love God without at the same time loving his neighbor (brother).

"I might urge many excellent reasons to influence your minds upon this question, but I prefer being as brief as I can, and trust to your own good sense, which with reflection will, I have no doubt, supply much that I have omitted.

"I must confess that I am extremely desirous that our differences should be amicably settled by ourselves. Let not our proverbial kind-heartedness be wanting towards each other, else it may become a mockery and reproach to us.

"With this feeling I shall confine my communication to Irishmen, and I wish that no one else be spoken to on the subject. And here I cannot help entreating you to turn your eyes towards Lower Canada, where Protestants, though greatly inferior in numbers, are not oppressed by the Catholics, and where, without any societies, all enjoy peace and live in harmony. If, therefore, the Catholics and Protestants cannot go on in the same manner here, it must be supposed, and I fear it will be said, that it is because they are Irishmen—which Irishmen should certainly be the last to admit—and they ought, therefore, no longer to pursue a course of conduct which must subject themselves to this reproach.

"This communication must be printed, because I cannot possibly spare time to make the number of copies I want, but I will take care that not a copy shall be sent but to an Irishman; and I particularly request that it may be circulated among those only for whom it is intended.

"Let your decision be what it may, I shall ever desire to be the true friend of every fellow-countryman, or, in other words, the friend of all such as I feel you must wish to be—worthy Irishmen.

"JAMES FITZGIBBON."

[EXTRACTS.]

"ORANGE PROCESSIONS.

"Mr. Brownlow, in rising to bring forward the motion of which he had given notice, said he was happy to bring this subject under the consideration of the House. He was anxious that the attention of this House should be drawn to the unhappy state of that country in this age of improvement of commerce, laws, government and trade.

"In the year 1825, the magistrates in the neighborhood of Lisburn were called on, at the instance of the Irish Government, to meet at Lisburn, to take into consideration the steps necessary to be taken in order to prevent the Orange processions on the 12th of July. This was done in consequence of the opinion of the law officers of the Crown as to the illegality of processions. . . . The Orangemen then proceeded to Lisburn, where a serious riot took place. . . . He did not make the present complaint as against Orangemen alone. He never would be ashamed to own that he had been once an Orangeman. The King had not a finer race of subjects, more independent, high-minded, determined, public-spirited, men more determined, in all difficulties and dangers, to do their duty, according to their sense of it, than these Orangemen of the north of Ireland. His motion was against that system which pitted one set of men against another, and stained the green fields of Ireland with blood. Hence, want of employment, burnings, massacres, and that state of irritation which rendered Ireland one immense madhouse of demoniac spirits, one mass ranging themselves under any man of distinction who was disposed to lead them on, and the other willing soldiers of anyone who had the hardihood to be their captain.

"The honorable member concluded by moving for copies of the correspondence which took place between the Lord Lieutenant and four magistrates of the county of Antrim; also copies of the correspondence with the Lord Chancellor of Ireland, and copies of the opinions of the law officers of the Crown.

"Mr. Plunket, the Attorney-General for Ireland, said that the members of the Government of Ireland were all equally disposed to suppress illegal associations of all kinds, both those of Orangemen as well as those connected with the Roman Catholic body. Between all the members of the Government, as well as between himself and his learned friend, the Solicitor-General of Ireland, with whom he differed on the question of Catholic disability as much as it was possible for him to differ with anyone, there existed a sincere determination to destroy all associations of an illegal character. Now, with respect to this particular case, he could only say that both he and his learned colleague had given a decided opinion that these processions were illegal. It had already been determined that the Orange societies were illegal, and it was of necessity a consequence that the processions of such societies were contrary to law. . . . It was his strong conviction that Orangeism was dying away in Ireland. Gentlemen were at length beginning to see the policy of discountenancing these lamentable divisions, and though occasions might occur again for popular excitement, yet, generally speaking, it was his opinion that before long it would subside, if it were not kept alive by vindictive recollections. These were disputes the memories of which ought to be buried.

" Sir John Newport said he had lived to witness many things connected with his unfortunate country, which wrung him to the heart. His right honorable friend had said that Orangeism was on the decay in Ireland. He doubted it. In 1811, when the subject of Orange societies was first brought under the notice of this House, the necessity of suppressing them was strongly urged by Lord Castlereagh, the President of the Board of Control, and almost every member of the Government, but it was answered that parliamentary interference was unnecessary, as party spirit was then declining in Ireland. Gentlemen might expect to see the same results in ten years more time, if something were not done. He earnestly prayed the House, as they regarded the well-doing and tranquility of Ireland, not to be insensible to the mischiefs of these processions. It was their nature to irritate and divide. Who could say that if the memory of the defeat at Culloden had been kept alive offensively by processions, Scotland would enjoy the tranquility with which she is now blest? The thing was impossible. Irritation must follow insult, and those

whose duty it was to extinguish provocation were
responsible for the consequences.

"Mr. Secretary Peel, after making several observations, said that for himself, being known to entertain
strong opinions upon the Catholic question, he could
only say that he had never heard a sentiment of disapprobation expressed, even by the warmest advocates
of the question, with respect to the impropriety of
Orange associations in which he did not most heartily
concur. It was his warmest wish that they were at
an end; and so far as that description of associations
was concerned, he believed they were gradually dis-
solving. With respect to Orange processions, he
agreed with the Right Honorable Baronet that it
would conduce much to the tranquility of Ireland if
they were given up, and he (Mr. Peel) would hold
those men higher who exerted themselves to discoun-
tenance these processions than those others, if any
there were, who gave them encouragement by their
example. If the imposition of law be necessary to
repress them, by all means let it be applied; but if
he (Mr. Peel) were a private gentleman residing in
Ireland, he would try what he could do by influence
and example to discourage them, and in these sentiments the House might count upon his sincerity.

"At a former period he expressed the opinion still
entertained by him, that these societies would yield
to the wishes of Parliament, and that loyalty could
compensate for the mischiefs resulting from the continuance of such societies and proceedings."

FitzGibbon's friendship for others, his interest in
the well-being and well-doing of the younger men
with whom he was thrown, and his prompt action in
interfering in whatever occurred within his cogniz-

ance whenever there appeared the remotest chance of such interference being for good, whether it was any business of his or not, according to the conventional reading of that expression, often led him to interpose where another, possibly more worldly-wise, might have passed by on the other side.

The world has long forgotten, if indeed the present generation has ever heard, the story of the sad quarrel between two young members of two of Toronto's oldest families. Chance threw FitzGibbon in the way at a moment when his interposition and forcible separation of two hot-headed youths, and the placing of one of them under his brother's charge, seemed the right thing to do. Unfortunately the sequel proved that others were less wise. When, however, some years later, garbled accounts of the affair appeared in one of the public prints, FitzGibbon, being appealed to, was able to bear testimony to the truth and exonerate one of the unfortunate actors from unmerited blame. That FitzGibbon was appealed to is evidence of the estimation in which he was held as one whose word, judgment and right feeling could be relied upon, and his integrity of purpose have weight with the public.

On June 8th, 1826, a raid was made upon the printing house of the *Advocate*, a paper published by William Lyon Mackenzie. The door was broken open, the press partially destroyed, and a quantity of the type thrown into the Bay; cases were "pied" and scattered over the floor, the furniture and other contents of the room left in a state of disorder and confusion. Mackenzie was absent at the time, having withdrawn to the other side of the line pending an arrangement with his creditors. The raid was perpetrated by a number of the young men, who, objecting to the utterances of the *Advocate* as disloyal and abusive, took the punishment of its editor and the destruction of the offending print into their own hands. Many of the ringleaders in this press riot were arrested; some of them, through FitzGibbon's active energy and assistance, were tried and heavily fined.

Although FitzGibbon agreed with the justice of the sentence and punishment for breaking the King's peace, he had no sympathy with the Radicals whose disloyal utterances had roused the hot-headed youths in the city into taking the law into their own hands. He might collar them and run them into prison to keep them out of mischief, but when the law punished them by the exaction of a fine, he was one of the first to assist in raising it. Impecunious himself, and unable to give it out of his own pocket, he had no hesitation in using his influence to get it out of those of others. It was but another of the characteristics of his nature. He could condemn the act, and actually sit in judgment upon it, but through his knowledge of human nature and youth, as well as his enthusiastic loyalty to the Crown, could condone the offence, owing to its cause of the provocation.

Mr. Dent, in his "History of the Rebellion in 1837,

is incorrect in saying that "FitzGibbon sympathized strongly with the boys, and regretted the result of the trial, and regarded them as martyrs."

He did nothing of the kind. The boys were justly punished, as all breakers of the peace and destroyers of other people's property should be, but the disloyal utterances of the Radicals provoked it, and it was but an instance, a practical illustration, of young blood being carried away by enthusiastic loyalty, which in later and calmer pulses made men staunch upholders of the British throne.

FitzGibbon volunteered to canvass the town for subscriptions towards discharging the fine. He succeeded in collecting the amount, but the names of the contributors never transpired. The list was burnt the moment it had served its purpose. The Radicals, hearing something of it, endeavored to make capital of it, and rumors were set afloat hinting at the heads of several departments of the Government as contributors, and sneering at the justice in which the judges levied a fine and then contributed to pay it. Collins went so far as to assert that Sir Peregrine Maitland's name headed the list opposite a large contribution.

FitzGibbon had been wise if he had taken no notice of this, but he was an Irishman and could not resist the temptation. In a letter published in the *Freeman* over his own signature, he distinctly declared Collins' assertion to be wholly untrue so far as the Lieut.-Governor was concerned. When Collins was arraigned for libel before Judge Willis, in his address to the bench he accused FitzGibbon of "begging the amount from door to door."

On May 4th, 1827, FitzGibbon succeeded Grant Powell as Clerk of the House of Assembly, being appointed to that office by Sir Peregrine Maitland, and on September 8th, 1828, Registrar of the Court of Probate of Upper Canada.

The salaries from these offices were small. The accumulation of debt and the requirements of his family made it almost an impossibility to confine his expenditure within the limit of such narrow means. The sale of his commission in the army in 1826 had relieved him temporarily from his embarrassments ; but FitzGibbon was one who, holding a public position, lived, to a certain extent, according to it, and not according to the disproportionate salary belonging to it. His correspondence was extensive. His popularity and well-known willingness to help his neighbor without fee or reward, brought many outside duties and responsibilities. His friendship for Sir Isaac Brock's family, and the undying gratitude he felt for his memory, for kindness which no after services of his to any one of his beloved colonel's family could ever repay, brought him the trouble and expense of trustee-ship, executorship, etc., the postage alone such offices entailed being a considerable item of expenditure. Among his papers are many letters acknowledging these efforts, and his generous assistance in managing their business matters.

In 1831, we find FitzGibbon's commission as Colonel

of the 2nd West York Regiment of Militia, ante-dated January 2nd, 1826, and redated March 19th 1831.

Party spirit in the Canadas, and particularly in the Upper Province, ran very high at this period. William Lyon Mackenzie, the talented leader of the party whose radical opposition to the Family Compact and its supporters terminated later in open rebellion, was the publisher and proprietor of the most outspoken radical organ. He was a member of the House, and had spoken forcibly against acts which he considered abuse of the executive power placed in the hands of the Government by the people.

Since the days of "I, Peter Russell, grant to you, Peter Russell" notoriety, members of the House had obtained grants of Crown lands, over which the Executive and not the Legislature held control, to the extent of from five hundred to two thousand acres each, on simply paying the fees exacted by the officials.* This was one of the grievances against which Mackenzie spoke. The grants were perfectly legal, but it was against them as a system which permitted of abuse that he strove. Although Mac-

---

* Grants of land were in the early days of the Province entirely subject to the discretion of the Governor-in-Council. Official dignitaries granted lands to their servants and other dependants, which, as soon as certain requisite forms were complied with, were transferred to themselves. When the Hon. Peter Russell held the office of Lieutenant-Governor of Upper Canada, he is said to have used his power to acquire lands in the manner quoted above.

kenzie was expelled the House on a question of
privilege, an Act was eventually passed to prevent
the alienation of Crown lands as rewards for public
services. How this Act affected FitzGibbon's fortune
will be seen later.

A brief epitome of Mackenzie's case may not be
amiss here, as it will explain FitzGibbon's share in the
events of that date.

While a member, he had at his own cost distributed
copies of the journals of the House, without note or
comment, unaccompanied by the appendix. For this,
as a breach of privilege, he was expelled.

The second time, a libel published in a newspaper,
and of which he acknowledged the authorship, was
made the ground of expulsion.

A third time, the House declared the previous
decisions rendered him incapable of taking his seat.

The fourth time, though unanimously elected, because unopposed, his election was declared void.

The fifth time he was not allowed to take the oath
or his seat, being forcibly ejected from the space below
the bar on a motion to clear the House of strangers,
and finally, after taking the oath, he was again
dragged from his seat by the Sergeant-at-Arms and
condemned to silence under threat of imprisonment.

Mackenzie and FitzGibbon had several passages at
arms over various matters connected with the printing
for the Government, which was done by the former's
printing-house. Some of those were based upon very
small provocation, if we may judge by letters extant,

on such apparently trivial items as the omission of certain blanks in the printed copies of the journals of the House on the score of an infinitesimal economy.

Mackenzie also complained in one of his petitions for redress to the Governor-in-Council, that Fitz-Gibbon had refused to administer the oath to him upon taking his seat, to which FitzGibbon replied by the assertion that he had not done so upon his own authority, nor could he administer the oath to any one on taking a seat that had been declared vacant by the Assembly.

After Mackenzie's second expulsion from the House, the vote being carried by twenty-seven to nineteen, he appealed to the people to resent the outrage as against their constitutional privileges. A sense of the wrong he conceived he had suffered at the hands of the Government goading him into the use of stronger language than he might otherwise have employed, and his eloquence being of a kind which attracted a turbulent class of followers, public feeling on both sides was roused to a height that threatened riot.

A stormy meeting was held in Hamilton on the evening of the 19th March, 1832, at which both sides claimed the victory. An attempt to assault Mackenzie was made the most of by rumor and excited sympathizers, and a meeting called for the 23rd, in York, promised to be a stormy one. The meeting assembled at the court house. Dr. Dunlop and Mr. Ketchum were respectively proposed as chairman, and both declared elected. Dunlop took the chair and the Reformers withdrew and organized an open-air meeting in front of the court house, making use of a farmer's waggon as a platform. When Mackenzie attempted to address this meeting, his opponents were not slow in expressing their antagonism, accentuating it by the material argument of stones and other missiles. The riot soon assumed an alarming aspect, and the sheriff, declaring himself unable to preserve the peace, begged Mr. Ketchum to bring the meeting to a close. Through the diplomatic suggestion that "The friends of the Governor might adjourn to Government House and cheer His Excellency," the attention of many was distracted.

During their absence Mackenzie addressed the meeting, and an address to the King being drawn up, setting forth their grievances, many signed it. Many who had not signed it before went with Mackenzie to the corner of Church and Richmond Streets, where, on tables in the street, four hundred and thirty-eight names were added.

So far I have quoted almost entirely from Mr. Charles Lindsey's "Life of William Lyon Mackenzie." The remainder I may now take from FitzGibbon's papers.

Rumors of the uproar reaching FitzGibbon, and hearing that the mob were not only threatening to burn Mackenzie in effigy, but intended to attack and destroy the office of the offending paper, he hastened to the scene. He found the streets full, the crowd denser and more excited as he approached the print-ing-house. A shot from one of the windows, answered by a volley of stones, was the signal for a general rush upon the building. FitzGibbon forced his way rapidly through the crowd, his height and strength, as well as his being recognized by all as one having authority, assisting his progress. Seizing two of the most excited instigators of the riot by the collar, he dragged them to the gaol close by, and returning took his stand on the steps of the house. Raising his voice that he might be heard above the noise, he called upon all the loyal and true men to aid him in making a stand against the rioters.

Mackenzie demanded that the military be called out. FitzGibbon flatly refused, assuring him that there were enough good men in the crowd to aid him to restore order without the intervention of the military, adding, however, an emphatic request that he (Mackenzie) would retire, as his presence was the chief cause of the disturbance.

"I will not retire, sir," replied Mackenzie, "I have as good a right to be here as you have."

"Very well," cried FitzGibbon, "if you do not I will put you in gaol, too."

"You dare not, I am a member of Parliament," shouted Mackenzie.

He little knew the man he had to deal with. Instead of replying, FitzGibbon proceeded to put his threat into execution and was actually dragging the future rebel to the gaol when two of his friends, also members of Parliament, appeared.

Appealing to them, FitzGibbon begged they would take care of Mackenzie, as he had no wish to imprison him; if they could persuade him to retire, he (Fitz-Gibbon) would protect them while doing so. Then turning to the crowd he called out, "Mr. Mackenzie calls upon me to order out the troops, but I will not insult you by complying with his demand. I will rather call upon you, and you, and you" (indicating individuals in the crowd), "and will find good men enough to ensure the keeping of the King's peace."

This appeal was answered by a shout of approbation. Mackenzie and his friends were then allowed to retire without further molestation. Upon reaching his house, Mackenzie, deceived probably by his immunity from attack while under FitzGibbon's protection, turned and wished to again address the mob. This was no part of the soldier's plan. Taking Mackenzie by the shoulders he put him forcibly but quietly inside and shut the door on him.

The two other members, Messrs. MacIntosh and Ketchum, again begged that troops should be called out, if only to be stationed in the court house during the night, but FitzGibbon was firm. The danger was over for the present, and he would himself incur the responsibility and remain at the court house with a sufficient number of special constables to see that all remained quiet. Apparently satisfied they left him.

A short time after, Colonel Foster, Assistant

Adjutant-General of the Forces in Upper Canada, galloped up and, alighting, desired FitzGibbon to mount and go at once to Government House, where the Lieut.-Governor wished to see him. FitzGibbon obeyed and found Sir John Colborne anxiously awaiting him. The two members, Messrs. MacIntosh and Ketchum, had just applied to him to order out the troops to keep the peace during the night, but before complying with the request the Governor had sent for FitzGibbon to learn if the troops were necessary.

"I pray of your Excellency," replied FitzGibbon, "to do nothing of the kind."

"Had I not better augment the guard on the Bay side, and have men at hand there?"

"Pray do not, sir."

"Well, then," said Sir John, "I will order a picket to be in readiness in the garrison, to turn out at a moment's notice if required."

"For God's sake, sir, do nothing of the kind. Give no order whatever. I am convinced that it is a great object with Mr. Mackenzie and his party to have the troops called out. They have been outnumbered and beaten to-day, and they now desire to have the troops called out, in order that they may be able to proclaim to the Province to-morrow, that "but for the interference of the troops they would have triumphed." No troops were called out, and quiet was maintained without them.

From the reminiscences of an old Upper Canada

College boy I have gathered something of the impression FitzGibbon made upon those about him at the time:

"I first went to college in 1831, my brother Lewis and I being the first sent from this district," writes William Wallbridge, of Belleville. "I remember Col. FitzGibbon well. He was a remarkable-looking man. I remember him in the House, for, not caring much to join my companions in their games, I used to find my way there.

"The Legislative Assembly then held its sittings in the old building opposite the market-place on King Street. I was particularly struck with the Clerk, a tall man, straight, upright, and decidedly military in his carriage, his clear incisive voice and prompt performance of his duties. I frequently met him on the way to the House, at the corner where St. Andrew's Church now stands, his height and soldierly appearance, as well as an eccentric habit he had of carrying his tall hat on the end of his cane, slightly above his head, instead of wearing it, that the air might circulate freely about his head, attracting my attention. His hair was always cut as closely as possible, a fashion more noticeable then than it would be now.

"In 1832, when the cholera was raging in Toronto —(it was bad in '34, but nothing to what it was in '32)—FitzGibbon was the prominent man. It was he who arranged and organized every plan for the care and comfort of the sick, and the decent burial of the dead. He was here, there and everywhere. He was

afraid of nothing, whether in the removal of the sick
to the hospital or in conveying the dead to the grave.
I remember seeing him once with two carts close to
the college, one for the dead, the other for the dying.
He was standing near, and with his own hands assisting in their removal. He seemed to have a charmed
life, to need no rest, and to be as exempt from conta-
gion as he had been from the enemy's fire on the
field of battle. He was not acting under any authority from the Government or city, but solely and
entirely on his own responsibility, and through pity
for the sufferers."*

[The General Hospital was west of the Upper Canada College on Russell Square; and it was opposite
this building, standing, as it does, slantwise to the
street, that Mr. Wallbridge remembered seeing Fitz-
Gibbon attending to the removal of the plague-
stricken people in 1832.]

"Toronto was a different place then to what it is
now. There was not a foot of pavement in the whole
city, except it might be a plank or two set down
between a few doorways. During the spring and
autumn, the streets resembled freshly ploughed fields,
the mud particularly adhesive and heavy.

"I saw FitzGibbon frequently during the years
1832, '33 and '34, and heard all about the political

---

* Dickson, in his "History of Upper Canada College," speaks of
FitzGibbon as "risking his life to labor night and day during the
cholera seasons of 1832 and 1834."

struggles of those days. I was in Toronto when
Mackenzie's meeting was held in the market-place in
1834. A fine new market-house had been built at
that time, with projecting hoods or roofs over the
butchers' stalls. Underneath these hoods great hooks
were fastened, on which the butchers hung their
quarters of beef. The meeting was such an exciting
one that every available place from which to hear
the speakers was crowded, and many of the lads
climbed upon these hoods. The one Geo. FitzGibbon
was on gave way, and in falling he was impaled on
one of the hooks beneath. He lived only a few hours
after he was extricated."

"On the coldest day in winter," writes another old
college boy, Mr. D. B. Read,* "Colonel FitzGibbon
walked into town carrying his hat in his hand. He
had, no doubt, an overheated brain, but it burned in
the right direction. He had uncompromising integrity
and undoubted courage."

FitzGibbon's simple faith that while he was doing
his duty, comprised in the broad creed of "doing good
to his neighbor," he was in God's hands an instru-
ment for His work, carried him safely through scenes
and sights their nervous fears unfitted others to cope
with. Firmness combined with the personal influence
courage gives over weaker minds, as well as the
almost superstitious belief of the poor in his immunity from death, ensured obedience to his direc-

---

*The author of the "Life of Simcoe," "The Four Judges," etc.

tions and reliance upon their efficacy. Excitable and impulsive when irritated by causeless opposition, he was prompt, cool and clear-headed enough in the moment of action to impress with confidence the men he led or the sick he succored. Many a terrified soul went home to its rest in the hope of mercy and forgiveness breathed into the ears of the dying body by the faithful soldier.

FitzGibbon's printed address to the Orangemen in 1826 had helped to induce them to desist from their processions in the public streets. For eight years none of the lodges in Toronto had held any such demonstration. In 1834, however, some recent arrivals from Ireland persuaded them to turn out again. Fitz-Gibbon anticipated the result, and took precautions to lessen the evil, although he could not prevent it altogether.

Early on the morning of the 12th, he called upon Sir John Colborne, Lieut.-Governor of Upper Canada, and communicated his fears to him, and the means he had employed to endeavor to prevent their being realized, reiterating his desire that every effort might be made for peace without the intervention of the military.

FitzGibbon speaks of the riot which occurred as much more serious than that of 1832, and one that required much greater effort on his part to succeed in quelling, although he was ably assisted by several of the magistrates. His greatest satisfaction appears

to have been in the fact that the riot was ended and
quiet restored without having to call out the troops.

It was during these years that Mrs. Jamieson, the
authoress, was in Canada, and became one of Fitz-
Gibbon's most intimate friends. Mr. Jamieson succeeded J. H. Boulton as Attorney-General, and though
unfitted for the post at such a critical period in
the affairs of the colony, was not very fairly treated
by the Government which placed him in that position.
Mrs. Jamieson's reminiscences of Canada in her
" Winter Studies," contain several anecdotes of Fitz-
Gibbon and her interest in " the simple-minded, generous, brave, capable, as well as remarkable man."

FitzGibbon's only daughter and eldest child was
often with the authoress, who was wont to say of
her that " she was one of the most truly ladylike and
aristocratic women she had met in Canada."

FitzGibbon had seventeen children born to him, but
only his daughter and four elder sons lived to grow
up. Of their childhood and the companionship of
their father, many pages might be written.

Knowing the value and advantages of education,
he not only availed himself of every opportunity of
obtaining it for them from outside sources, but
endeavored, by entering into their studies, to make
them practical and entertaining. In his life-book the
definition of a gentleman was, " one who would not
hurt another's feelings by word or deed, but was ever
ready to lend a courteous hand to help in time of
need." His manner was as courteous and kind to the

humblest as to the highest among his acquaintances.
A story told of him, or rather a remark made by one
of his greatest admirers, a canny Scot, to whom he
owed money, goes to show how this pleasant manner
often stood his friend :

"Ay, ay, the Colonel is a fine mon; he'll aye shakit
ye verra kindly by the han', but na word aboot the
pay."

FitzGibbon lived at this date (1831 to 1840) in a
two-storied rough-cast house at the south-west corner of what is now Queen Street and Spadina Avenue.
The house stood a hundred feet, more or less, back
from the road.   Four large willows* grew by the
edge of the roadway before it.   The usual route followed by the colonel to his office, and the boys to
college, was along the shore of the bay.

Upon the morning the new buildings of the college
were opened, the boys were in great haste to set out.
Their father walked with them.   Some of their school-
mates, many of whose names are first on the list of
"old boys" of Upper Canada College, lived in the
opposite direction, east of the college, their route
also being along the shore on the space between Front
Street and the lake, known afterwards as the Esplan-
ade.   Each party catching sight of the other at the
same moment, when about equidistant from the college, the same idea seemed to occur to both.

"Run, boys," cried the colonel, "and we'll beat

---

* These willows have been taken down since 1870.

them." A race ensued, the dignified Clerk of the House racing along with the boys as keenly interested in the result as they were, and no whit behind them in speed.

"And we won, too. We got in first, though by little more than a neck," says one of the boys; "and my father was prouder of that half-dozen steps than if we had beaten by a dozen yards."

In 1832 or 1833, a woman had a small house or shanty built in the rear of the college in McDonnell's field. The house was not more than fifteen feet square. In this she kept a tiny shop or stall for the sale of apples, sugar-sticks and other such school-boy delights, finding her principal customers in the college. Every one of the boys knew the old dame. She was often teased and chaffed by the "young gentlemen," all of which she took in good part, resenting only what she designated as "fine airs."

One day, one of the FitzGibbons apparently offended her in this way. She retaliated by the taunt that "their father was not a gentleman, he having risen from the ranks and was only a common soldier."

Furious with indignation, the boy ran to his father to deny it. Amused, yet knowing the old woman must have had some provocation, FitzGibbon questioned the boy, and learned that he had really been rude and overbearing. On reaching the college the next morning he took the boy to the old woman's stall.

"Good morning, Mrs. ———, I have brought my

lad with me to apologize for his rudeness to you yesterday, that you may believe his father is a gentleman, though he did rise from the ranks, and cannot allow his son to prove himself anything else."

On the 6th of March, 1834, the town of York had its limits extended and was erected into a corporate city, and its original name Toronto restored to it.

There has been much controversy at various times over the origin and meaning of this name, Toronto. I think it is not difficult to find. T-wan-to, pronouncing the letters as if French, is the Ojibeway word for "shelter from wind," virtually "a harbor." The present pronunciation of the word and its consequent spelling is due to the preponderance of the Irish among the residents and legislators, when the name was first pronounced and written by the aborigines' successors.*

On the 15th, a proclamation was issued calling a poll for the election of aldermen and common councilmen on the 27th. In this election the Reformers had the majority, and chose Wm. Lyon Mackenzie as their mayor.

Owing to the necessity of funds for municipal expenses, it was requisite to obtain a loan. To meet this demand of the city treasury, a rate of 3d. in the pound was levied. This was deemed an exorbitant

---

* The name "Toronto" is to be found on old maps of Upper Canada at various points on the lakes, where the Indians sheltered their canoes. (See Bouchette's History of Canada.)

tax, and roused such popular indignation that a meeting was called to enable the corporation to explain the necessity, and give an account of the city debt and required expenditure.

The meeting was a stormy one, and was finally adjourned until the following day, July 30th, to be held in the market-place. This was the meeting referred to by Mr. Wallbridge.

Mr. Lindsey, in his " Life of Wm. Lyon Mackenzie," tells us this " building was a parallelogram, and over the butchers' stalls a balcony to accommodate spectators was hastily run up.

" When the sheriff (Jarvis) was addressing the meeting in support of his vote of censure on the conduct of the mayor, he said:

" ' I care no more for Mackenzie '—then looking about him at a loss for a comparison, he, school-boy like, looked upwards, and seeing a crow flying overhead, added—' than that crow.' "

" This elicited a cheer and a stamping from the crowd on the balcony, many of them mere lads, who naturally turned about to see what sort of crow it was that had come so opportunely to the sheriff's assistance. The hastily built erection strained and collapsed, precipitating the crowd upon it to the ground, breaking limbs and bruising many, and impaling others upon the great hooks of the butchers' stalls beneath."

The last was the unfortunate fate (before alluded to) of FitzGibbon's third son, George, a fine promising lad of sixteen, whose ready wit and brilliant sallies were the life of his school-mates, and whose abilities promised future success at the Bar, the profession to which he had been early destined by his father.

FitzGibbon's grief and horror were great. The boy lived only a few hours, but in such agony that the bereaved father was grateful to see the bright eyes close in death and the agonized limbs at rest.

In 1835, FitzGibbon's eldest son, Charles, left home for the first time. He had studied for the Bar and passed his examination, but a visit to Dublin, where FitzGibbon's father and brothers were then residing, and an offer of a post in an uncle's business there, seemed to promise more speedy returns than the practice of the law in Canada.

The following letter was written upon receipt of the tidings of his son's change of plans:

"MY DEAR CHARLES,—I have but a short time to commit to paper a few items of advice for your future guidance. Attention to some of these has helped me much to conquer the many difficulties which ever beset the path of him who has to ascend by his own unaided exertions.

"Spare no pains to acquire a thorough knowledge of the business in your uncle's establishment, and conduct his affairs as much as you possibly can exactly as you think he wishes to have them conducted. Remember that in proportion as you succeed, you will lighten the burden of his cares and anxieties, and increase his kindness and affection towards you.

"Comport yourself towards your aunt with affectionate deference, even to the minutest attentions, and to the children be affectionate and kind; and be the same to the Martins" [other cousins]. "Confine yourself to the circle of acquaintances to which your uncle will introduce you, and studiously decline every other. For, be assured that it is incompatible with due attention to your business to cultivate society at all while in the early part of your progress.

"Against smoking and against drinking I need not, and against any other vice, I almost flatter myself, I need not warn you. But the passions require to be guarded against with great diligence. I therefore recommend you to fight the battle against them, one and all, at first and in the outset. To keep the high and happy ground of innocence is much more easy than to return to it, if once you take a downward step. I wish I could convey to your mind a part of the impression made on mine by the many melancholy examples I have seen in the army, of young men who could not abstain from what they called pleasure, but which soon brought them to disappointment, misery and a wretched end. Every temptation you successfully resist will strengthen your moral courage, and you will soon find yourself to be of too much value to your parents, to your relatives and to yourself, to become an unworthy and degraded being. Be assured that the Almighty will guide you from usefulness to eminence and happiness, if you carefully and devoutly turn to Him for help and support.

"Attend punctually to the duties of your Church, not for form's sake, or for the approbation of the world, though this is well worth having,—but for strength from above to enable you to resist temptation and to do good. Your good example has already helped to improve your younger brothers, and the continuance of it will still ensure our gratitude to you; but especially for your mother's and Mary's sake and mine, do all you can to make us rejoice in you.

" The last words my father spoke to me, when I first parted from him in Glin were, 'The greatest consolation I have, James, on your leaving me, is that I feel confident you will never do anything to disgrace me.' And you must tell him that I write these words now with tears of satisfaction that I never forgot them, and am sure I never shall, and that I hope the blessing which attended them will be seen to extend to his grandson under his own eyes in his old age. Be to him what my brothers and I were to our grandfather, and may God Almighty bless you all.

" TORONTO, UPPER CANADA,
       " *September* 11th, 1835."

In November of the same year, FitzGibbon's second son was called to the Bar of Upper Canada.

Riotous proceedings having occurred among the laborers employed in the construction of the canal below Cornwall, Sir Francis Head sent FitzGibbon to restore peace among his excitable countrymen. Fears were entertained that advantage would be taken of their antagonism to their French fellow-laborers during the elections of 1836, and more serious trouble be the result.

FitzGibbon was ordered to take fifty stand of arms and ammunition from Kingston to distribute to the local militia in the event of requiring their assistance.

The service was, however, successfully performed,

and the elections, which were important, party feeling
having been excited almost to rebellion by the questions at issue, passed without riots.   As on former
occasions, FitzGibbon trusted to his personal influence, and did not require the aid of the militia.

He was appointed Justice of the Peace for the
Eastern District about this date (June 18th, 1836),
probably in order to give him authority to enforce
the law against the riotous workmen he was sent to
pacify.

When he sold his commission in the army in 1826,
FitzGibbon had purchased eighteen acres of land in
Toronto, on the west side of what is now Spadina
Avenue, and south of Queen Street.   He knew that
Canada was a land of great promise, and time alone
was required to develop her resources.   Toronto was
one of the earliest settled cities, and had a population
whose descendants were likely to reap a rich harvest
from their small sowings.   Knowing this, he considered this purchase one that would in time be an
ample provision for his children and grandchildren,
and was anxious to retain it at all cost to himself.

Dent (in his "History of the Rebellion of 1837")
speaks of FitzGibbon as "a persistent office-seeker."
He was, indeed, active and energetic in mind as well
as body, and was always ready to undertake more
work.   The expenses of living, as well as of carrying
on the various schemes (small though they might be),
that he considered incumbent upon him as a loyal
officer of the Crown and a true subject, required

means to defray their cost, and FitzGibbon doubtless refused no honest opportunity of earning what was required. He held several posts, but the aggregate salary was not a large one.

The following letter from Sir John Colborne, through his Secretary, evidently refers to one of these offices:

" GOVERNMENT HOUSE,
    " TORONTO, *Jan.* 20th, 1838.

" SIR,—With reference to your letter of the 12th inst., I am directed by the Lieut.-Governor to assure you that His Excellency is so fully persuaded of your zeal and active services while he has been in the Province, that he has long been desirous of having an opportunity of conferring on you an appointment which might in some respects be more in accordance with your views and wishes.

" His Excellency thinks it but due to you to express his thanks for your exertions on many occasions in the public service, and to notice the sacrifices which you have made of your time and health, in carrying on the various duties which you have been entrusted to discharge.

" I am also to add that His Excellency will leave a copy of this letter with his successor, in order that your character and services may be made known to him.

" I have the honor to be, Sir,
        " Your obedient servant,
                " W. ROWAN.
" JAMES FITZGIBBON, ESQ."

CHAPTER IX.

THE year 1837 was an eventful one, not only in the history of Upper Canada, but in the life and fortune of our hero.

"It was at once," he writes, in a letter to Sir Augustus d'Este in 1844, " the most successful as well as the most disastrous of my life. What occurred then enabled me to accomplish something towards the saving of the city of Toronto and the overthrow of the rebels—having no thought of reward, other than the saving of bloodshed—and the spontaneous and unanimous vote of my fellow-citizens to reward me for what I had done, roused such hopes of freedom from my pecuniary difficulties that their defeat well-nigh imperilled my reason."

It is difficult for the present generation, brought up under a *régime* of self-government, to understand the system of colonial management as carried on from Downing Street.

To men who had, in the end of the previous century, given up home, friends and property for the sake of loyalty to the Crown, the defence and maintenance of rights asserted on behalf of their sovereign was the highest of political duties, and they had brought up their children in that faith. In many it fell little short of the loyalty of the Cavaliers to the

Stuarts. Self-government by the people was Round-head, Puritan, Yankee—things they had fought against and fled from.

They sought for property and influence at the hands of the monarch and his ministers, as a reward for their sufferings in his cause and the defence of his American dominions, just as the Cavaliers sought redress of their wrongs and reinstalment in their old rights by Charles II.

To these Loyalists came active British Radicals, such as Gourlay and Mackenzie, while reform was working its way through the times of difficulty and distress which followed the close of the great war, bringing Catholic emancipation, municipal and parliamentary reform in England, and revolution in France.

Many others followed Mackenzie and Gourlay to Canada filled with the same ideas and proud of their success in the old country.

They could boast of no services for the Crown such as those of the U. E. Loyalists. Their sufferings and aspirations had all been for popular rights.

The necessity of opening up and cultivating the wild lands throughout the country, and the encourage-ment offered to emigrants, had brought many settlers from the United States, whose notions of govern-ment had been formed in the Republic.

An alliance between these two bodies against the Loyalists and their leaders in the Family Compact was as inevitable as was the strife which grew up between these opposite forces Downing Street rule was, for the most part, in conformity with the views and wishes of the U. E. Loyalists in Upper Canada, and with the great body of the English-speaking minority in the Lower Province.

Unfortunately Sir Francis Bond Head was not capable of coping with these rival constituents. He was not a military man of any standing or experience, and recognized none of the signs of rebellion patent to those who were, or who were more in touch with the inevitable advance of reform; and when the rebellion, in the imminence of which that "paragon of eccentricity and blundering" (*vide* Bryce) so repeatedly asserted his disbelief, actually broke out, he only added inaccurate statements and boastful accounts of his own over-weening confidence and prowess to the blunders already committed.

FitzGibbon wrote several accounts of the outbreak of the rebellion in Upper Canada, and of Mackenzie's intended (attempted) attack on Toronto in December, 1837. "An Appeal to the People of Upper Canada," published in 1847, is perhaps the most exhaustive as regards his own share in the defence of the city. The "Appeal" was written after successive events had robbed him of the reward voted to him by the unanimous voice of the House of Assembly, and the publication of Sir Francis Head's garbled account in his despatches to the Colonial Office had thrown discredit upon his services and bade fair to "make the colony over which he (Sir Francis) held so brief a rule, little more than a nation of liars."

Stung to the quick by Sir Francis Head's assertions, his entire silence on some points, half-truths on
others ; impetuous, harassed by the difficulties which
his pecuniary circumstances rendered unavoidable,
sick at heart from hopes long deferred, and embittered
by disappointment, FitzGibbon rushed into print
before time had enabled him either to look at the
facts calmly and state them with such diplomatic
tact as might ensure success, or to learn with what
credence the Lieut.-Governor's account would be received.

Had FitzGibbon allowed Sir Francis to fall into the
pit he was so persistently determined to dig for himself, and had taken no precautions against the danger
he knew was imminent; had he merely shrugged his
shoulders and allowed the Lieut.-Governor to take
the responsibility of leaving the city unprepared, and,
when the principal buildings were in flames, and the
rebels armed with the muskets Sir Francis refused to
place at the service of the loyal defenders, had he
then stepped in, and at the cost of valuable lives and
property won a pitched battle, and driven out a
greater number of rebels, he would probably have
been knighted, or had other honors paid him.

To do this, however, was not FitzGibbon's nature.
He had seen too much of the sad scenes of war, knew
too much of its realities, was too generous and noble-
minded to profit by another's folly, to run the risk of
such bloodshed and devastation. He saw on all sides

evidences of the imminence of an outbreak of rebellion against the authorities.

From the year 1815, when Sir Francis Gore, by his policy as Lieut.-Governor of Upper Canada, had sown the seeds of future trouble, FitzGibbon had watched the course of events with interest, and from 1824 with ever-increasing anxiety. He communicated this anxiety to Sir John Colborne in 1834, and was requested by him to carry out one of the suggestions he offered, as a precautionary measure—the formation of a corps of young men in Toronto, ostensibly for the purpose of instruction in drill, that they might be better fitted for commissions in the militia when required. The corps was limited to seventy, that being the number of rifles available from the military stores. During the summer months of the three successive years, FitzGibbon drilled these lads twice a week, and in order to encourage them to equip themselves in correct military style, went to the expense of procuring rifle uniforms for himself and eldest son. This might well be called the first military school in Canada.

Perhaps the happiest hours of those years were spent in this labor of love. He was a soldier before everything. He loved the very rattle of accoutrements, and took a genuine pride in the improvement and smartness of his company. He valued drill not only as a means of making a man upright in his carriage, prompt and vigorous in his movements, but as calculated to regulate his mind, strengthen his character for uprightness, honesty, obedience and straightforward simplicity, and draw out latent resource and talent. Add to this the confident expectation that his efforts would not be thrown away, but in the hour of need the time spent in drilling would bear fruit, and we may understand the pride of the soldier in his "boys."

"It may not be irrelevant to observe in conclusion," writes one of the corps, the late Walter Mackenzie, "that your previous instructions assuredly enabled many members of the rifle corps to render efficient service at the critical period in question (the outbreak). For myself, I may assert that my appointment to the command of one of the four principal divisions organized in the Market Square of this place, on Tuesday morning, the 5th of December, 1837, must have arisen from my connection with that body, and that my confidence in assuming the charge was materially increased by finding myself under the guidance of an officer of your ardent zeal and distinguished services." (Letter from the late Walter Mackenzie to Colonel FitzGibbon.)

The tidings of the rising of the French-Canadians in Lower Canada in 1837 added certainty to Fitz-Gibbon's forebodings, and induced him to redouble his efforts to persuade his friends and fellow-citizens to join him in preparing for the like contingency.

That the members of the Government at that date were not only swayed by the opinions and will of the Governor then in office, but were practically governed by him, the light of the present day, thrown upon the events of the past, shows plainly. Where, as in 1837, the Governor was a narrow-minded, self-opinionated and obstinate man, it mattered little of what constituents his council was composed. Good and true men as many were, they were either overruled by the Governor's authority and determination, or silenced by doubt, or fearful of incurring the responsibility of dissension or acting without his authority. In such a man the rebels recognized their most useful ally, and in his obstinate, contradictory nature and his persistent disregard of the advice of the few who saw the probable result of such culpable blindness, able assistants.*

---

*That FitzGibbon was not the only one who endeavored to warn Sir Francis of the threatened danger and urge the need of precautions being taken, is shown by the following extract from a letter written from Cobourg by the Rev. Egerton Ryerson to a friend in Kingston : "You will recollect my mentioning that I pressed upon Sir Francis Head the propriety and importance of making some prudent provision for the defence of the city, in case any party should be urged on in the madness of rebellion so far as to attack it. He is much blamed here on account of his over-weening confidence, and foolish and culpable negligence in this respect."

Again, when telling his brother William of the efforts to induce Sir George Arthur (Sir Francis' successor) to commute the sentence of Lount and Matthews, two of the rebels condemned to death, he repeats : "I also mentioned to the Governor that you and the Rev. J. Stinson had waited on Sir Francis about four weeks previous to the insurrection ; that you informed him of insurrectionary movements about Lloydtown and other places, which you had learned from me ; that you had strongly urged Sir Francis to raise volunteers and put the city and other places in a state of defence ; that

FitzGibbon's way to his office in the Parliament buildings lay, as has been said, along the Bay shore on the stretch of land below Front Street. Here he frequently met Sir Francis Head on his way to walk for exercise on the long wharf near the garrison.

These meetings led to long and animated conversations on many subjects, but chiefly upon the state of the Province and political parties. The Governor's opinions differed greatly from FitzGibbon's on many

---

you and I had waited on the Attorney-General next day, and that we had urged these things on him in a similar manner, but that these statements and advice had been disregarded, if not disbelieved."

Again, after expressing his decided opinion that "punishments for political offences can never be beneficial when they are inflicted in opposition to public sentiment and sympathy," Dr. Ryerson adds: "The fact is, however, that Sir Francis Head deserves impeachment just as much as Samuel Lount deserves execution. Morally speaking, I cannot but regard Sir Francis as the more guilty culprit of the two." (Extract from "The Story of my Life." Ryerson.)

Again, after speaking of the evil effects of Sir F. B. Head's arbitrary conduct upon the country, and the state of dissatisfaction everywhere evident, William Ryerson says: "After all we know but little of the calamities and miseries with which our once happy land is now afflicted, and yet Sir Francis, the most guilty author of this misery, escapes without punishment; yes, with honor and praise. How mysterious are the ways of Providence; how dark, crooked and perverse the ways of men."

Colonel Foster, the Assistant Adjutant-General, also repeatedly urged Sir Francis Head to retain a small regular force in the Upper Province, and he also wrote to Sir John Colborne, representing the mischief that was likely to be the result of the withdrawal of all the military quartered in Upper Canada, particularly Toronto and its vicinity.

important points. Fearful that Sir Francis might think he threw himself in his way, or finding the arguments their conversation often ended in irksome, FitzGibbon, upon seeing him approaching, would sometimes turn aside in another direction, that he might avoid meeting him. Sir Francis, however, frequently called to him, or, if out of reach of his voice, beckoned him with his stick to wait for him.

FitzGibbon has left no details of these morning chats, only the general idea that he, too, took the opportunity of urging upon Sir Francis the great need of making some preparation, or taking some measures to ensure the safety of the city and the prevention of loss of property; and by being in readiness to put down any rising, practically prevent it. FitzGibbon, confident that his fears were not groundless, saw it coming; the Governor, determinedly shutting his eyes, refused to believe it either probable or possible.

When Sir John Colborne asked Sir Francis Head how many of the troops then in Upper Canada he could spare for service in Lower Canada, he answered " All."

When the last detachment, consisting of a sub-altern and thirty men, were on their way from Pene-tanguishene through Toronto, FitzGibbon begged the Lieut.-Governor to keep them in the city, " if only as a nucleus for the militia to rally round."

This he also refused, saying, " No, not a man. The doing so would destroy the whole morale of my policy; if the militia cannot defend the Province, the sooner it is lost the better."

"Then, sir," exclaimed FitzGibbon, "let us be armed and ready to defend ourselves."

"No," replied Sir Francis, "I will do nothing. I do not apprehend a rebellion in Upper Canada."

Six thousand stand of small arms with ammunition had been sent a short time before to Toronto from Kingston, and deposited by the Lieut.-Governor's orders in the market buildings, under the keeping of the civic authorities, the two constables being on guard over them at night. FitzGibbon considered this protection, under the circumstances, insufficient. He called upon and urged Sir Francis to allow him to organize a guard from his rifle corps to prevent any attempt on the part of the rebels to obtain forcible possession.

This offer was also declined, the Lieut.-Governor emphasizing his refusal by the assertion "that were it not that he disliked to undo what he had already done, he would have the arms brought to Government House and entrusted to the keeping of his own domestic servants."

In despair of being able to induce Sir Francis to realize the need of action, FitzGibbon desisted and withdrew. Before reaching the passage he was recalled by His Excellency in person, and requested to "make the offer in writing."

This FitzGibbon was very willing to do, the manner of the request leading him to hope that his offer would then be accepted. His surprise, therefore, may be understood, when the following day's issue of the Toronto *Patriot*, the Tory organ, contained a printed copy of the offer made to His Excellency.

Had FitzGibbon been self-seeking, or anxious only for self-aggrandizement, he might have turned this to his own advantage, but he saw only that Sir Francis used the offer of a guard, for which he had asked in writing, to publish to the Province that he had no fear of rebellion, and to throw odium on the man who urged preventive measures being taken. Although such blindness seems incredible, Sir Francis doubtless calculated to be able in the event of there being no rising, to boast of how much more correctly he had estimated the political situation than the more anxious of his advisers.

But this was not all. Sir Francis not only made an ungentlemanly use of this offer, but, knowing how unlikely it was that a copy of the *Patriot* would ever reach the eyes of the officials at home, he entirely ignored the offer in his despatches to the Colonial Office.

Some little time previous to this, FitzGibbon had been transferred from the command of the 4th Regiment of York Militia to that of the 1st Regiment of the city of Toronto. In this regiment FitzGibbon found many vacancies. True to his nature to do at once work that lay close to his hand, and which he considered from the circumstances required attention, he made out a list of candidates for the vacant commissions and submitted it to His Excellency. Believing it would ensure more speedy consideration being paid to it, he carried the list to Sir Francis personally. The Lieut.-Governor took the paper, read the list it contained and handed it back to FitzGibbon, declining positively to do anything until the following summer. Exasperated by what he thought extraordinary folly, yet unable to act in this manner without authority, FitzGibbon racked his excitable brain to devise means by which to make some preparation, however small, to meet and hold the rebels in check until, when the Governor's eyes were opened by finding them at his door, proper and more effective measures would be taken to defeat them.

It must be remembered that FitzGibbon's popularity, the devotion to him personally he had won from many he had at various times befriended, sympathized with, or saved from getting into trouble or sorrow; the friendly word and kindly smile he had always ready for the most insignificant, his intense individuality, his ready interest in others and the sort of hero worship his daring deeds and reputation had won for him in the minds of the lads of the next generation, put him in possession of means of information which he might act upon but could not betray.

He had also been the first provincial acting Grand Master of the Freemasons in Upper Canada, and though he had resigned that office in 1826, he was still a prominent member of the fraternity. He had lived in neighborly contact with his fellow-citizens for over twenty years. He had been valued and honored by his commanders and superior officers through the war of 1812-14.

He had known York in the days when it was little more than a garrison, and, in consequence of the civil appointments he had held in the intervening years, had not only had the opportunity but the will to know every additional member of the increasing population.

Sir Francis, on the other hand, knew little or nothing of the colony he had been taken from comparative obscurity to govern—knew little in fact of men or politics—had no tact, but was amply provided with insular prejudice, without the knowledge which ennobles it or robs it of an obstinacy of which the only designatory adjective is *pig-headed.* Nor, it may be said, did Sir Francis know anything of FitzGibbon beyond what a man of his limited penetration could learn in the short period of his residence in the Province. The obstinate contradictoriness of his nature resented being argued out of preconceived opinions by a man of FitzGibbon's excitable temperament, and one who made no secret of having risen from the ranks of a line regiment.*

---

* The impression made by FitzGibbon's repeated assertion of this fact has led to many blunders on the part of his biographers, who state that he was "the son of a poor cotter on the Knight of Glin's estate," "of humble origin," etc.—blunders which only careful search among family papers, a visit to the ruins of the old house on the hill above the towers of Glin, and the Knight's corroborative testimony, gleaned from his title deeds and family records, has effectually corrected.

His anxious desire to take some precautionary measures receiving no encouragement, but distinctly the reverse, from Sir Francis Head, FitzGibbon determined upon acting on his own responsibility.

Enumerating the men in Toronto upon whose loyalty he knew he could rely, to the number of 126, and taking the list to Government House, this irrepressible defender of his home showed it to Sir Francis, with the intimation that he "intended to warn each of the men on the list to be in readiness to come armed to the Parliament House, at any hour of the day or night, upon hearing the college bell ring the alarm," and "that he also meant to ask the Mayor of the city to warn all his loyal friends east of Yonge Street to rally to his aid at the City Hall upon the ringing of the cathedral bells."

Pausing for a moment, but not long enough to allow His Excellency to utter the refusal he feared was on his lips, FitzGibbon added: "For the doing of this I desire to have your Excellency's sanction, but permit me to tell your Excellency that, whether you give me leave or not, I mean to do it."

Sir Francis looked at him with indignant surprise as FitzGibbon continued: "I say so with all due respect to your Excellency, as the representative of my sovereign, but you are so convinced that we are in no danger that you will take no precautions; but I, being fully convinced that the danger is most imminent, am determined to take every measure in my power to devise for the protection of my family and friends."

Sir Francis did not reply immediately, but, after a pause of doubt and uncertainty, he at last gave a reluctant consent, much as if it was forced from him by the soldier's determined words.

Whether willingly or unwillingly given, it was still consent. Thanking His Excellency, FitzGibbon withdrew. He went at once to the City Hall, where, in the presence of Alderman Dickson (Dixon?) he communicated the result of his interview with Sir Francis, and asked the Mayor to co-operate with him and undertake that someone should be at hand to ring the bells of the cathedral when warned by the ringing of the college bells.

Sir Francis was not the only one who thought FitzGibbon over-anxious and over-zealous in thus taking timely precautions against surprise by the rebels, who, he knew, were arming and being drilled in the outlying districts about Toronto. When he called upon the Chief Justice he met with something of the same opposition he had received at the hands of the Lieut.-Governor. Upon stating his object and expressing his fears, the Chief said : " Colonel Fitz-Gibbon, I cannot partake of your apprehens'ons, and I am sorry you are alarming the people in this way."

FitzGibbon repeated what he had said to Sir Francis, and again reiterated his determination not to be persuaded by anyone to desist from taking what precaution he could against being surprised by an undisciplined rabble such as he expected the rebel force would be. He, however, yielded so far to the Chief Justice as to agree to warn the heads of families only.

The insurgent forces were gathered, the rebellion broke out, and the college bells rang the alarm before FitzGibbon had time to warn fifty of the one hundred and twenty-six men whose names were on his list.

Although the following letter was written some two years later, I think I cannot do better than insert it here. FitzGibbon never blamed the men who at this time were so incredulous. They had as deep interests at stake as any could have, and would have been as prompt to defend them had they not been blinded by the false security in which Sir Francis had wrapped himself, and apprehended no danger of any actual rebellion. The conduct of the Chief Justice after the event was, however, that of a generous man. It contrasted very favorably with that of the Governor.

(Extract from the letter of Chief Justice Robinson.)

"My Dear Bishop,—I think Colonel FitzGibbon may feel assured that the Government has a just sense of his faithful and valuable services. If I had any doubt of this, I would most readily repeat in writing what I have taken occasion to say to the Secretary of State on that subject.

"During the many years that Colonel FitzGibbon has resided in Upper Canada, his resolute character, his ardent loyalty, and his active and intelligent mind, have led him and have enabled him to render important services to the Government and to the Province, and on several occasions when I think it would have been difficult to find anyone else who could have discharged the same duty so efficiently.

"With regard to his services in 1837, I have no doubt (and I should be happy to state this on every occasion where it could be useful to him) that his earnest conviction before the outbreak that violence would be attempted, and the measures of precaution which he spontaneously took in consequence of that impression, were the means of saving the Government and the loyal inhabitants of Toronto from being for a time at least at the mercy of the rebels; and I believe that the most disastrous consequences would have followed the surprise which Colonel FitzGibbon's vigilance prevented. His conduct also, when the crisis did occur, was most meritorious.

"The Legislature has shown a strong sense of this service, and a great desire to reward it; and I am persuaded that no one would receive more pleasure than the present Lieut.-Governor of Upper Canada and his predecessor, from any measure of Her Majesty's which should have the effect of recompensing Colonel FitzGibbon in such manner as may be most agreeable and useful to himself.

"(Signed)   JOHN B. ROBINSON."

[Enclosed in a note from the Lord Bishop of Toronto, dated London, 83 Sackville Street, 16th August, 1839.]

On Saturday, December 2nd, a man whose name is not given in any of the papers, either printed or in manuscript to which I have had access, came to the Adjutant-General's office and asked to speak with FitzGibbon in private.

At this interview FitzGibbon obtained further information concerning the movements of the disaffected, and of arms being sent from all points to the north of Toronto. He endeavored to persuade his informant to repeat it to the Governor and his Council, but without success. The man declined positively. He had revealed what he had seen and heard to FitzGibbon as to a fellow-mason, and refused to run the risk of losing life or property at the hands of the rebels by permitting his name to transpire. They (the rebels) knew that he had come into town upon urgent private business, and believed it was for that alone he was there. He could not depend upon anyone else keeping his name secret, and if it was betrayed, assassination upon his return, or destruction to his property if he remained in town, would be the inevitable result.

Knowing how much more satisfactory this information would be if delivered first-hand to the Lieut.-Governor, instead of through him, FitzGibbon urged it by every argument he could advance, but only succeeded so far as to induce the man to say where he might be found, if Sir Francis should demand his presence.

The tidings warranted the belief that the outbreak was as imminent as FitzGibbon feared, yet such was the opposition he met with both from the Governor and his assembled Council, to whom he lost no time in communicating it, that the man was summoned and interviewed by Sir Francis and the Attorney-General, and the intelligence discussed for nearly six hours without any definite conclusion being arrived at or any orders issued to meet even a possible emergency.

In vain FitzGibbon urged the necessity of some precautions being taken, some preparation being made to guard against surprise. Neither the Lieut.-Governor nor his Council would consent, the Hon. Wm. Allan alone advocating FitzGibbon's advice being taken.

In reply to Sir Francis' weak objection, that the man's report had not made the same impression on his mind as it had apparently upon Colonel Fitz-Gibbon's, the information he brought being at third and fourth-hand, FitzGibbon reiterated the question :

" ' What impression does it make on the man's own mind ? Has he not seen in a blacksmith's forge bags filled with what he has no doubt are pike-heads ? Has he not seen the handles already made, and the timber prepared for more, which, he was told, were intended for hayrakes or pitchforks ? And has he any doubt at all of the object of all the preparations which he, from day to day, has seen making in the neighborhood ? '

"Whereupon the Hon. Wm. Allan said : 'What would you have, gentlemen ? Do you expect the rebels will come and give you information at first-hand ? How can you expect such information but at second, third or fourth hand ? I am as long in this country as most of you, gentlemen. I know the people of this country as well as most of you, and I agree in every word spoken here to-day by Colonel FitzGibbon, and think that an hour should not be lost without preparing ourselves for defence.'

"After Mr. Allan had done speaking, I turned to His Excellency and said : 'In short, sir, when I came here this morning, I expected that your Excellency would give me leave to go into the streets and take up every half-pay officer and discharged soldier I could find in the city, and place them this very day in the garrison to defend it.'

" To this His Excellency answered : 'What would the people of England say were we thus to arm ? And besides, were we to pass the militia by, they would feel themselves insulted.'

" To which I replied : ' Pardon me, your Excellency ; they would rejoice to see me organize the military to be a nucleus for them to rally round.'

" When I withdrew from this meeting or council, and reflected on all that had passed, I did fear that I should be looked upon by those present as a presumptuous and arrogant man, for I spoke with great earnestness and fervor." ("An Appeal to the People of Upper Canada.")

This meeting was held on Saturday. Nothing was done until Monday morning, when FitzGibbon being sent for, Sir Francis read a militia general order, appointing him Adjutant-General, and ordered him to sign all general orders and documents issuing from the Department as Adjutant-General.

After a moment's hesitation, FitzGibbon declined putting himself into what would be a false position. The law allowed only one adjutant-general, and as Colonel Coffin still held that post, another could not legally be appointed. Reflecting, however, that even the nominal holding of such a position would enable him to do much upon the authority of his office that would otherwise be impossible, FitzGibbon consented, provided the words " Acting Adjutant-General " were allowed to follow his signature. There was another reason for his reluctance to accept this appointment, in the fact that some time previously Sir Francis had questioned him upon the condition of the working of the Adjutant-General's department, and the state of things was such that he had been obliged to report neglect and inefficiency on the part of the official holding that position; and his being a personal friend made it a sin against the *noblesse oblige* of his race to appear to supplant him. Now, however, he saw no alternative but to do so to some extent, or lose the one chance that offered by which he might obtain the power to do what he was so confident the safety of the country required. It was a sacrifice of personal feeling for the benefit of others, the loss of one for the gain of the many. That the friendship between the two men was unbroken by it is but one more proof of the estimation for integrity of purpose and loyalty to the truth in which FitzGibbon was held by friend and foe alike.

Sir Francis consented to the proviso, and immediately prepared a militia general order, appealing to the officers commanding regiments and corps in the Province, and conveying instructions for their guidance in the event of that which FitzGibbon now believed was inevitable—the possible outbreak of rebellion.

FitzGibbon carried a copy of this order to the Queen's printer the same day, but it was not ready for circulation in time to be of much use as a precautionary measure. The outbreak occurred on the night of the same day in which it was placed in the printer's hands.

Though FitzGibbon, in writing of this memorable day, December 4th, has given no positive detail of information obtained which served to increase his apprehensions of the imminence of the outbreak, his actions go to prove that he believed it but a question of hours. Mackenzie had attacked him personally in the columns of his paper, and was probably kept informed by his friends of FitzGibbon's appeals to Sir Francis, as well as of the Lieut.-Governor's refusals to provide against surprise.

On the afternoon of the 4th, the discovery that suspicious-looking characters had been seen lurking about the neighborhood of his house, led FitzGibbon to believe that he might be especially marked for the rebel vengeance.

There is a dim recollection in my mind of a story told me when a very small child—so dim, however, it is, that I do no wish to advance it here as authentic in the remotest degree. If, however, there is even the least foundation of truth in it, FitzGibbon's certainty of the advance of the rebels and their singling him out for especial attention would be explained.

The story was told us in the nursery, and belongs to the treasured traditions of my childhood. One of the young men, returning from an outlying district in the early dusk of the winter twilight, happened to pass by a low house in the northern outskirts of the city. A light in an upper window and the mention of FitzGibbon's name heard through a narrow opening, the sash being raised on a reel of cotton, attracted his attention. He stayed to hear more. His horse's feet making no sound upon the soft, wet grass, the gentle creature, obeying his hand, drew close to the window in silence. Half a dozen men were in close converse in the room, discussing the intended march on Toronto that night, and their confidence of success.

Waiting to hear no more, the lad walked his horse until out of hearing from the house, then hastened into the city to report what he had heard to Fitz-Gibbon. Whether in confidence, or whether the informant was one of his own sons, and he feared the lad's interest and excitement had exaggerated the importance of what he had overheard, and did not wish his name mentioned, my memory fails to recall; the chief item impressed on my childish mind being that some important intelligence was obtained through a window sash propped open with a reel of cotton, and that the rider had such loving control over his horse that he was enabled to ride away undiscovered, and convey the tidings to the colonel.

FitzGibbon merely says that as night approached he became more apprehensive of impending danger, and consequently determined to sleep at his office in the Parliament House until he considered the crisis over. Late in the day he invited several of his friends to spend the evening with him, an invitation readily accepted. Although they might not share his apprehensions, many were willing to share his vigils. FitzGibbon was an excellent *raconteur*, and is frequently spoken of as "one of the most entertaining and amusing men of his day." Few of the men of his acquaintance would refuse to spend the night with him.

About ten o'clock, some other incident occurring, the detail of which he does not give, FitzGibbon deemed it as well to inform His Excellency of his fears for the night, and his intention of remaining at the buildings. He found upon reaching Government House that Sir Francis had retired for the night. Looking back now upon the insistence of the man, one cannot but acknowledge that he must have been regarded as an intolerable nuisance by those who did not share his apprehensions, and this disturbing of vice-regal slumbers a great annoyance.

In vain Mrs. Dalrymple protested that her brother

was fatigued, and that it was hard that he should be disturbed. FitzGibbon insisted, and the Governor came down in his dressing-gown to hear what he had to say, and no doubt returned to his rest in nowise more convinced than hitherto, and possibly in no very amiable mood. An hour later, information was brought to FitzGibbon that the rebels were actually approaching the city in force from the north.

Sending Mr. Cameron, one of his rifle corps, to ring the college bell, FitzGibbon mounted a horse belonging to the House messenger and kept in a stable close at hand, and galloped from house to house in the west end of the city, warning the occupants and bidding them hasten to the Parliament buildings, armed, as the rebels were then approaching the city. The college bells were rung, but the city bells were still silent. Annoyed and anxious lest nothing but a confused, unarmed body of citizens should assemble, to fall an easy prey to the rebels, and knowing that even momentary success would swell the rebel ranks, FitzGibbon rode to the cathedral. Finding the doors still locked, he shouted for someone to run for the keys; then, when to his impatience the messenger seemed long in returning, he called for axes to break open the doors. The keys, however, arrived in time to prevent other means being resorted to; the doors opened and the bells rung, but not until half an hour of what might have been valuable time was lost. FitzGibbon had relied on the promise given him by the Mayor, that the city bells should be rung as soon as the ringing of the college bells gave the alarm.

Giving directions that the cases containing the arms in the City Hall should be opened, and their contents distributed to the men as they came in, Fitz-Gibbon, accompanied by two students, who were also mounted, rode up Yonge Street to ascertain what progress the rebels were making toward the city. Reaching the ravine opposite Rosedale without encountering any rebel force, FitzGibbon began to fear that his alarm was premature, and that he had laid himself open to ridicule by his extraordinary proceedings and excitement. He determined, however, to guard against possible contingencies and carry out his plans. He saw there would be time to place a picket on Yonge Street, to check the expected advance of the rebels, but before turning to retrace his steps, he expressed a regret that he had not a few more mounted and armed men with him, as he might then have ridden on to Montgomery's, the reported headquarters or rendezvous of the enemy, and reconnoitred his position more satisfactorily. The two lads eagerly volunteered to do so, but FitzGibbon was very reluctant to allow them to undertake such a service. One of them, Mr. Brock, had been sent out to Canada and placed under his especial care by his father, Major Brock, who had served with FitzGibbon in the 49th, and had since proved himself a most generous and kind friend.

Not wishing to expose his friend's son to unneces-

sary danger, FitzGibbon at first refused, but the lads
were so anxious and so confident no harm would
happen them, that he at length consented and returned
to the city without them. He had not ridden many
yards before he met Mr. Powell, one of the city aldermen, and Mr. McDonald, the wharfinger, also riding
out to learn what truth there was in the rumors of
rebels mustering at Montgomery's. FitzGibbon hailed
them with satisfaction, begged them to ride on quickly
and overtake Mr. Brock and Mr. Bellingham, and
continued his way, relieved of some of his anxiety
concerning the lads. FitzGibbon's surprise was therefore great upon arriving at Government House a short
time after to find Mr. Powell there before him. Mr.
Brock and his friend had been met and taken prisoners
by the rebels within a few minutes of their parting
with FitzGibbon and Mr Powell, encountering them
directly after, had been summoned to surrender himself also. Instead of complying, he had fired at and
shot their leader, then turning his horse had galloped
back to town. Finding the toll-bar shut, and no one
replying to his shout, fearing pursuit, he had left his
horse and made his way across the fields to Government House, where he found the Governor still in
bed, the clamor of the bells not having disturbed him.
Mr. Powell's report roused him to the reality of the
impending danger, and for the first time he was ready
to take FitzGibbon's advice, though it was only to
dress himself and come with him to the market-place.

While FitzGibbon was thus escorting the Lieut.-

Governor to the centre of defensive operations, the City Hall, Judge Jones, who had grumbled at the over-zeal of FitzGibbon when wakened by his messenger an hour before, had also realized the necessity for action. He had formed a picket, and marched it out to the toll-bar on Yonge Street. Riding thither, FitzGibbon learned that the rebels, alarmed by the fall of their leader and the ringing of the city bells, had returned to Montgomery's. Sentries were then carefully posted. The remainder of the night was spent in arming and organizing the citizens.

One of the first men FitzGibbon had roused when warned of the approach of the rebels was the Assistant Adjutant-General, Colonel Foster. To him, more than perhaps to any other member of the Government, was due the rapid and effective organization of the mass of excited citizens—who had rushed unarmed, and in many cases panic-stricken, to the market-place—into an orderly defensive force.

FitzGibbon speaks in one of his letters of this night as one of the most anxious he ever spent. If we consider the nature of the service required of him, we may realize his anxiety. He had to deal with an excited mob, hastily aroused from their beds, many of them sympathizers with or themselves unavowedly rebels, crowding to the City Hall unarmed, but ready to seize the weapons served out (without any possibility of distinguishing friend from foe), and use them either in attack or defence, whichever side scored the first success and turned the scale; but recently, almost at the eleventh hour, appointed to the command, having no regular soldiers, men who fall into the ranks mechanically at a word and obey orders in silence; with militia regiments insufficiently officered amid the darkness, the clamor of the bells mingled with the excited exclamations of the mob; the panic caused by the flying rumors and exaggerated reports of the extent of the outbreak (rumors circulated by Mackenzie's friends and sympathizers), and the feeling of certainty that if the rebel force struck the first blow with even partial success, hundreds who now appeared loyal would join the standard of revolt. Under such circumstances, we can not only realize FitzGibbon's anxiety, but can understand the value of the few old military officers and men upon whose technical and practical knowledge, as well as loyalty, he could rely.

The militia certainly deserved the chief credit and great praise for service rendered under most trying circumstances, but the assistance of men like Colonel Foster was a large factor in the organization of the people into a force capable of guarding the city. FitzGibbon speaks later of Sir Francis Head's desire to act through the militia rather than through those who had any pretensions to military experience, as if regardless of the injury he must do by neglecting to avail himself of the professional services at his disposal, giving as an instance in point Sir Francis' refusal to accept an officer formerly belonging to the 68th Light Infantry as his aide-de-camp, requesting

that FitzGibbon should send him a militia officer to
act in that capacity on Thursday, December 7th.

This policy of the Lieut.-Governor may in a
measure account for the absence of many names in
the various accounts of that period and the promin-
ence given to the militiamen in the excitement in
Toronto during the first few days of the rebellion in
Upper Canada.

By sunrise on Tuesday, the men were formed in
platoons in the Market Square, the one gun, a 6-
pounder, mounted and loaded in front of the City
Hall.*

Rumors reaching FitzGibbon that the rebels, having
retired to Montgomery's, were felling trees and forti-
fying their position, he rode out to ascertain what
truth there might be in the report. He was accompanied by Captain Halkett of the Guards, Sir Francis'

---

*Extract from William Ryerson's letter to Dr. Ryerson, Decem-
ber 5th, 1837 :

" Last night about twelve or one o'clock the bells rang with great
violence ; we all thought it was the alarm of fire, but being unable
to see any light we thought it was a false alarm, and we remained
quiet until this morning, when on visiting the market-place I found
a large number of persons serving out arms to others as fast as they
possibly could. Among others, we saw the Lieut.-Governor, in his
every-day suit, with one double-barrelled gun in his hand, another
leaning against his breast, and a brace of pistols in his leathern belt.
Also Chief Justice Robinson, Judges Macaulay, Jones and McLean,
the Attorney-General and Solicitor-General, with their muskets,
cartridge boxes and bayonets, all standing in ranks as private
soldiers, under the command of Colonel FitzGibbon." ("Story of
my Life," p. 177.)

aide-de-camp and four others. The rumor was without foundation, the road was open and the position of the rebels such that FitzGibbon felt confident a prompt attack would certainly disperse them without much, if any, loss. Full of this opinion he returned, and going at once to Sir Francis, begged to be allowed to march three hundred of the five hundred men then in the Market Square, with the 6-pounder, to attack the enemy at once. To his surprise and indignation Sir Francis replied: "No, sir, I will not fight them on their ground; they must fight me on mine."

In vain FitzGibbon urged the advisability of making an attack upon the rebels before their number increased. In vain he represented how much less the loss of life and property would be if the rebels were defeated or dispersed before they entered or attacked the city—how much less difficult to surround and defeat them on their own ground, or to defend one entrance to the city, if they should be even partially successful in resisting the attack, than to guard and watch the many approaches by which their most powerful weapon, incendiarism, might enter it.

Sir Francis would listen to none of his arguments or entreaties. Finding that persistence only aroused irritation, FitzGibbon reluctantly desisted.

Tuesday was spent in further preparation. The picket posted by Judge Jones on Yonge Street had been withdrawn in the morning, and as the evening approached FitzGibbon undertook to form another to mount guard during the night.

While selecting and drawing up the men, Sir Francis saw him from a neighboring window, and sending for him demanded, "What are you doing?" Upon FitzGibbon replying that he was forming a picket to place on Yonge Street, he ordered him peremptorily not to send out a man. FitzGibbon urged not only the importance but the absolute necessity of not leaving the road open and unguarded. Sir Francis only reiterated his command.

"We have not men enough to defend the city. Let us defend our posts, and it is my positive order that you do not leave this building yourself."

FitzGibbon protested against such an arbitrary command, but Sir Francis only repeated it. Disgusted at such ignorance, and annoyed that he should be the victim; feeling that he was being treated like a child who had been given a task to do, and then told he was incapable of attempting it, FitzGibbon left the room—not, however, to obey. He was not a man to give up what his knowledge of military tactics and night fighting, as well as the possible designs of the rebel force, such as had flocked to Mackenzie's standard, told him was the right and best course to pursue. The picket posted on Yonge Street was a necessary precaution, and, Sir Francis' commands to the contrary, he meant to so post it. He only did out of His Excellency's sight what he would otherwise have done under his eyes. He formed the picket, placed it under the command of Sheriff Jarvis, marched it out, and posted it himself.

Upon his return, he went directly to Sir Francis, reported himself and told what he had done. Sir Francis rebuked him angrily, but in milder terms than he had expected.

An hour afterwards, when tidings were brought to Sir Francis that the sheriff and his picket had been taken prisoners by the rebels, he turned to FitzGibbon and reproached him bitterly for his disobedience. But the soldier scoffed at the report. The sheriff was no fool; the pickets had been well posted, and directions for their guidance too carefully given for such a result; and though Sir Francis' wrath was somewhat appeased by the arrival of a second rumor that the picket had escaped, FitzGibbon was as incredulous of it as of the first. When, a short time after, Mr. Cameron came from the sheriff to report to the Governor that the enemy had approached the picket, been fired upon and fled, leaving several of their men dead upon the road, Sir Francis acknowledged, by desisting from his reproaches, that FitzGibbon had acted advisedly.

A few minutes later, an anonymous letter was handed to Sir Francis, warning him that the rebels intended to come in before day and set fire to the city in several places simultaneously, in the hope of distracting its defenders or driving them from their positions, especially their stand at the City Hall, where the arms and ammunition were stored.

It was ascertained the following day that the party

driven back by Sheriff Jarvis' picket had been despatched by the rebel leader for this purpose.

Alarmed by this letter for the safety of the spare arms, Sir Francis gave orders that they should be removed to the Parliament Buildings, which, being isolated, were less accessible to an incendiary. There were no wagons or other means of transport available. It was midnight, cold and dark, the roads were bad, and the men weary from watching and excitement.

FitzGibbon knew that if Sir Francis Head's plan of ordering the men to leave their loaded weapons at their posts, shoulder half-a-dozen of the spare unloaded arms and convey them to the Parliament House, was carried out, nothing but confusion and probable disaster would be the result. Uncertain of the loyalty of many of the men armed to defend the city, if opportunity arose of helping the rebels; certain that they were surrounded by spies and sympathizers who would advise their friends of any such proceedings, FitzGibbon opposed the Lieut.-Governor by every argument and persuasion he could think of or advance.

Sir Francis persisted, and remembering how recently his orders had been openly disobeyed, he appeared the more obstinately determined that this one should be executed. FitzGibbon was in despair. He continued to remonstrate, assuring Sir Francis that if he would allow the arms to remain where they were till daylight, he would himself undertake to place reliable men in positions that would enable them to keep the rebels at such a distance as would ensure their safety, for he apprehended the very worst results from such a movement as Sir Francis ordered being made in the dark.

Fortunately at this moment a shout from the street announced the arrival of Col. Macnab, with upwards of sixty men, from Hamilton. Turning to the Lieut.-Governor, FitzGibbon said: "Now, sir, we are safe till morning, for with this reinforcement you can guard every approach to any distance from which we can be injured." Sir Francis yielded, although Fitz-Gibbon had seized upon the arrival more as an argument by which he might gain his point, than because he thought the additional number made any appreciable difference in their security from the fire-brands of the rebels.

The remainder of the night passed without disturbance, and on the following day the arms were transferred to the Parliament Buildings.

During the day (Wednesday) volunteers and militia came in from Hamilton and Niagara by water, and from the country by the eastern and western roads. The city was soon crowded. There was not a sufficient commissariat for the moment, supplies were not conveniently available, the householders had to hide away their provisions to ensure a bare subsistence for themselves, and the danger of a famine was more to be dreaded than any attack from the rebels. It became an imperative necessity to attack them, to defeat their enemies and disperse their friends with the least possible delay.

During the day the Attorney-General met Fitz-Gibbon in the corridor of the Parliament House, and showed him a militia general order appointing Colonel Macnab to the command of the militia in the Home District, to which his (FitzGibbon's) name was affixed. Indignant at finding his name appended to a document he had never before seen, FitzGibbon was about to demand, in no measured terms, who had dared to act for him; but reflecting how important it was that he should not add to the already great difficulties which must arise where such a number of men and officers from all parts of the country had come together, and, without any regular organization, were to march against the common foe, he said nothing.

Night came on and no orders were given by Sir Francis for the attack.

FitzGibbon waited until eight o'clock; then, too anxious and impatient to delay longer, he went to Government House in search of Sir Francis Head, and was told the Lieut.-Governor was at the Archdeacon's.

On returning to his office he met the Hon. William Allan and Mr. Draper. He asked them to go with him to Sir Francis and urge an attack being made on the following morning.

After discussing the matter for nearly two hours without arriving at any conclusion more definite than a promise from Sir Francis that he would give orders to attack the rebels on the following day,

FitzGibbon rose to leave.   Sir Francis had, unknown
to FitzGibbon, promised Colonel Macnab the command.
FitzGibbon, naturally concluding that, as Adjutant-
General and the man upon whom so much had
devolved, he was in command, could not understand
His Excellency's hesitation in giving him the necessary orders.

Now, although his attention was drawn to it by
Mr. Allan, the question was still undecided when he
left to attend to other pressing duties.

After visiting the pickets and guards FitzGibbon
went home.   He had had no rest since Sunday night.
Learning that some suspicious-looking people had
been fired at in the neighborhood of his house, he
deemed it wiser to return to his office, where he slept
until four o'clock on Thursday morning.

Believing that he should eventually be given the
command, he spent the first half-hour on awaking
in drawing a rough memorandum for the attack.   As
it may be interesting to those curious about such
details to give this roughly-sketched memorandum
here, I copy it from the original draft.   It is written
on coarse foolscap and docketed

December 7th, 1837.

ROUGH SKETCH OF DISTRIBUTION FOR THE ATTACK
THIS MORNING:

Colonel Macnab.
Lieutenant Nash......1st Company......Advance Guard.
  "   Coppinge ..2nd   "   ......   "
  "   Garrett....3rd   "   ......   "
Major Draper.
Henry Sherwood.

Two Guns.

Captain Wm. Jarvis.......1st Company......Battalion.
" Campbell..........2nd "
" Nation............3rd "
" Taylor............ 4th "
" Jno. Powell ....5th "
Henry Sherwood...........6th "
Henry Draper ....7th "
Donald Bethune............8th "
Colonel Samuel McLean ....Lieutenant Cox to aid.
Lieut.-Colonel Geo. Duggan.
Major Jno. Gamble.
Judge Macaulay.
Colonel McLean.
" Jones ....For the left Battalion.
" Jno. Macaulay.
Captain Macaulay.
" Durnford.

Artillery.

Captain Mathias.
Major Carfrae.
Captain Leckie.

Dragoons.

Three Companies in front.
One Gun, Major Carfrae.
Four Companies :
The men of Gore, under Colonel Macnab.

One Gun.

Four Companies :
Right flank under Colonel S. Jarvis.
One Company Men of Scarboro' in the woods with
Colonel McLean (Allen).
Left flank under Colonel McLean (Archibald).
Two Companies under Colonel Jones.

Whether or not this disposition of the force was afterwards adhered to, there is no record among FitzGibbon's papers. It may have been altered.

We find when Sir Francis declined to accept the
services of Captain Strachan as his aide-de-camp for
the day, that FitzGibbon sent Henry Sherwood in
his stead, and asked Captain Strachan to remain near
him during the attack upon the rebels.

Trifling as these details appear to us now, they are
indicative of the antagonism and irritating friction
between the two men, as well as finger-posts pointing
out the cause of much misunderstanding. They also
show the influences under which each acted according
to his knowledge or characteristics, or was swayed
by the impulses of the moment.

The question of who should be given the command
was still unanswered. FitzGibbon would not ask it
himself, yet no one else seemed to be moving in the
matter. While in this uncertainty, Judge Macaulay
and the Hon. John Macaulay came into his room,
anxious to learn what were the plans for the day.
FitzGibbon told them what had passed at the Archdeacon's the previous evening, and asked if they
would go to Sir Francis, who was sleeping in a room
near by, and ascertain his wishes. A few minutes
later, FitzGibbon was sent for. He found Colonel
Macnab also by Sir Francis' bedside.

The scene must have been a curious one: the
dishevelled, half-roused Lieut.-Governor resting on
his elbow in the camp-bed, the rival commanders on
either side of him; the two Macaulays, one of them
an old comrade and friend of FitzGibbon's early days
in the country, one who had fought beside him in

the campaign of 1814, and knew his military abilities and reputation, standing by, interested spectators
of the scene. Here, too, was an opportunity for
the exercise of the Lieut.-Governor's fondness for
"rounded periods" and "love of epigram."* He did
not lose it. FitzGibbon says: "He raised himself up
and said that he 'found himself in a painful position,
having as rivals before him two officers of equal zeal,
of equal bravery, and of equal talent, competing for
the command.'"

The last comparison roused our hero's indignation.
Colonel Macnab's pretensions to military knowledge
or talent were drawn from a cadetship of one year,
an ensign's commission for less, and no rank at all in
the militia until after FitzGibbon had held that of
full colonel. No wonder he stepped back and looked
at Sir Francis. The situation was dramatic. One
regrets that some sketch or cartoon of it has not
come down to us from the pen of one or other of the
two witnesses. The result of the interview was a
request from the Lieut.-Governor that FitzGibbon
and the Macaulays would leave him to settle the
question with Colonel Macnab. After waiting half an
hour in the corridor, they were recalled, and told that
Colonel Macnab had released him from his promise,
and the command was given to Colonel FitzGibbon.

Without a single thought or reflection on what

---

* Lord Melbourne's speech in the British House of Commons, on
Sir Francis and the Rebellion.

might be the terms of such a surrender, FitzGibbon
shook hands with Colonel Macnab, and hurried away
to do what he thought had been already delayed too
long—to organize the force for the attack.

FitzGibbon never blamed Colonel Macnab in any
way for this rivalry, if so it can be called—he
but did as he was told. The two men were always
great friends; Sir Francis' extraordinary behavior
roused no jealousy nor caused misunderstanding between them. Although Colonel Macnab received the
honor of knighthood at the hands of Her Majesty
and a sword from the colonists for his share in quelling the rebellion, FitzGibbon was at the time about
to be rewarded in a manner more adequate to his
needs, and the fact that he never received it caused
no more than a passing comparison with Colonel
Macnab's better fortune. That Macnab was equally
generous will be seen later.

Few whose knowledge of Canadian militia is limited
to the fine body of well-drilled men forming any of
our city regiments of to-day, can realize the difficulty
of forming the militia of 1837—many of them but
raw levies from the scattered settlements throughout
the country—into an effective attacking army. The
moment the column marched, FitzGibbon's spirits
rose. He was confident of success—success, too, without much, if any, attendant bloodshed. He had no
doubt but the rebels would fly after a brief resistance,
if they stood their ground at all. These expectations
were, as we know, realized. The rebels fled in haste;

the attacking force broke their ranks and pursued in such disorder that it was little more than one crowd running after another.

Fearing lest the rebels might take advantage of the disorder in the ranks of their pursuers and rally, FitzGibbon kept well in the advance, that in the event of his fear being realized, he might make an effort to re-form at least a portion of his men. It was not required; the enemy fled in all directions. Their leader, Mackenzie, being very closely pressed, left his horse and took to the woods on foot.

Giving up the pursuit and returning, FitzGibbon met a party of about forty men. Asking the officer in command where he was bound for, he received the reply that they had been ordered to burn Gibson's house. Montgomery's was already in flames, having, much to FitzGibbon's regret, been set fire to by some of the more excited of the loyalists, but Gibson's house, being out of the way some two miles, had hitherto escaped.

Believing there must be some mistake, as nothing could be gained by such action, the officer repeating that he had positive orders, FitzGibbon rode rapidly after the now returning main body, in order to ascertain from Sir Francis if he had given the command. Before reaching him he was met by Mr. Sherwood, Sir Francis' aide-de-camp, with the intimation that " the Lieut.-Governor wished the men recalled who were going to burn Gibson's house, as he did not wish it burned." Sending Capt. Strachan to overtake the detachment and countermand the obnoxious order, FitzGibbon rode on himself to the main body.

A few minutes later he was called and told that His Excellency wished to see him immediately at the head of the column. FitzGibbon obeyed the summons and to his surprise the order to save Gibson's house was countermanded. He endeavored to remonstrate, but Sir Francis was obstinate. He laid his hand on FitzGibbon's arm as he rode along beside him, and repeated, authoritatively:

"Hear me; let Gibson's house be burned immediately, and let the militia be kept here until it is done." Then setting spurs to his horse, he rode on rapidly towards town.

It was late. The men had had a fatiguing day; they were cold, weary and hungry. There was no necessity to keep the entire force waiting while the order he so utterly disapproved of was carried out. Fitz-Gibbon reigned back his horse until the main body had passed, wheeled out the last division, and sent them northward. Turning to the field officer, whose name he does not give, he bade him take the command and see the order executed.

"For God's sake, Colonel FitzGibbon," the officer replied, "do not send me to carry out this order."

"If you are not willing to obey orders," said the colonel, "you had better go home and retire from the militia."

"I am very willing to obey orders, but if I burn that house, I shall be shot from behind one of these fences, for I have to come over this road almost every day in the week."

In the meantime the two men were left alone, the main body returning to town, the detachment wheeled out for the special service on the way north. There being no other officer at hand to whom to entrust the command of the latter, FitzGibbon determined to undertake it himself.

Sir Francis Head's despatch to the Colonial Office December 19th,* so misrepresented his action with regard to the burning of Gibson's house, that upon perusing it in the following April, FitzGibbon wrote a clear statement of the truth to Lord Glenelg,† with the result that Sir Francis was obliged to append a footnote to the page in his "Narrative," acknowledging the falsehood contained in his despatch. Curt as are the words, " By my especial order," they suffice to show how reluctant the writer was to proclaim his former statement to be false—to prove that, had there been a loop-hole of escape, he would have seized it.

---

* " The militia advanced in pursuit of the rebels about four miles until they reached the house of one of the principal ringleaders, Mr. Gibson, whose residence it would have been impossible to have saved, and it was consequently burned to the ground." (Sir Francis' Despatch, December 19th, 1837. See Appendix VII.)

† Although this statement was written on April 17th, and placed in Sir George Arthur's hands to be transmitted to Lord Glenelg, FitzGibbon was persuaded by his friends to withdraw it; but upon reading a further production of Sir Francis' pen published in May, FitzGibbon could no longer withhold his letter. A copy of the original will be found in Appendix VIII.

FitzGibbon always deplored this act. It was not only unnecessary, but impolitic and petty. Had the order been given him in private, or before a limited number, as other of Sir Francis' commands had been, FitzGibbon would have taken the responsibility of disobeying it, as he had done before. But an order given by a commander-in-chief to his second in command, in the hearing of a number of subordinate officers, and in the presence of the men, has no alternative : it must be obeyed, however reluctantly.

The deed was done, the rebel Gibson's house razed to the ground, and FitzGibbon returned with the detachment to town. Dismissing the men, and ascertaining that the guard at the Buildings had been relieved, he turned his steps to his own house. He was weary, mentally as well as physically. The restless excitement and anxiety of the past few days, the want of sleep, the irritation and annoyance caused by the Lieut.-Governor's behavior, the heart-sick disgust he felt at having been forced to do a deed his very soul abhorred—one that seemed to him unchristian and beneath the dignity of a true British soldier—and the long hours in the saddle unheeded during the excitement, told upon him now that the need for action was past. By the time he reached his own door, late on that winter evening, he was unable to dismount without assistance.

So bitterly did he feel the treatment he had received at the hands of the Lieut.-Governor, that on the following morning, finding himself unable to rise

from his bed, he sent a verbal message to Sir Francis,
resigning the recently bestowed appointment as
Adjutant-General. The blow had fallen, the rebellion he had so persistently and in the face of opposition and ridicule prophesied, had broken out, but,
owing to his foreknowledge, energy and determination, had not succeeded. The country was now
thoroughly roused to a sense of the reality of the
rebellion, there were men willing and anxious to
defend their homes and prove their loyalty to the
British Crown, and his services were no longer indispensable or necessary.

"I could not," he writes, "serve the Province advantageously to its interests under the immediate
command of such a man as His Excellency, and I felt
constrained to resign an office in the Provincial service which, above all others, I desired to hold. Its
duties were familiar to me, and to their efficient
performance I could cheerfully have devoted my
best energies."

Sir Francis, without one word of regret or enquiry
of the cause, accepted the resignation, and appointed
Colonel Macnab to succeed him.

Ill enough to be confined to the house for several
days, his youngest child dying, his wife ailing, the
long coveted position given up, and entirely neglected
by the Lieut.-Governor, who did not pay him the
ordinary courtesy of conventional enquiry, we may
understand something of the soreness and disappointment felt by the generous, loyal, enthusiastic heart.

In 1847 Sir Francis Head's policy in Upper Canada was attacked in the Edinburgh *Review*, the writer, in an article of some length, blaming him for disregarding FitzGibbon's advice.

Sir Francis' reply contained the following statement, the gross falsehood of which FitzGibbon was fortunately able to prove:

"It is therefore necessary that I should disabuse the public by reluctantly stating, what was perfectly well known throughout Upper Canada, namely, that the gallant militia colonel in question, from excessive zeal and loyalty, gradually became so excited that on the day after the defeat of the rebels, it was necessary to place him under medical treatment; that during his illness I in vain endeavored by every possible act of personal kindness to remove from him the strange idea that I was his enemy; and that, although he eventually recovered, this idea continued to haunt him so incessantly that when, a year afterwards, on his visiting England, I was, from feelings of regard, about to call upon him, I was earnestly requested by a Canadian, now in Toronto, not to do so." (Letter from Sir Francis Bond Head in the London *Sun.*)

CHAPTER X.

THE year 1837 closed in gloom and sorrow for FitzGibbon, but the beginning of the new year had brighter days in store for him.

The people saw with regret the way in which he had been set aside by Sir Francis. The loyal among them knew that to him they owed their escape from the rebel designs on the city, and were anxious to show their gratitude in some tangible form.

On January 23rd, 1838, the matter was brought up in the House of Assembly, and the following resolutions passed unanimously:

"*Resolved*,—That James FitzGibbon, Esquire, having rendered signal services to this province in a military capacity on various occasions, when he was a regular officer of the regular forces of the empire during the late war with the United States of America, and subsequently in several civil capacities, and also very recently as Colonel of Militia on the breaking out of the rebellion in the Home District, it is a duty incumbent on this House to recognize, by some public expression, his brave and faithful conduct, and to use such means as may be in its power to procure to be granted to him by his sovereign some lasting token of the royal bounty, as an acknowledgment of the estimation in which these services are held by the people whom it represents.

"*Resolved,*—That this House do humbly address Her Majesty, praying Her Majesty will be graciously pleased to grant to the said James FitzGibbon five thousand acres of the waste lands of the Crown in this province, as a mark of Her Majesty's royal favor, for the honorable, efficient and faithful services of that gentleman during a period of twenty-six years."

Upon these resolutions, an address to the Queen was passed by the House, and sent to the Legislative Council, which House also passed it with only one dissenting vote.

With what feelings of gratitude did the soldier receive this spontaneous act on the part of the Legislature! He had asked no reward for his services, had expected none, had endured his anxieties and trials as well as he could, and, although he had felt Sir Francis Head's treatment of him keenly and resented it indignantly, he had no expectation of relief from his troubles reaching him in so gratifying a manner. Whatever the Lieut.-Governor thought of him, the people were grateful. He forgot all the clouds, turned his back on all his troubles; his sanguine nature anticipated the sunshine; he saw his debts paid, his children provided for, and himself an honored and valued citizen of the place he had done his best to save from fire and sword.

The address was forwarded to the Secretary of

State for the Colonies, accompanied by a letter from the Lieut.-Governor, the following copy of which he ordered to be sent to FitzGibbon:

> "UPPER CANADA, TORONTO,
> "*March* 8th, 1838.

"MY LORD,—I have the honor to transmit to your Lordship a joint address to the Queen from the Legislative Council and House of Assembly of Upper Canada, praying that Her Majesty would be graciously pleased to grant to James FitzGibbon, Esquire, five thousand acres of the waste lands of the Province, as a mark of Her Majesty's royal favor for the honorable, efficient and able services of that gentleman during a period of twenty-six years.

"I beg leave respectfully, but most earnestly, to join in this recommendation, and I can assure your Lordship that a braver, a more loyal and devoted servant than Colone FitzGibbon cannot exist in Her Majesty's dominions.

"In time of war as well as in peace, he has admirably performed his duties, and I am confident that the boon which is solicited in his favor by the Legislature of this province, would be most gratefully acknowledged by Her Majesty's loyal subjects in Upper Canada.

> "I have the honor to be, etc., etc.,
> "(Signed) FRANCIS BOND HEAD.

"To the LORD GLENELG, etc., etc."

It is difficult to describe the effect of such a complete contradiction of his former behavior. The over-strained laudation of services he had pre-

viously ignored or denied, disgusted the honest-
hearted soldier.

Sir Francis was now as civil as he had before been
uncivil. He professed himself ready and anxious to
do anything and everything in his power to further
the wishes of the Assembly, to ensure the address to
the Queen being received with favor by the Colonial
Office; assured FitzGibbon he had always valued his
services and abilities and had "noticed him·in his
despatch." He bade him go to the Surveyor-General's
office and pencil his name on five thousand acres of
any vacant land he desired, "provided he did not ask
for town lots."

These attentions, paid after the two Houses had
passed the address, are probably the foundations for
Sir Francis' assertion in his letter in the *Sun*. A man
of FitzGibbon's character was not likely to receive
such false blandishments with much cordiality.

On March 12th, FitzGibbon was appointed Judge
Advocate on the militia general court-martial for the
trial of alien invaders, or such persons as should be
brought before it charged with levying war against
Her Majesty in the Province.

The court met at the Garrison in Toronto on the
13th March. FitzGibbon ably discharged the duties
of his post. At this court-martial General Sutherland,
the American officer who had been actively engaged
with the rebels on Navy Island, was arraigned. In a
volume published by him later, he gives a full account

of his own trial from his point of view. Among the documents quoted is a letter from FitzGibbon in his capacity of Judge Advocate. Sutherland took exception to his acting as such, but as he did likewise to the appointment of the majority of the commission, it may be taken for what it was worth.

At the end of March the Home Government accepted Sir Francis Head's resignation, and the evening before his departure he invited FitzGibbon to dine with him.

Reluctant as he was to accept the invitation, Fitz-Gibbon did so. The Lieut.-Governor's evident desire to conciliate him and his own naturally forgiving disposition made it seem the right thing to do.

The only other person present was the Lieut.-Governor's private secretary. Again Sir Francis reiterated his wish to see the boon asked for in the address granted, and he parted with FitzGibbon promising to use his best efforts on his behalf upon his return to England.

In May, when his despatch of December 19th, 1837, was published in Toronto, the "mention made of FitzGibbon" in it was greeted by an indignant protest from the citizens.

A public meeting was called and resolutions passed by a crowded gathering, embodying their strong sense of the injustice done FitzGibbon by the Lieut.-Governor.

Alderman Powell was called to the chair, and in spite

of the effort of an enthusiastic gentleman by the name of McMillan, who wished the chairman to divide the honors of December 7th with the colonel, further resolutions were carried, to apply to the Provincial Government for a grant of one acre of land within the city limits, and that steps should be taken to place subscription lists in the banks and other houses of public business in order to raise funds to defray the cost of building a suitable house for the man to whose exertions and forethought the citizens owed the preservation of their homes.

There are very few files of the daily papers of this date now extant in our libraries, what there are being but odd numbers scattered over several years, the fullest being those of the Reform organs. From the wholesale abuse and ridicule levelled at Fitz-Gibbon, whole columns of these rebel papers being devoted to him, the widespread admiration and enthusiasm felt for him by the loyal may be more truly realized than from the partial praise of friends.

The assent to the address from the Legislature had not been received, and the more cautious of FitzGibbon's admirers and friends feared a second and more local petition would neutralize the first (from those authorized to speak for the Province at large), for which reason it was considered advisable to drop it.

In June, the answer was received, and the following letter was sent to FitzGibbon:

"GOVERNMENT HOUSE,
"TORONTO, *June* 23rd, 1838.

"SIR,—I am directed by the Lieut.-Governor, as it is a matter in which you are particularly interested, to inform you that he has received a despatch from the Right Honorable the Secretary of State, acknowledging the receipt of the joint address to the Queen from the Legislative Council and Assembly of this Province, praying that a grant may be made to you of five thousand acres of the waste lands of the Crown, and stating that on its being laid at the foot of the throne, Her Majesty had been pleased to express her gratification at the honorable testimony borne to your services by both branches of the Provincial Legislature.

"His Lordship adds, that if it should be the pleasure of the two Houses to mark their sense of your services by a pecuniary grant, it will afford Her Majesty much satisfaction to give her assent to any Act which may be passed for that purpose ; but Her Majesty is advised that, consistently with the terms of the recent Provincial Act on the subject of the alienation of the waste lands of the Crown, and the principles on which that Act proceeds, Her Majesty could not make you the proposed compensation in the form of a grant of land.

"I have the honor to be, Sir,
"Your most obedient, humble servant,
"JOHN MACAULAY.
"COLONEL FITZGIBBON, etc., etc."

Thus the Act passed to put an end to the promiscuous granting of lands—an Act forced through the Houses by the clamors of the Reformers—defeated the unanimous vote of the same Legislature to reward

the man who had been instrumental in putting down
the rebellion raised by the principal men among these
Reformers.

The joke was a grim one, but it did not lessen the
severity of FitzGibbon's disappointment. His hopes
had been so buoyed up by anticipations of release
from debt and dreams of better days, that the reaction
was great. But his friends had not given up his
cause. A bill authorizing the House to legalize the
grant passed both Houses. This, it was hoped, would
receive the ready assent of the Governor-in-Council.
They were again disappointed, the bill being reserved
for the consideration of the Crown.

Fearful lest it should meet with the same fate as
the address, FitzGibbon was advised to cross the Atlantic, and by bringing the influence of such friends
as he had in London to bear upon the Government,
ensure it being granted. It was, however, useless.
The Home Government had had their eyes opened
to the abuse of privileges by former officials in Upper
Canada, and they were determined that no more
Crown lands should be granted to individuals for
public services.

FitzGibbon had two interviews with Mr. Labouchere,
the Under Secretary of State, but without any satisfactory result. Reluctant to give up all hope of
obtaining the consent of the Crown, he lingered on
in London. I have been unable to ascertain where
or in what part of the great metropolis he lodged
during the six months he remained there. The only

mention of his private life in the letters of that date extant is an incidental assertion that he "was very hard up, and lived in quiet, cheap lodgings, as inexpensively as possible."

The letter given below belongs to this time. His intercourse with the Brock family had never been broken off. The kindly services he had been glad to render them in return for their brother's kindness to him, were again returned with kindly interest by the friendship and affection of Sir Isaac's brothers and nephews. Savery Brock, in particular, remained a loving friend until death parted them. Among the correspondence of FitzGibbon's later years are one or two letters, written in the shaking, uncertain hand of extreme old age, their expressions of love and friendship as strong and true as in their palmiest days. Nor did the feelings find expression only in words. Savery Brock lent his friend money without interest until better days dawned, and FitzGibbon was able to pay it back in full. Whether the visit to Guernsey, mentioned in this letter, was paid or not, we have no record :

" GUERNSEY, *July* 1st, 1839.

" MY DEAR FITZGIBBON,—I have received your letter of the 26th ult. The packets, Government steamers, leave Weymouth every Wednesday and Saturday evening (nine o'clock) for this island, and are about seven hours running over. Every Tuesday and Friday evening at seven o'clock, from South-

ampton, starts a very fine steamer, the *Atlanta*, that
makes her passage in ten or eleven hours.

"On Monday, Wednesday, Thursday and Saturday,
a steamer quits Southampton at seven o'clock, and
comes over in twelve hours—all good boats. The
railroad to Southampton trains quit London every
day about noon, and reach Southampton in time for
the steamboats. With these accounts, you cannot be
at a loss to come over here, and you may be assured
of a hearty welcome by me. I have a bed for you,
and nothing can give me more pleasure than seeing
you.

"Let me hear from you on receipt of this. I am
anxious to learn that you have got over your difficulties. I suggest nothing. You know how parties
run, and the Ministers will not be sorry to be
informed on many points by you. They will, I
think, grant you the land in question. I know they
ought to do so, for without a few such men as you
are, they would have no land to grant.

"I send this to the Colonial Office to hunt you out,
as you have not given me your address or the address
of Mr. Price.

"Yours faithfully,
"JOHN SAVERY BROCK.

"COLONEL FITZGIBBON.

"Should you come here direct from London, I
advise you to come by Southampton; if from Ireland,
by Bristol, then by Weymouth; but I know you will
come and see me."

Returning to his lodgings after the second fruitless visit to the Colonial Office, FitzGibbon had
almost given way to despair, when his eye fell upon

a letter of introduction given him years before by an officer of the Guards (Sir John Eustace), who had served with him on the Niagara frontier in 1814. The letter, which was a sealed one, had been entirely forgotten, and only the overturning of other papers in the morning had brought it thus opportunely to light. Although FitzGibbon had little hope of this letter being of any use to him, he determined to deliver it at once. The address took him to a distant part of the city, 35 Upper Berkeley Street, Portman Square. Sir Augustus d'Este was not at home. FitzGibbon left the letter and his card, then, having nothing to do, went for a long walk across the park into the country to the west of London.

Returning to his lodgings some time after four, he was surprised to find his call had been returned at two o'clock. Sir Augustus d'Este, not finding him in, had left a note expressing his disappointment, and a hope that he should be more fortunate the following day at the same hour, when he meant to do himself the pleasure of calling again.

From the first hour of their meeting until his death, Sir Augustus d'Este was one of FitzGibbon's best and most valued friends. He helped him with interest, with valuable introductions, and, above all, with a devoted love and admiration that found expression in long lover-like letters and many a kindly service. The dress sword worn by FitzGibbon in later years, and shown in the portrait which forms the frontispiece to this volume, was given him later by Sir Augustus, with the loving words that he hoped its having been worn by himself would not lessen its value in the eyes of his friend.

The scabbard is crimson velvet, with the armor of various dates in gold raised in relief upon it; the hilt a gold-winged dragon; the handle ivory, capped by a helmet of gold; the blade, which is a scimitar in shape, is a beautiful specimen of enamelled steel in blue and gold, the designs representing different coats of arms and mottoes. The belt is of crimson leather embroidered with gold thread, and linked together by lions' heads—the buckle an interlaced dragon's head of the same metal. The velvet of the scabbard is frayed at the edges, proving that it was no mere ornament, but had been worn by its noble donor.*

---

* Sir Augustus d'Este was the son of H. R. H. Prince Frederick Augustus (Duke of Sussex), the sixth son of George III., and the Lady Augusta Murray, second daughter of the Earl of Dunmore.

They were privately married in Rome, on April 4th, 1793, and, lest there should be any doubt raised of its legality, though not from any apprehension of the first ceremony being insufficient, they were again married by banns, in the Parish Church of St. George's, Hanover Square, London, on December 6th, 1793. Yet a decree afterwards passed the Court of Doctors' Commons declaring the marriage unlawful and void. This decree separated the husband and wife.

Prince Frederick Augustus, in his will, dated "Berlin, September 15th, 1799," expressly declares that "I feel myself still not less bound by every obligation of law, conscience and honor, to consider her as my lawful and undoubted wife in every respect, as if that decree had never taken place, and that I consider, and

FitzGibbon remained in England until nearly the close of the year, when he returned to Toronto.

Soon after the meeting of the last session of the last Parliament of Upper Canada, in January, 1840, an address was voted by one of the Assemblies praying that His Excellency the Governor-General, the Right Honorable Charles Poulett Thomson, would "be pleased to inform the House if the royal assent had been given to the bill passed last session, entitled 'An Act to enable Her Majesty to make a grant of land to James FitzGibbon, Esquire.'" (See Appendix IX.) The reply to this address was practically the same as to the former, and though further discussion of the matter resulted in an Act being passed by both Houses to repeal the Act providing for the disposal of public lands of the Province so far as to enable Her Majesty to consent to the grant to FitzGibbon, it also was

---

ever shall acknowledge, our son, Augustus Frederick, who was born after both these marriages, as my true, lawful and legitimate son."

In 1830, papers fell into his son's hands which convinced him beyond a doubt of the legality of his claims. He was, however, unsuccessful in establishing them, and refused to accept any other title from the Crown than the simple one of knighthood. He died unmarried. His sister, Lady Augusta, married Chief Justice Wilde, but left no children.

Sir Augustus gave FitzGibbon a complete copy of all the documents and papers connected with his case.

The marriage was doubtless annulled on the ground of absence of license from the Crown, that, according to the law of Great Britain, being necessary.

reserved for Her Majesty's consideration and received no further attention.

The following extract from the debate in the House on January 25th, taken from the columns of one of the most bitterly antagonistic Radical papers, the Toronto *Mirror*, shows with what feeling the question was discussed. The editorial column of the same issue, containing some virulent abuse of Fitz-Gibbon, leads one to suppose that the report of the proceedings in the House would not be more partial to his cause than the necessity of the case obliged.

"Mr. Burwell brought forward a resolution praying Her Majesty to grant from the casual and territorial revenue to James FitzGibbon, Esquire, £2,500 for important services rendered to this province by that gentleman.

"Mr. Boulton opposed the resolution. He respected Colonel FitzGibbon, but considering the present state of the country and the embarrassed state of our finances, he thought £1,000 quite sufficient to compensate him for any services rendered. A bill passed this House granting him five thousand acres, which, at four shillings an acre, the price paid by Government for United Empire rights, would amount to £1,000.

"Mr. Burwell believed, under Divine Providence, the safety of the country was owing to the gallant colonel, But for him the city would have been taken. The sum proposed was only equivalent to the land.

"Mr. Gowan wished to know how the gallant colonel had saved the country, before so large a sum should be taken from the pockets of the people to reward him.*

" Mr. Thomson said the financial affairs were in a very embarrassed state, but at the rate they were going on, it would not appear so. He called upon the Chairman of Finance to inform the House if their affairs were in a flourishing state. He would recommend to members to pay their honest debts. Sums were advanced by people for the repair of roads and bridges, and they were allowed to suffer.

"Mr. Kearnes reminded them of the poor man who asked a bishop for a guinea, which was refused; he then asked him for a crown, which was likewise refused; and last of all, he asked for a penny. That was also refused. He then asked the humane bishop for his blessing. ' Yes,' said the bishop, ' kneel down, and I will give it.' Because the blessing cost him nothing, he was willing to give it, but he would not give the money. The £2,500 proposed would be given to the colonel on account of his great and meritorious services, and his attention and anxiety when preserving the city and the lives and property of the people of the Province. There was not a dissenting voice against the 5,000 acres of land voted to him, and the despatch said he could not get it; and now they were going to remunerate him in money. Would they raise a man high in his expectations, and then depress him? Would it be honorable to do so? He saved us from ruin, and £2,500 was very little for his services to the city of Toronto.

" Mr. Merritt said that at the time the disturbance

---

* Mr. Gowan had evidently not forgotten FitzGibbon's address to the Orangemen, nor his influence in preventing the processions and demonstrations which he (Gowan) had made every effort to revive.

took place here, the gallant colonel had preparations made quietly, and but for that Mackenzie would have been in and taken the town.

"Mr. Gowan said, if he was to judge of the preparations by the event, he could not go with him. It was all done by surprise. There were other individuals who deserved reward as well as Colonel FitzGibbon He thought £1,000 quite sufficient a reward for the services performed. Several other persons distinguished themselves in 1837, and they were not to get anything.

"The Speaker (Colonel Macnab) did not think it was generous to make enquiries as to the services rendered. A grant was made at a time when his services were fresh in the memory of every member. They addressed the Government to give him 5,000 acres of land, and he was deeply grateful for the consideration which this House laid on him; and what did they do? They made good their pledge by passing an Act of Parliament, and it passed unanimously in both Houses. To that bill the Queen's assent was withheld; but they were told they could make good their pledge by an appropriation from the casual and territorial revenue. Have they got that sum in the casual and territorial revenue? You may grant it. You pledged yourselves, and you cannot retrace your steps without disgracing yourselves. It would be unjust to hold up this hope, and then cut it off. They might give the 5,000 acres, or give a sum of money. In the last American war he served his country faithfully. In the late rebellion he commanded the militia and he (the Speaker) served under him, and he was active and zealous.

"Mr. Rykert said the House was pledged, and he would support the resolution.

" Mr. Gowan had no objection to the £1,000, as the House was pledged. He moved that £1,000 be granted to Colonel FitzGibbon in order to compensate him for his meritorious services.

" Mr. Cook thought he was deserving, but plenty of land could be had at five shillings an acre.

" Mr. Kearnes moved the House to rise, report progress, and ask leave to sit again.

" Mr. Backus said the casual and territorial revenue was not yet surrendered; he hoped some communication would be laid before the House upon that subject. He was for granting the land.

" Mr. Thomson said they should be careful how they granted money out of the ordinary revenue of the Province.

" Mr. Merritt said it was nonsense to argue about the price of U. E. rights. Some land was worth two dollars an acre.

" Mr. Rykert said they should not retract their vote; they should give a sum equivalent to the land.

" Committee rose, reported progress, etc., etc."

This debate called forth a further storm of rage and indignation from the Reform press. Part of the editorial columns of the paper from which the above is taken contained, as has been stated, the most virulent abuse of the "gallant colonel."

Lord Seaton interested himself in FitzGibbon's behalf, and wrote to Lord John Russell on the subject. In the following letter to FitzGibbon he enclosed the reply he had received :

" I acquainted Lord John Russell that I presumed he had received a report of your conduct at the time of Mackenzie's menaced attack on Toronto; that you had constantly exercised your influence over your countrymen settled in Canada, with great advantage to the public, and that the local authorities had made use of your influence in times of difficulty and danger.

"I regret that my application has not produced a more satisfactory result, but I shall have great pleasure in being able to render you any assistance in my power.

"I remain, very faithfully yours,

"SEATON."

The letter enclosed was but a repetition of the former refusal of the Colonial Secretary to allow the alienation of public lands.

During Lord Sydenham's administration nothing was done. The union of the two provinces absorbed the attention of the Legislature and the Governor to the exclusion of private questions, and though Fitz-Gibbon in a private letter, thanking him for the offer of an appointment for his son in Quebec, drew His Excellency's attention to his case, he felt how small a matter his embarrassments were in comparison with the larger interests of the Province, and made no further effort to obtain redress.

FitzGibbon's eldest son had given up the business post he held in Dublin, and returned to practise at the bar in Toronto, bringing with him a cousin who had recently been left an orphan. She became as a daughter to her uncle, and to her tender care the

comfort of FitzGibbon's declining years was largely
due.

After the death of his wife, on March 22nd of
this year (1841), FitzGibbon removed his family to
Kingston, that being the next stopping-place of the
perambulating Government of the day. He was
there appointed commissioner for administering the
oath to members of the Legislature, June 5th, and
Clerk of the Legislative Council on June 10th.

The house on Queen Street was left in charge of
the gardener for a time. There were still five acres
about it free from mortgage or incumbrance, all that
remained of the eighteen acres purchased in 1826.
Knowing its value, FitzGibbon made every effort to
retain it. Although deeply in debt, he was willing
to pay high interest rather than lose this one bit of
landed property, and from appearances all he was
ever likely to hold. The house was a good one as
houses were in those days; the garden was well kept
and the fruit and flowers plentiful; the lawn included
a bowling alley, which was a source of much pleasure
to his sons as well as to friends and neighbors.

Of FitzGibbon's life in Kingston we can glean very
little. Casual mention of his name in letters, references to him in the local papers, reminiscences of
pleasant chats and walks with him by the one or two
of his friends who survive him, and two indifferently
well executed portraits, are all that we have.

The portraits have unfortunately been cut down

and the name of the artist lost.* We have only a shadowy outline of the story of how they came to be painted. How or where he found the artist is uncertain; but, knowing FitzGibbon's kindly interest in the poor, who were struggling to earn a living, his sympathy in the sufferings of his fellows, and his quick observation of whatever crossed his path, as well as the ever-present wish to do some little good to his neighbor, we can understand how an expression of suffering or despair on an intelligent face would attract his attention and induce him to follow and learn whether a hand might not be stretched out to help.

"I do not know who the artist was," writes his daughter-in-law, years afterwards, "but I always understood that the colonel found him in a garret starving, that he fed him, visited him, and when strong enough, found him work, beginning with his own portraits, for which he paid seven pounds ten each. I believe what the man was able to earn through the colonel's influence provided him with funds to take him to New York, where he afterwards did better and commanded good prices for his portraits."

The portraits of FitzGibbon are more than life-size, which gives the likeness a startling effect and the

---

* From the occurrence of the name Krœbel in the public accounts of the Legislature in 1842 to 1845, it is not unlikely that he was the artist of FitzGibbon's portrait.

impression that they are coarse representations of the original, the crudeness of the drawing giving the face an unnatural fulness, and both nose and upper lip a greater length than the face of a photograph taken twenty years later possesses.

A lithograph print taken from one of these portraits was published in the *Anglo-American Magazine* for September, 1854. The smaller size robs it of some of the defects of the painting. FitzGibbon found no fault with it. In a letter to his nephew, Gerald FitzGibbon, dated January, 1855, he says:

" I have just received a Canadian magazine from Toronto, to which is prefixed a print of my rough old face, to my great surprise; and having in it, also, a brief biographical sketch of my military life, but not a word of my having saved Toronto, which, however, may be reserved for a future number. . . . I thought I had been entirely forgotten by the provincials, but it is not quite so."

Sir Charles Bagot, Lord Sydenham's successor, took up FitzGibbon's cause with interest. He read the facts from an outsider's point of view, and lost no time in drawing the attention of the House to a case in which he " considered the colonel an extremely ill-used man." As a result, an Order-in-Council was made, recommending an issue of land scrip to Fitz-Gibbon to the amount of the Government price of the land, which he might have procured had the bill granting the land received the royal assent.

Unfortunately, the value of the land scrip at the

time this Order-in-Council was made was about half
what the land was worth. By accepting this way
out of the difficulty, and being obliged to sell at once,
the Government would have had to disburse two
thousand pounds in order that FitzGibbon might
receive one thousand, the purchaser or speculator
pocketing the difference. The upset price of the land
having been fixed by the Government at ten shillings
an acre, it would be obliged to redeem the scrip at
that price, irrespective of the sum received for it by
FitzGibbon. To this FitzGibbon objected, both for
his own sake and because it gave an opportunity for
that which savored of jobbery.

The session closed, however, without the message
being sent down to the House. A few days after,
FitzGibbon met Sir Charles Bagot in his official
capacity. The Governor took the opportunity to
express his regret that he had not been able to
bring the matter to a satisfactory termination for
FitzGibbon; he "wished to send the message down
but had been overruled."

Sir Augustus d'Este, about this time, drew up a
short, concise, but clear statement of all that had
occurred in connection with the business, and had
taken an opportunity of reading it himself to Lord
Stanley, then Secretary for the Colonies. He writes
(in March):

"MY DEAR FITZGIBBON,—On the 28th, the last
day of last month, I was in the chair upon the occa-

sion of a dinner which was given to Sir Charles Metcalfe, previous to his departure, by the Colonial Society. After dinner, I requested the favor of being allowed to call upon him, which request was readily granted, and yesterday, March 1st, I read over to him almost the whole of the accompanying statement, which had been prepared for and presented to Lord Stanley. I also furnished him with a copy of it, which he promised to read over during the voyage.

"When you have read the statement, you will be aware of the exact extent of Sir Charles Metcalfe's knowledge concerning your services and their contemplated acknowledgment by the two Governments. Hoping that you will approve both of the statement and of the measure of my reading it over to your new Governor-General, I shall for the present conclude, renewing the assurance of the sincere regard of,
"My dear FitzGibbon,
"Yours most truly,
"AUGUSTUS D'ESTE."

When speaking of his friend elsewhere, Fitz-Gibbon says: "To him also I was indebted for a special introduction to Sir Charles Metcalfe, whose conduct towards me during the short remainder of his most valuable and exemplary life was extraordinary even for that extraordinary man."

The new Governor did, indeed, take a deep interest in the soldier and his difficulties. When he found the Government would neither pay over the sum granted to FitzGibbon, nor advance any portion of it to enable him to meet the most pressing of his debts, he insisted upon advancing sufficient out of his own pocket, generously doubling the amount named by FitzGibbon.

Lord Metcalfe sent FitzGibbon's memorial to the Council, but it went no further, and another session passed without any settlement. The resignation of a number of the Executive Council necessitated the prorogation of the House, and yet another session passed without any settlement being reached. Lord Metcalfe, however, obtained a report from the Council, which he forwarded, with a favorable recommendation, to the Colonial Office. (See Appendix X.)

When the new Parliament assembled in January, 1845, the matter was again brought to their notice, and in March, when the estimates were laid on the table, the sum of £1,000 was inserted and recommended in payment of the long outstanding reward for his services, so enthusiastically voted him by the unanimous voice of the Assembly in 1838. The protracted anxiety and uncertainty, alternate hope and despair, so affected FitzGibbon's health, that when the seat of Government was removed to Montreal, he applied for leave of absence and remained in Kingston.

Finding the state of his health still unfitted him for a faithful discharge of his duties, FitzGibbon tendered his resignation in May, 1846. It was not accepted at once; a Committee of the House addressed the Governor-General to allow FitzGibbon to retire on a pension of three hundred pounds (Canadian currency) a year. This was at first refused, but upon

a second and third address being presented, stating
that in consequence of inability of the clerk to perform his duties, he having produced medical certificates
to that effect, the office was in danger of becoming
a sinecure, and the work of the House not being done
satisfactorily by a substitute, the petition was granted
and FitzGibbon allowed to retire.   Thus in June,
1846, ended twenty years' service in the Canadian
Houses of Parliament, and forty-six years of active
life in the country.

(Copy of Dr. Widmer's Certificate.)

" TORONTO, *April* 3rd, 1845.

" It is now thirty years since I became acquainted
with Captain FitzGibbon, then in the Glengarry Light
Infantry.   The war with America had then just
concluded, and the whole community of Upper Canada, civil and military, was full of applause in regard
to the conduct of Captain FitzGibbon, during the
course of the preceding campaigns.

" It was justly pronounced that his services had
been of the highest order, and contributed to stamp
his corps with the character of vigor, vigilance and
valor.

" During a long series of years of peace, the same
qualities which rendered him conspicuous as a military
man, were productive of an effective and highly
honorable discharge of the duties of the offices he
held in civil life.

" And thus would the useful and faithful course of
Captain FitzGibbon's career have terminated in civil
engagements, but for the occurrence of the unnatural
attempt of the rebels to sever the country from British

connection, in 1837. At this crisis the foresight and
energy of Captain FitzGibbon saved the city of
Toronto from destruction, and were the means of
shortening a struggle that might otherwise have been
protracted. For these services alone, the gratitude
of the Government is eminently due to Captain Fitz-
Gibbon. His expectations of a release from pecuniary
embarrassments have been raised by a vote of the
Legislature for a grant of land grounded on the high
value at which it estimated his services during the
rebellion. These expectations having failed in their
accomplishment, to my knowledge, has had a powerful effect in destroying the healthy tone of his mind,
and has rendered him incapable of performing the
active duties of his office, and almost unfitted him for
the social intercourse of his friends and acquaintances.

"(Signed) C. WIDMER."

(Dr. Winder's Certificate.)

" These are to certify that my knowledge of Colonel
James FitzGibbon, Chief Clerk of the Honorable the
Legislative Council, extends over a period of thirty-
three years. Gifted with a constitution naturally
good, and of abstemious habits, he has nevertheless
a temperament highly sanguine and nervous, and this
acted upon, primarily, by an active life spent in the
military and civil service of his country, and second-
arily, by disappointments and distresses of no ordinary
character, has produced such a state of mental irritation, prostration and despondency, and loss of memory,
as at times to render him quite incapable of the
efficient discharge of the duties of his very important
office. In addition to the foregoing circumstances, I
would observe that Colonel FitzGibbon has nearly
attained the age of sixty-five years, forty-seven of

which have been honorably passed in the public service; and advancing age has brought with it an increase of physical infirmities, some of them indeed of long standing, which greatly add to the causes of incapacity above mentioned.

"On the whole, then, it is my deliberate opinion, founded on facts which have come to my knowledge from so many years' personal friendship and intimacy with Colonel FitzGibbon, that he is, from causes quite beyond his control or power of avoidance, physically and mentally incapable of further public duty, and that his perseverance in the attempt to perform the arduous duties of his present official station, will greatly aggravate the constitutional maladies under which he now suffers.

"Given under my name, at Montreal, this fifth day of May, 1845.

"(Signed)   WILLIAM WINDER, M.D.

Thus had the repeated disappointments, hopes deferred, and accumulation of debts and difficulties brought about the very disability to perform his duties in 1845 which Sir Francis Bond Head had falsely asserted of FitzGibbon in 1837.

CHAPTER XI.

FITZGIBBON'S second son, William, had been appointed Clerk of the County of Hastings in 1842, and had taken up his residence in Belleville, his sister and cousin accompanying him. His father, although in Montreal several times during the sessions, spent much of the intervening months with them.

The square house in which they lived, with a broad verandah round two sides of it, is still standing.* It is situated in the low part of the town, near the river mouth, known as the Flats, and is not now a very healthy locality, owing to the spring floods which sweep down the ice and inundate the low-lying lands on that side of the Moira. Here, as the colonel's health improved, and he was able to take exercise again, he astonished his neighbors, and gained a character for eccentricity, by his athletic performances.

Club swinging, horizontal bar, and other kindred athletic exercises were not so common then as now, and the spectacle of a man turned of sixty-five years of age, clad in jerseys, swinging himself from a bar fixed across the supports of the verandah,

---

* The house has been turned about by the force of the spring floods, and its outward appearance also much altered.

doubling himself up into a ball, jumping through his hands, or hanging by his feet, drawing his body up by sheer strength of muscle, and anon leaping over chairs arranged in rows, was quite sufficient to obtain him a certificate of insanity from the majority of his neighbors.

"On the bright moonlight nights in the summer, the colonel would spend an hour or two taking such exercise," writes an old resident of Belleville. "He had a splendidly developed muscle and a fine physique. A crowd of boys and half-grown lads would congregate on and along the fence that divided the narrow strip of garden in front from the road. It was as entertaining as a circus to them. He never saw or took any notice of these spectators, but, on the contrary, appeared quite unconscious of their presence. When literally dripping from the effect of the violence of his exertions, he would wipe the drops from his face, and 'thank Providence that he lived in a quiet neighborhood.'"

His brother Gerald, the Master in Chancery in Ireland, had lent FitzGibbon £1,000 in 1841. This, with the grant voted by the Assembly to him in 1845, enabled him to discharge a considerable portion of his debts, but the long delay and the unavoidable renewal of notes, etc., and other law expenses, had increased them to a total far exceeding the original sum. Among the letters from Sir Augustus d'Este is one which shows that the debts upon which no interest was accumulating were the first to be discharged. After acknowledging the receipt of a bill of exchange for £100, Sir Augustus says, " with which sum it was my happiness to have been able to accommodate you at a time when it was useful." Th's, as indeed every other letter FitzGibbon received from this kind friend, breathed love and friendship, and an admiration that was almost exaggerated in expres ion.

Lady Simpson, in a letter to FitzGibbon, then in Montreal, December 18th, 1845, while regretting that illness prevented his being with them that day, also speaks of " the affectionate regard in which you are held by our dear and estimable friend, Sir Augustus d'Este, whose whole life seems to be one continued act of goodness. I have already heard from his own lips much of your history, and had with him lamented the coldness and ingratitude of those in power, who, while claiming for themselves the merit of putting down the rebellion, appear to have forgotten or overlooked the one to whose judgment and valor that happy event was mainly attributable.

"The kind heart of your excellent friend can well feel for those who have suffered, for cruelly and deeply has he been wronged, and much has his noble spirit endured, but you are doubtless well acquainted with the merits of his own case, and it is therefore needless for me to dwell upon a theme which ever fills my mind with sorrow and indignation.

> "With our united kind regards,
> "Believe me, my dear sir,
> "Yours very sincerely,
> "FRANCES K. SIMPSON."

FitzGibbon returned to England early in the year 1847, but in what part of London he lived until July, 1849, we cannot ascertain. Lady Seaton addresses a letter to him at that date, to 56 Stafford Place, Pimlico, and it is probable he had been there for some time. Charles Mackay speaks of him at that time as "his friend Colonel FitzGibbon, living for six months in London on sixpence a day, fourpence of which was spent in bread, one penny for milk, and the remaining penny for sugar, and assuring him (Mackay) that he never felt so well in his life."

This story has been repeated many times as an illustration of cheap living, some of the variations indulged in by the different narrators being widely different from the original.

The pension granted in 1846 was not paid until September, 1847, and then only from the beginning of that year. FitzGibbon had gone to England in June in the confident expectation of receiving the first half-year's payment in or by the end of July. Its non-arrival left him very short of funds, and he wrote to enquire the cause. Calculating the time that must elapse before he could receive a reply, he counted his cash and found, after paying for his room, he had just sixpence a day to live upon, until he might reasonably expect to receive a remittance from Canada. His success in this extraordinary economy was so satisfactory that after the money did reach him, he spent most of it in defraying the cost of the publication of several tracts and pamphlets on infant education, and in helping to further the establishment of night schools in the poorer parts of London.

Miss Strickland, who knew him very well at this time, speaks of him as "starving himself in order to publish some papers or articles he had written on infant training." That these papers attracted some attention the following letters show:

"AMBLESIDE, *November* 11th, 1848.

"SIR,—I have read your pamphlet and letter with great interest; and I think it will please you to hear that they arrived just as I was writing the concluding portion of my papers on 'Household Education,' which are, I suppose, the papers you have seen of mine. I was actually writing upon the 'Power of Habit;' and I have taken the liberty of quoting a passage from your tract. I knew you would not object, as the object of us both is to rouse the minds of parents, in every possible way, to see the truth.

"I am not likely to go to London this winter, but I should like to send you my volume on 'Household Education' when it comes out. I don't know exactly when that will be, but it goes to the publisher (Mr. Moxon) next week, and it will not be very long printing.

"Unless I hear that you will have left England by Xmas, we will say, I will desire Mr. Moxon to forward a copy to the same address with this note.

"Be assured I sympathize warmly with your earnestness in regard to the important subject you have treated, and am, Sir, with much respect, yours,

"H. MARTINEAU."

"BUCKINGHAM PALACE,
"*May* 5th, 1849.

"Miss Murray presents her compliments to Colonel FitzGibbon. She was so pleased with the 'Remarks' by 'A Colonist,' which he was very obliging in sending to her, that she has taken some pains to penetrate through the veil under which the opinions were concealed. The subject is one which has for a great many years attracted the attention of Miss Murray, and she is at this moment much engaged in considering the best mode of checking juvenile delinquency by inducing the Government to take a reformatory and educational charge of each child upon their first conviction in a court of justice. This would check the evil at its very commencement, and totally prevent the frequent recommitment of young offenders."

In the following letter from Miss Strickland, whose niece had become engaged to FitzGibbon's eldest son, a pamphlet from his pen is mentioned, which, I regret to say, I have been unable to find in any library or public depository of such works:

"AVENUE LODGE,
"BAYSWATER, *Aug.* 6th, 1849.

"DEAR COLONEL FITZGIBBON,—I have read with the strong interest natural to my family connection in Canada, your pamphlet received this morning, for which I return you my thanks. Nothing can be clearer or more concentrated than its composition. It is thoroughly readable by an idle person ignorant of the subject. Every one of that species of reader will be as much charmed as I was at the conduct of the Ohio volunteers. But, query, was their most

original behavior to their captain caused by his lack
of governing power, or the impracticability of his
respectable squadron? Equal portions of both contributed to the result, *I guess.*

"The business part of your pamphlet appears to me
a most salutary warning. If our Government will
not listen to the voices of its veteran officers possessing experiences both military and civil, they must
e'en take the result. Perhaps if the warning of
friends will not be heeded, they will listen to that of
enemies. The enclosed has, I doubt not, excited some
alarm in our colonies, although no one seems to have
noticed it here.

"As a woman, I feel that my opinion on such matters is out of place, and as a historian my thoughts
seldom dwell on any matter younger than two hundred years; but I think that the federation you
propose would become more palatable to the Nova
Scotians, New Brunswickers, etc., if each colony were
invited to cause a resident minister to be selected
from among their own representatives to sit in the
British Parliament as a referee, to give information
on any statistic matters under legislation. The condition that such person must be a Nova Scotian, New
Brunswicker born, or French-Canadian, etc., would be
gratefully received, I am sure; the pride of the colonists would be mightily gratified, the utility would
counterbalance any trouble, the colonists would tax
themselves in a trifle of £500 per annum or so, to
maintain their resident minister, and the situation
would be a stimulus to obtain English attainments in
education, and a bond of the strongest nature as to
the affections of the colonists. I know personally
something of the Nova Scotians and Newfoundland
natives, and I know their pride is adverse to the

federation with Canada, but if they were patted and soothed as high-blooded horses are tamed, they might be led anywhere, provided their nationality be owned."

On the same sheet of note paper, written the reverse way of the sheet, is the following:

"*Aug.* 13th.

"DEAR COLONEL FITZGIBBON,—I am sorry to say that I discovered this note unposted, when I thought you had had it some time ago. Such is, I am sad to own, the fate of many of my epistles. Writing them is almost a suffering to me, and when written, something I must attend to demands me, and away they go among my papers. I own I cannot keep up anything like a correspondence; my friends are obliged to come and take my epistles *viva voce,* and agree not to think me savage if I do not write.

"I have, however, written to Lord Aylmer, for I owe them a long score of apologies for invitations not accepted, not noticed indeed, and calls unreturned; therefore I am doing neglected devoirs as well as mentioning your work. Will you enclose one with Colonel FitzGibbon's compliments to Lord Aylmer, and the other to Lady Aylmer, she being literary, and he a firm friend to Canada.

"I am, yours very truly,
"ELIZABETH STRICKLAND.

"P.S.—Lord Aylmer is, I am sure, from home, but if you enclose my letter with the pamphlet to the Eaton Square address, he will receive them in time.

"I have no objection to receive a quiet visit on Sunday. I was at church and dining out with an old friend the day you called. I dine out to-morrow and Wednesday; on Thursday I shall be glad to see you."

Miss Jane Strickland, the author of " Rome, Regal and Republican," and many tales from Roman and Eastern history, met FitzGibbon frequently at her sister's cottage in Bayswater, and in her beautiful old age* was never weary of talking of the charm of his conversation, his intense individuality and love of humanity.

"I have told him repeatedly," she said, in speaking of this date, "that he should write a history of his campaigns; but no written page could convey the life and vim of the relation, a mere body without a spirit that gave it such indescribable charm. He was plain, decidedly plain, but he carried himself well, was a fine-looking man, and the moment he began to talk, all else was forgotten."

Despite Miss Strickland's avowed aversion to letter-writing, there are several letters from her among FitzGibbon's papers, and of his among hers, which betray a mutual admiration and affection for each other, expressed in the courteous, dignified language of their day.

Miss Strickland introduced FitzGibbon to Mr. John Ollivier, the editor of the *Home Circle*, a magazine then in good circulation in England. Several articles and papers from his pen on infant training were published in its columns. Ollivier also published a pamphlet for him which attracted the attention of George Combe, the phrenologist, and the following

---

* She lived to be eighty-eight, retaining her faculties and wonderful memory to the last hour of her life.

letter was the beginning of a pleasant correspondence and friendship between the two men. The letter is addressed to " A Colonist " (FitzGibbon's *nom de plume*), " to the care of John Ollivier, Esq., 59 Pall Mall, London." It is written in a firm, clear, copper-plate hand, the lines straight and the words well separated—a hand that must have been a pleasure to his printers and proof-readers :

" 45 MELVILLE ST., EDINBURGH,
" *November* 13th, 1848.

" SIR,—I have read with much pleasure your ' Remarks on the Advantages of Early Training and Management of Children,' and admire the spirit in which they are written. Apparently, however, you have not had an opportunity of learning what has been written on the subject of education since you left England. Robert Owen taught us so long ago as 1820, the identical proposition contained in the third paragraph of your pamphlet, and tried to realize it in practice on a great scale at New Lanark in Scotland, and with only partial success.

" Having written and published a good deal myself on human nature and education, I beg to enclose an advertisement of my books, in some of which, particularly the ' Constitution of Man,' you will find some ideas congenial to your own.

" I am, Sir,
" Your very obedient servant,
" GEO. COMBE.
" To 'A COLONIST.' "

Through Lord Aylmer, Lord Aberdeen, Lord Seaton and others interested in Canada and Canadians, and in FitzGibbon personally, he was appointed one of the Military Knights of Windsor, Lower Foundation, on May 20th, 1850, and on January 8th, 1853, was removed to the Royal Foundation of the same Royal Pension.

The Military Knights of Windsor were founded by Edward III., in the twenty-second year of his reign, 1348, for the support of twenty-four soldiers, " who had distinguished themselves in the wars, and had afterwards been reduced to straits." Appointments are in the gift of the Crown. Each member is paid a small annual stipend, and an allotted residence in the walls of the Lower Ward. The only service required of them is the attendance of a certain number daily at the religious offices in St. George's Chapel, where they occupy stalls at the feet of the Knights of the Garter. The dress is a long dark blue cloak, with a scarlet collar and a Maltese cross of the same color on the left shoulder; a short, straight, two-edged sword or rapier with a Maltese cross-shaped hilt and a scabbard of dark leather.

The residence is a cottage interior with low ceilings and deep window sills, built in the walls of the castle on the right of the main entrance towers. A tiny gate-way and narrow path lead to the low doorways which face the beautiful St. George's Chapel, where these "poor Knights of Windsor," the original designation, pay their daily devoir.

The installation is a very simple ceremony. After the first lesson of the service for the day is read, two

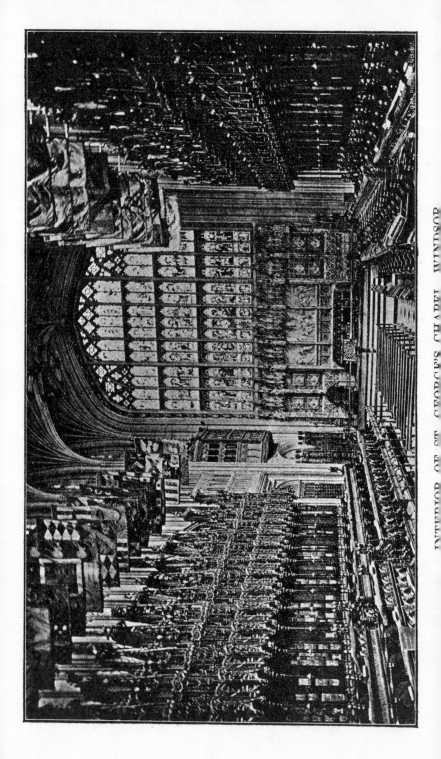

INTERIOR OF ST. GEORGE'S CHAPEL WINDSOR

knights, the latest installed, go out, and hand in the new one. As they enter, all three bow to the altar, turn, and bow to the dean; the new knight is then led by the hands and placed in the stall he is henceforth to occupy.

I will not attempt to depict the beauty of the chapel, its lofty grandeur, the exquisite perfection of the carving on screen and stalls, the great east window, through whose softly-toned tints the light falls in such mellowed tenderness; the historic associations of the rich emblazoned banners pendant from the rafters above the stalls of the Knights of the Garter; the historic arms and mottoes of those who have left their impress on the history of their country recorded on the panelled walls; the full notes of the organ above the screen, and the clear, sweet voices of the chorister boys from away down the long northern cloisters, growing clearer and clearer as they approach, until the sweet sounds rise above the aisles, and fill the grand nave beyond with melody.

Six of the knights are obliged to attend service once a day for a month, except in the case of sickness or leave of absence.

The pension attached to this royal bounty was small, only one shilling a day, and upon the appointment of a new Knight of the Garter, each military knight received a fee of one pound.

The chief benefit derived from it is a settled residence among their compeers, and under the immediate protection of the Crown they have served. There is also a certain prestige about the position which helps to smooth the rough places made by poverty for those who have done their work well, without adequate worldly reward—those who, in the common language of the times, have "seen better days."

Here they have congenial society, the quiet which old age seeks, coupled with the advantage of keeping in touch with the questions stirring men's minds; out of the tumult and strife, but within the circles of the echoes roused by the advance of science, literature and art; within reach of the tidings from the political world, and in the time of war, of the latest news from the army.

Can we not picture their excitement and interest in the tidings from the Crimea?

What unedited accounts of bygone battles fought and won, of retreats well conducted when the day had gone against them, of marches made, deeds of daring done, hardships endured, could the walls of the knights' quarters tell? How often the "only course" left for the men in command was laid down, argued over, and emphatically advocated by the knights as they paced the ramparts in friendly converse after service.

How every appointment was canvassed and commented upon, each bringing his knowledge of the name or man to bear upon the approval or disapproval of the "action at headquarters." How they rejoiced when a favorite or familiar regiment, or name which represented "one of the youngsters" of their day, was mentioned in the despatches, and grieved over the untimely fall of those who had shown promise of ability in their profession.

Can we not realize how each knight represented his own old corps among them, and received the congratulations or condolences of his fellow-knights as its representative ?

FitzGibbon was an early riser now as ever, and an excellent pedestrian. A favorite walk was to Frogmore, then the residence of the Duchess of Kent. Sir George Cooper, Her Royal Highness' secretary, whom FitzGibbon had known well in Canada, had obtained him the privileged entrée to the park and gardens.

FitzGibbon was never weary of this beautiful place, and went there frequently for the pleasure of sitting under the trees and walking over the perfectly-kept sward. It was also a show-place, to which he took his friends and visitors. His sister, Mrs. Washburn, who spent some weeks with him in the summer of 1851, speaks of going to Frogmore with her brother, of the loveliness of the park, and the "delicious feel of the velvety grass which made it such a pleasure to walk upon."

Another long and favorite constitutional was down the Long Walk to the statue at the end, a distance of three miles, or in the Lower Park towards Ditcham and back.

The great Exhibition of this year brought many colonists to London, and many of his old Canadian friends found their way to the knight's quarters—

some glad of the opportunity of seeing him again, others, on sight-seeing intent, very willing to visit Windsor Castle and an old acquaintance at the same time.

The Baroness de Longueuil was among the former. She had written a warmly expressed letter of congratulation to FitzGibbon upon his appointment, and Her Majesty's kindness to his daughter,* and now took advantage of being within easy access of London to visit her old friend.

Several of his former brother officers, whom he had not seen for years, but whose friendship he had retained through all the changes and chances of their lives, also came to see him.

Among these, Captain Brackenbury, of the 49th, one of the tutors of his barrack-room university (see page 50), was one of the most welcome. They had not met since they were young men in Canada. The afternoon spent together was all too short in which to recall the old days and their recollections, or tell of all that had happened to either during the intervening years. The intercourse thus renewed was never again broken off.

He had also other visitors about whose names still lingers more or less of interest. Miss Agnes Strickland, accompanied by the artist, Melville, and her

---

* I regret much that I have been unable to ascertain the particular nature of Her Majesty's kindness, but the reference to it in the Baroness de Longueuil's letter is evidence of the soldier's gratitude to his sovereign.

publisher, Colburn, when on a visit to the Castle in order to have one of the portraits there copied for her "Lives of the Queens of England," spent the evening at No. 9; the Rev. H. Hawtree; Major Clarke; I. Kitterminster, who writes in glowing eulogy of the happy hours spent in "the quiet, snug room in the Castle, while the brave old man swung to and fro in his Yankee chair, relating scenes of bygone days, living life over again in all its delights, forgetting the sorrows that attended them;" of the "stroll on the ramparts watching the sun go down in a blaze of glory;" their "walks by the river-side, exchanging thoughts of this and other worlds;" of the "beauty of the landscape dressed in all the pride of spring," "the song of the lark and murmur of the river," accompaniments of their "fondly remembered intercourse."

Other friends, unable to come to Windsor, invited FitzGibbon to dine with them in London.* These invitations, however, were generally declined, and the alternative of breakfasting with them offered. He preferred going up early to returning late, or incurring the expense or inconvenience of remaining all night at an hotel.

He had been elected a member of the Highland Society of London in 1842, and always received a card for the annual dinner held in the Freemason's Tavern, Great Queen Street, on March 22nd, in com-

---

* Among these was Sir Allan Macnab.

memoration of the battle of Alexandria, but even this invitation was only once accepted.

He had also been admitted as a Royal Arch Mason, Ionic Chapter, Toronto, on January 12th, 1848, and to the Supreme Grand Chapter of London, England, on August 6th, 1850; and though there is no note among his papers of his attending the lodge meeting in London, the position in the craft gave him additional means of influence, and enlarged his opportunities of making himself heard when occasion required it, or when his advocacy could be used to benefit others.

FitzGibbon went several times to town to the Crystal Palace in Hyde Park, going up by an early train and returning in time for dinner at seven, meeting many friends and calling upon others. Such a day is briefly described by his sister, who went with him on September 10th :

"Up to London by the 9.02 train ; walked to Miss Strickland's from Paddington. Miss S. had a small cottage and garden at Bayswater. She showed us the largest apples I ever saw, that had grown on her trees. Took a biscuit and glass of wine. Miss S. showed us out a short way. We walked to the Crystal Palace through the park, a most pleasant and not a long walk. We entered the Palace at half-past eleven, and stayed there until three. Met Egerton Baines from Toronto, who told us his mother was in town. Although we were pretty well tired, we walked to Brompton Row (could get no conveyance) to Lady

Barkley's. She had asked us to stay a few days with her, but we could not. We stayed nearly an hour, then took an omnibus to Regent's Circus, where we intended to take another to Paddington Terminus, but we were too late ; the omnibus had just left, and there would not be another for an hour. Took a cab, and got in in time for the half-past five train, and home by half-past six."

The first years spent at Windsor were, however, years of real privation and poverty. Small as his income was, FitzGibbon devoted the larger portion of it to the payment of his debts, reserving only what was barely sufficient for actual subsistence. There are letters extant from friends, some of them of rank, breathing friendship and affection for him ; and while at the same time acknowledging the receipt of various sums they had induced him to accept as loans during the trying time between 1838 and 1845, reproaching him for being in such haste to draw upon his so lately augmented but still narrow means.

His daughter and niece, who, with his son William, joined him in England in 1850, shared his privations, seconding his laudable ambition and enabling him to realize it.

His brother Gerald was soon his only remaining creditor, and with the exception of the last sixty pounds due, the thousand pounds lent by him in 1841, principal and interest, was paid in full before FitzGibbon's death. This sixty pounds was generously forgiven him by his brother at a time when the approach of the infirmities of age rendered him so anxious lest he should die in debt, that the fear affected his health injuriously.

These years brought other and greater griefs in their train. His son William's health had been failing for some time. The sea voyage and change had not the beneficial effects they had hoped for. He returned to Canada early in the autumn, and died at Belleville, in October, 1851. FitzGibbon felt this loss keenly, but another and a greater blow was soon to fall upon the brave old man. His daughter Mary, the dearest companion of his life, was slowly dying, although as yet her father's eyes could not see it.

In March, 1852, he writes to Miss Strickland of a visit from an old brother lieutenant, "one of my old corps, the 49th, who sold out in 1810, and returned to England to the study and practice of medicine. So strong does his friendship for me continue that he has taken upon him the management of my Mary's health, and came here to study her case for a few days."

Dr. Anderson ordered her to drink goat's milk, and later on FitzGibbon writes : " Every alternate day I walk about six miles out and home to bring to Mary a soda water bottle of goat's milk from the beautiful Cashmere goats belonging to Prince Albert, on one of the farms in the Park."

His youngest son, James, died in 1852. After having served but a few years in the 24th Regiment, he sold his commission and returned to Canada to devote himself to the study of the law. He practised in Belleville, Ontario, and stories are still extant there of his wit and eloquence at the Bar.

Mary did not long survive her brother, and the year closed in sorrow for the bereaved father.

There are several letters of this date from his old friends and brother officers, full of kindly friendship and sympathy. In one of these, from Captain Brackenbury, a remarkable dream is referred to, which dream had at the time so comforting an influence on FitzGibbon's mind that he had it printed, in the hope that it might benefit others.

"In my dream I fancied myself standing in front of a golden column, brightly burnished, in which I saw my own face most clearly reflected. Delighted with the brilliant appearance of all around me, I gazed intently upon the reflected face, and soon it appeared to expand, to be enlarged, to become more expressive, beautiful, sublime, beyond all I had ever imagined of the human face. Filled with a delight beyond all power of language to express, it flashed upon my mind that I was in heaven. The first impulse was that I should prostrate myself in profound gratitude to the Almighty for having created me for such a blissful destiny. I vividly remembered the Scripture which says, 'Eye hath not seen, nor ear heard, neither hath it entered into the heart of man, the things which God hath prepared for them that love Him;'

and here I felt that it was more than realized to me, and the crowning joy of it all was that it would never end. My mind became, as it were, expanded to a vast extent, looking into eternity with mental power never before imagined by me, and with an awful impression of its boundless, its infinite extent.

"In the midst of these ineffable thoughts my mind was suddenly turned to earth, and there I saw my wife lying on a sick bed, with her five children in tears standing around it. Here then was the very state of sorrow and suffering I had so often in imagination dreaded. Yet my happiness was not in the least affected by it. Before this dream I could not have conceived how this insensibility to their suffering could be, but now I clearly comprehended why I was not so affected. I mentally exclaimed: 'Oh, it matters not, they will be here immediately;' and whether the intermediate time were five years, or fifty years, or five hundred years, did not then appear to me worth an anxious thought, so brief did all time appear to me compared to the eternity which then appeared before me.

"And so, in truth, it really is to a mind expanded as my mind then was. And this comparison and the consideration of it now appear to me as fraught with a consolation to suffering minds here on earth, which no other consideration is at all equally calculated to give. And, therefore, while my mind is thus so intensely and blissfully impressed, do I hasten to record this vision, before it fades from my memory in the slightest degree.

" Now, I trust I shall not be thought superstitious by anyone to whom I may communicate what I have here written. I am delighted with the dream, because it proves to me that even in this life I possess a capacity for enjoyment of blissful happiness of which before now I had no adequate idea, and because it convinces me that in heaven no consideration of things on earth can diminish my happiness there. And here I take for granted that the Almighty has in like manner endowed every human being with latent capacities for increased happiness, whenever in His merciful will He pleases thus to exercise those capacities.

" Thus a new field for thought appears to be opened up before me, in which my mind may be further improved, and I be enabled to increase its powers and enhance its happiness. Now, more plainly than ever heretofore, do I understand and feel that man is a progressive being, and that it is his duty to avail himself of every circumstance, occurrence, or means which may enable him to advance himself in usefulness, in virtue, and piety; and with the view, especially, of further enabling him to do good to his neighbor.

" Anyone, at the hour of death, leaving behind wife, children, or other beloved relatives, exposed to poverty, sorrow, or other suffering, having such an absolute conviction of mind as I then had, of the shortness of all things of time here on earth, as compared with eternity, must surely, under such conviction, be nearly, if not altogether, relieved from much mental suffering, and enabled to depart in comparative peace, and even with hope and joy and confidence in the goodness of God.

"That this account of my dream may occasionally soothe and cheer the anxious spirits of persons so circumstanced, I humbly hope and fervently pray.

"AMICUS."

CHAPTER XII.

FITZGIBBON was never idle. His old energy and anxiety to be of use to someone—to do what little good might be within his power—never flagged. He read all the papers with avidity, making notes of interesting items, clipping paragraphs containing information suitable for the acceptance of some of his youthful correspondents among his nephews and friends; occasionally, where a reminiscence of his own was *apropos*, replying to or writing articles for the press, military matters especially attracting his attention.

The following is, perhaps, as apt an illustration of this interest and the "grist he sent to the mill" as anything among his papers:

"MONDAY, *November* 22nd, 1852.

"SIR,—In the supplement to the *Weekly Despatch* of yesterday, I have just read the following words: 'And never let us forget to honor and care for the 'humblest soldier who has done his part of the great 'task in the faithful spirit of his chief. The indivi-'dual honors cannot be his, and he knows it. He is 'proud to see decorations on the breasts of his officers, 'they are tributes to his valor; his bayonet helped 'to win them; his discipline, his firmness held the 'ground; his energy was in the last decisive charge.' I cannot withhold from you the statement of a simple fact which, I think, beautifully illustrates the truth of your hypothesis.

"The battle of Queenston, in Upper Canada, was fought on the 13th of October, 1812. Captain Dennis, of the Grenadier Company of the 49th Regiment, commanded the post at the beginning of the battle, and for about an hour afterwards. Major-General Brock arrived from Niagara, and was killed, and Captain Dennis was wounded, but he still kept the field. The invaders were all killed or taken prisoners; among the latter was Lieut.-Colonel Scott, the present Commander-in-Chief of the American Army.

"In three months after, a general order was read at the head of that grenadier company, which promoted Captain Dennis to the brevet of Major.

"On the company being dismissed, one of the soldiers tossed his musket high above his head, and cried aloud, 'Hurrah, boys, we have done something for the old Roman at last!'

"That Captain Dennis is the present Major-General Sir James B. Dennis. Because of his zeal and his daring in battle, his soldiers usually called him 'the old Roman.'

"The tribute you have paid to the memory of the Duke and to the army, and especially to the privates of that army, is most gratifying to me, having been once a private soldier myself, and I am most grateful to you for it. I wish every soldier in the army had a copy of it. The study of it would add to his just pride, would increase his devotion to the service and nerve his hand in the day of battle.

"May I request of you to give this effusion a place in a future number of your journal.

"I am, Sir, your obedient servant,

"AN OLD GRENADIER OF THE LAST CENTURY."

The mention of an old comrade would again lead to a renewal of intercourse or letter of enquiry.

The following is a reply so evidently characteristic that we give it. The top of the page has unfortunately been mutilated by some enthusiastic collector of crests for the impression of the coat of arms:

"I am, indeed, my dear sir, the same Tom Mansel who shared with yourself the glory of victory at Nelson's ever-memorable battle of Copenhagen, but certainly not possessing the youthful bearing which then animated my aspiring spirit, as both body and mind are fearfully, in the present stage of progressive old age, fast approaching the lee-shore of beam-end position, yet I endeavor to preserve an even keel as long as remains a shot in the locker to keep off the *ennui* of natural infirmities. As I intend, in the course of a short time, to clinch the tow-rope of pleasure by hailing your snuggery at Windsor Castle, I therefore cut my pen yarn short, and will spin one as long as the main top bowling when we meet to talk in good earnest, and fight our battles of glorious record o'er and o'er again.

"Believe me to be,
"My old comrade and friend,
"Yours very faithfully,
"TOM MANSEL.

"P.S.—If you happen to visit the gallant Naval Knights of Windsor, will you kindly convey my royal mast-high regards to Lieut. Henslow, who served under my command some years gone by; a gentlemanly, exemplary officer thus I held him in estimation, and no mistake."

His correspondence with George Combe led to an enthusiastic study of phrenology. He was a firm advocate and believer in the science, and in many of his letters speaks highly of its influence for greater contentment and increase of hope in the future improvement and development of good in humanity.

He was also a great reader, and many of his letters of this date contain his opinions and impressions of the books he was at the time perusing. In July, 1857, during the mutiny in India, he refers to the life of Sir Charles Napier as "the most exciting work I have ever read."

He understood the antagonism of the directors of the East India Company to Sir Charles Napier's measures. Sir Charles' difficulties were a more extensive reproduction of his own in Canada prior to the rebellion. He believed that had Sir Charles "been duly supported, the present mutiny would never have occurred. For years he had warned the Indian Government of their danger. He had prevented mutinies, and pointed out clearly how to govern all safely and well, but as his counsel involved changes in the civil departments, which affected the vast abuses of patronage, he was treated as an intolerable nuisance, and driven from the country.

"Were it not for the destruction and ruin consequent upon this mutiny, I would rejoice at it. Never have men so well deserved disaster and punishment as these directors."

He paid one or two visits to Dublin before the year

1855, but though he made many plans and promises to repeat them later—promises which he was, however, careful to speak of as "conditional only"—he was unable to fulfil them. He valued and loved his sister-in-law (wife of his brother Gerald) highly, and his letters are full of kindly, grateful reminiscences of her hospitality and affection for him. It is to her care of his correspondence we are chiefly indebted for the details necessary for the last chapter of our veteran's life.

The night schools and classes established in the town of Windsor were also of great interest to Fitz-Gibbon. He frequently addressed the boys, and while entertaining them with graphically depicted accounts of incidents in his own experience, anecdotes of men and soldiers he had known, he drove home many a lesson and maxim of value. He never lost an opportunity of impressing upon them the desirability of cultivating truth, sobriety, courtesy and kindness to the least of God's creatures. He noted everyday incidents in the streets, trifles which others passed by unheeded, and turned them to account in his friendly talks with the boys.

He was always ready to drill a score of ragamuffins, and halfpennies never stayed long in his pockets when others' need seemed to demand their expenditure.

During the last few years of his life, while still able to go up to town for the day, it became necessary to see that he had a return ticket on the railway;

otherwise his soft heart for a hungry lad or sympathy for a doleful tale of want would have left him
without the means to pay his fare back.

He was repeatedly called upon by the Dean to act
as trustee for the widow or orphan daughter of a
deceased brother knight, or for advice and assistance
in preparing pension papers and arranging their
affairs.

Although he corresponded with many friends in
Canada during these first few years of his life at
Windsor, none of his letters has come within my reach
except the following to the late Mr. Walter Mackenzie,
of Castle Frank, Toronto. He had been one of Fitz-
Gibbon's rifle corps organized previous to the rebellion
of 1837, and ever remained one of his most devoted
friends and admirers. In this letter a strong love for
Canada is expressed, and one cannot but regret that
his version of the history of the war of 1812 was not
written for the benefit of those now so deeply interested in that little known period of Canadian history.

"LOWER WARD,
"WINDSOR CASTLE, *May* 10th, 1855.

"MY DEAR MR. MACKENZIE,—I must begin this
answer to your interesting letter of the 14th ultimo,
by making an admission, or more properly a confession, that I really am unequal to making it an adequate return to your epistle. Your idea that the
'Celt being especially distinguishable from the Saxon
by retaining the fire of youth amid the snows of
winter's age,' is no longer fairly to be entertained by

me. It is true that my physical condition is now far better than ever hitherto I could have hoped for. I can jump and dance with as light and elastic a bound as at any period during the last forty years, and certainly more so than during any period of the last ten years. But I cannot say so much for the mental energy. Would that I could guide, aid or forward in any way your efforts in the cause of Canadian advancement, either historically, politically or socially. In fact, my desire is so strong in this direction that it requires an effort to make me refrain from making you an offer of help wherever you may think I could render it. But in justice to you I dare not. The only way in which I can concoct anything like an adequate answer to yours is to go over it paragraph by paragraph and say something to each.

"Should Dr. Widmer not have left Toronto before you receive this, pray charge him from me to come to Windsor, which he can do in less than an hour by rail, or if he cannot from any cause, that he will write me to come to him. I think the meeting would make us both a year younger.

"Our 'tilt' with the Dean and Canons is now fully in the lists before the Chancellor. Whether we, like the slender Ivanhoe, shall roll their Reverences in the dust, as he rolled the brawny Bois de Guilbert, time alone can tell. Your letter shows me that we have the good wishes of one honest heart. The gentlemen of the long robe are now actively employed in preparing questions and answers, replies and rejoinders, and all the usual prolonged fence of such gladiators. The last note to me, as chairman of the Knights' Committee, from our chief champion, is very encouraging. Still I will not indulge in much hope, and I am pursuing my own course without any reference to aid from that quarter. If it come, *tant mieux*.

"For the honor and prosperity of old England, I grieve to see its clergy so grasping and avaricious. No class of this nation is doing so much injury to the public mind, and it pains me to learn that a like spirit is manifesting itself in your thriving province.

"I have not a copy left of the letter you mention. I believe it was the substance of a paper I wrote at the request of Lord Seaton, in 1849, and which I had soon after printed in London. I have been sometimes urged to give my version of the war of 1812, but I could not reconcile myself to do so; because, if I did, I could not refrain from telling all the truth, and this would expose to public blame, if not shame, some I would fain not wound. But at this long distance of time I might say much without reluctance which then I would decline. Therefore, should you ever enter upon a sketch of Canadian chronicles, and would call on me for an account of any single occurrence or series of events known to me, I could give you detached sketches, some of which may help to fill up or amplify a narrative for you.

"It is interesting to me to learn that you went to Sir Francis Head, with Judge McLean, to urge him to attack the rebels on Tuesday morning, because I also went to him soon after sunrise and entreated of him to give me three hundred out of the five hundred then armed in the Market Square, and with the only 6-pounder then brought from the garrison, I promised in two hours to disperse the rebels. His hurried answer was, 'Oh, no, sir, I will not fight them on their ground; they must fight me on mine.' I could not help mentally exclaiming, 'What an old woman I have here to deal with!' (Perhaps you have a copy of a pamphlet which I had printed and published in Montreal in 1847, 'An Appeal to the People of Upper Canada;' if you have not, pray obtain one if you can; I suppose Rowsell may yet have some unsold.) At that moment I considered it of the highest importance to disperse them with the least possible delay, that the news of their defeat should accompany, if not precede, the news of the outbreak, and thereby paralyze and confound all other disloyal men in the Province before they could act in concert; and had the rebels the presence of mind and the daring which their first steps indicated, the Upper Province might have fallen under their power. The steps taken by you and me and our other few friends, such as the shooting of Anderson by Powell and the ringing of the city bells on Monday night, gave the first check.

"As to the Navy Island campaign, it was disgraceful to us. The rebels and sympathizers were on the island like rats in a trap, and the moment the detachment of the 24th joined at Chippewa, an attack should have been made. Elmsley had boats enough, and a descent upon the island was easy and certain to succeed. But there was no will and therefore no way. So far from thinking you not the fit person to record the events of that outbreak, I know no man who knows more of its details, or observed them with so earnest a zeal and spirit as you did—no, not one.

"And here I must break off to attend the summons of Margaret to tea—as you broke off to attend the summons to 'tax costs.'

"What you say as to your lack of love for your profession brings vividly to my remembrance the case of the only son of old Col. James Green, long secretary to Lieut.-General Peter Hunter, once Lieut.-Governor of Upper Canada. He desired above all things to go into the army, but his father sent him to Oxford, to be educated for the Bar. He was called to the Bar in Lower Canada, and took up his post, not of exercise, but of practice, in Three Rivers. The headquarters of the 49th were then there, in 1810, and young Green told me that when in Portsmouth, England, on his return to Canada, he was on the point of enlisting as a private soldier, which, however, he did not, but returned to Canada. We invited him to become an honorary member of our Mess, where I became most intimate with him. His life became a most unhappy one, and although he became Clerk of the Peace at Quebec, he died early, as I believe, of something like a broken heart, He was a high-minded, noble and generous young man. (Mrs. Grasett is his daughter, or other relative of his.)

"But surrounded by such 'specimens of humanity' as you mention, you must cultivate cheerfulness, self-confidence and perseverance for their sakes, and not sink, nor even bend, beneath the burden of mortified feelings or disappointed hopes. For Mrs. Mackenzie's sake and their sakes, cheer up and cherish a manly pride and a lofty resolution to meet and surmount every obstacle to a final success and independence.

" I would gladly see you employ such spare time as you can command in literary exercises which may be most agreeable to you. I dream of preparing some essays for the guidance of the young in Canada in the exercise of their social and political duties, adding now and then a few hints on the parable of the Good Samaritan, with special reference to my discordant countrymen, the Orangemen, and their adversaries, the Romanists, who mutually dishonor our common Christianity by their almost total want of the great Christian virtue, charity. From time to time I fear much for the future harmony and prosperity of Canada.

" But I find my firmness of purpose becoming, day by day, less firm, or rather more feeble. It just occurs to me that if I were near you I would give you leave to exercise authority over me, which, if sternly exercised by you, might produce some fruit; for I really have the needful health and physical strength, and lack only the strong will to bring all into active operation.

"The first *Anglo-American* magazine you sent me, and the only one I have received, I lent to the Earl of Albemarle and have not received it back. As chairman of the Committee of the Military Knights of Windsor, I have been in correspondence with his Lordship for some months, he being our advocate in the House of Lords. On seeing the appointment of Lord Bury to an office in Canada, I have from time to time sent to the Earl Canadian papers of various descriptions, finding they are acceptable to him and to other individuals of the family.

"You say, 'Last week I sent you one containing a second article on the same subject, which I took complimentary but somewhat mistaken notice of,' but this I have not received. I fear that all things sent by post are not surely delivered. Occasionally I send newspapers to Canada, and know not if they ever reach. I cannot enter into a correspondence to ascertain if they do. Last week I sent you a *Times*, and occasionally I may obtain one to send you hereafter, though uncertain if they ever reach you. But the Provincial papers, no doubt, republish all, or nearly all, that can interest you Provincials.

"I cannot think of offering you any comment on the thousand and one errors and blunders of our great men here. The public prints say much more than any private correspondent possibly could; to them, therefore, I must refer you. In November I was on the point of addressing a letter to the *Times*, giving sage counsel to Lord Raglan. (What presumption!!!)

The letter which I thought of writing, I was sure the *Times* would not publish. Nevertheless, I am since sorry I did not then write it, as it would have actually foreshadowed almost every evil which has since been inflicted on that doomed (as it then appeared to me) army. I, who witnessed three campaigns in the winters of Canada, might well foresee the horrors in store for those gallant fellows. But the horrors have been so patiently, so heroically borne, that the soldiers of that army have added a new and beautiful ray of glory to the character of the British arms, or I should rather say, to the character of the British soldier. I consider this result as almost an equivalent for those losses and disasters—and the like, I say, of the insane charge at Balaclava, ordered by Lord Lucan. The men who made that charge have earned a place for themselves in history above that of any of their predecessors. These two examples will bring forth good fruit in due season.

"The Roebuck Committee's report will be printed by order of the House, and, I suppose, sold as usual. I will, if I can, procure a copy for you.

"You talk of blind and brainless men. Query: Have we any other now, after forty years of systematical exclusion of all talent, as such, or if any one of the favored class did possess natural talent, had he any encouragement to cultivate his talent? Or would he not have exposed himself to ridicule had he seriously attempted it? Now, however, we are on the eve of changes which as yet cannot be clearly seen.

"Being now old, and no more work in me, I often imagine myself as if standing on the top of the flag-staff on the Round Tower of this castle, and surveying all the passing displays of folly and wisdom exhibiting on the surface of this globe of ours, and sapiently commenting thereon. I often wish to record my imaginary comments, but it is too late in the day. Of the views and objects of the Royalists, the Aristocrats and the Democrats in Europe, I entertain opinions which I believe to be clear and well founded, but to detail them would be too much for me to write, and perhaps for you to read. But I am convinced that the period is approaching when Napoleon's saying at St. Helena will be verified, that "in fifty years Europe will be Republic or Cossack," and I think the danger is greater of its becoming Cossack than Republic. The despots everywhere are armed and well prepared to pounce upon the first uprising of any of the peoples, who are everywhere isolated and, as it were, prostrate. I sometimes exclaim, 'Thank God, I have Canada to fall back upon.' Its future seems to me more full of promise than that of any other section of the human family. I long to be among you. I think I could make my pen useful to you all, but this hope is not a very strong one.

"Tell Mrs. Mackenzie that if I go to Chatham, I will call upon Major Durie. But this is not likely, unless I can obtain more money from the Dean and Canons; for I have reserved to myself only the bare means of subsistence, and have appropriated all else towards paying off my remaining debts. How cruel of this heartless Government to stand between me and the grant of land three times voted for me by the two Houses of the Upper Canada Parliament! And yet they assented to the Rebels' Losses Bill, and voted to Papineau $4,500 which he had forfeited by his acknowledged rebellion. I sometimes lose my patience and my temper. God bless you and yours.

J. F.G.

Although the letter to the *Times* of which Fitz-Gibbon speaks was not written, the following extract from one to his nephew Gerald, of a later date, may be interesting as a soldier's opinion on the cause of some of the disasters in the Crimea. The letter is dated Monday evening, 5th February, only, but from the context we may conclude the year to have been 1856.

" My indignation against those who have caused so many unnecessary evils to our army in the Crimea was boiling over when I wrote my last note to you, and I therefore forgot your request as to the Toronto magazine. It was then lent, and has not yet been returned to me, but when I receive it back I will send it to you by post. The charge will be sixpence only.

" From all I have now read, I am confirmed in my opinion that those evils have been chiefly caused by the want of a good road from Balaclava to the camp. The want of that road I ascribe chiefly to Sir John Burgoyne, the commanding engineer there. Next to him I would blame Lord Raglan himself, who should early have foreseen the necessity for such a road. I consider that every officer on his staff, certainly the Quartermaster-General, Lord de Ros, and every general belonging to that army, as most shamefully wanting in military skill and foresight. They were there for weeks before the bad weather set in, during which time I wonder the want of a winter road does not appear to have occurred to them; or if it occurred to the juniors, they, perhaps, had not courage to offer an opinion to a senior. For many of our commanders I have known to have met such advice, or even suggestion, with a contemptuous repulse. General de Rottenburg gave for answer to a suggestion offered to him by an excellent officer in Canada, in 1813 : 'Colonel Nichol, when I want your advice I will ask you for it.' Yet if the colonel's suggestion had been acted upon, Buffalo would have been taken during the following week, and all the stores for the approaching campaign captured or destroyed, which would have made it impossible for the Americans to invade the Province that summer. They, however, did invade it, and we lost Fort George and the lives of many hundreds of our officers and soldiers, together with many valuable stores and much provision.

"I rejoice that the French army is side by side with ours, thus to prove, beyond all doubt or denial, our shameful mismanagement, which would be stoutly and insolently denied were our army acting alone, for it would be impudently said that such evils were inevitable."

His knowledge of Canada and Canadian life brought many to him for information or letters of introduction for themselves or friends about to emigrate. All sorts and conditions of men came to him; some he could put off with his card to be exhibited in Canada, but the majority requiring more particular attention, occupied much of his time and increased his correspondence extensively.

The following letter, addressed to Mr. Stayner, Post Office Inspector of Upper Canada, and sent to the care of FitzGibbon's eldest son, is a specimen of the many kindly letters of introduction he wrote to old friends in Canada in behalf of parties in whom he was interested :

"9 LOWER WARD,

"WINDSOR CASTLE, *Sept.* 24th, 1859.

"MY DEAR SIR,—I can hardly expect that you can recall me to your memory, for I never had the honor of an intimate acquaintance with you. I first saw you in Montreal in 1807 or '08, when you married the daughter of Mr. Sutherland, with whom I was then acquainted. I was then the Adjutant of the 49th Regiment.

"I am now impelled to address you in behalf of a young gentleman (son of one of the Military Knights of Windsor, Capt. Douglas, a neighbor of mine) who has ventured to identify his fortunes with the Province of Canada, and is now employed in the Provincial post office at Toronto. The Hon. W. H. Merritt, of Upper Canada, spent a day with me here this week, of whom I enquired if you were yet at the head of that department in Canada, and he thought you were, as he had recently seen you.

"Capt. Douglas is now an old man, as all these Military Knights are. He has three daughters here with him. At his death I fear these three young ladies will be wholly unprovided for. They have two brothers. One is employed in the Post Office Department here in England, usually in taking charge of the mails to Alexandria and other ports in the Mediterranean. His conduct has given so much satisfaction that he has recently been promoted in the Department. This brother remits to his sisters all he can possibly spare from his income. That his brother in Canada is equally desirous of aiding them I entirely believe.

"The interest I take in these young ladies impels me to address you; they are intimate with my two nieces who reside with me and keep house for me, and I am therefore acquainted with the particulars which I thus communicate.

"Should the brother in Canada be really deserving of your favorable consideration, may I venture to bring him to your notice, in the anxious hope that he may be soon enabled to contribute his share to the support of these excellent girls.

"The only apology I can offer for thus trespassing upon your benevolent attention is my desire 'to do good to my neighbor;' and my impression of you makes me believe that my appeal will not be unacceptable, but rather the contrary, if you can depend upon my judgment and discretion in making this statement. And I venture to hope that the recollections of those days, and of the 49th Regiment, will be pleasing to you, especially of the family of the late Dr. Robertson and Mrs. Robertson, who were intimate friends of Mr. and Mrs. Sutherland.

"Do not take the trouble of acknowledging the receipt of this letter. I write it in the hope that you are yet at the head of the Department in Canada, and that it may possibly be in your power to advance this young man should his good conduct deserve your patronage.

"Should Mrs. Stayner be yet alive to bless you, pray offer my kind remembrances, for I well remember her while she was at school.

"Very truly, my dear Sir, yours,

"JAMES FITZGIBBON."

This kindly letter was never delivered. Mr. Stayner had been succeeded by Mr. John Dewe, and he being a more intimate friend, and the letter being unsealed, its contents were conveyed to him verbally.

In the postscript to the letter to his son, FitzGibbon says :

"Since writing the foregoing I have looked over a Canadian almanac, and see that Mr. Dewe is Inspector of the Department in Toronto. He called on me here a few days ago in company with Mr. Vankoughnet, of Toronto. I knew him in Kingston formerly, and I feel confident he would willingly oblige me. Show him my letter to Mr. Stayner, and I think you had better follow his advice in regard to young Douglas. He may be able to do more for him than anyone else."

FitzGibbon's energetic service did not stop here. A short time before his appointment a question had been raised by the knights over the appropriation of the revenues from which their pensions were paid.

Few among them had influential friends who cared to exert themselves in their behalf. They could only bemoan their wrongs and condole with each other over the iniquity of those who had deprived them of their just rights, the supineness of those who had benefited by it, and the coldness of the Government that could not be moved to take any action in the matter. They were literally " poor knights," although the march of manners had altered the title to "Military and Naval Knights," and were proving the worldly wise maxim that " those who cannot command friends at Court, find it hard to obtain them by begging."

But FitzGibbon was not one to rest content under a wrong without making an effort to right it, especially when he could thereby benefit others. Though poor in purse, he was rich in friends, in resource and ability. Fortunately for the success of his efforts, one of the next vacancies among the knights was filled by the appointment of Sir John Millais Doyle. Sir John was a man of family and position in the army. He seconded FitzGibbon's efforts, and brought many influential friends to bear upon the question. They worked together, and succeeded in making such a stir, both through the press and in Parliament, that the knights' cause was taken up and carried into Court.

The correspondence the case entailed fell principally on FitzGibbon. The business carried him frequently to London to interview those whose interest could further the settlement of the claim of the lawyers who had taken it under their charge.

Sir John Doyle knew little of business matters other than military, and he was willing enough to leave it to his more enthusiastically energetic friend. Lord Albemarle took a great interest in it, and friendly letters passed between him and FitzGibbon on the subject. The latter's letters to Dublin from the years 1851 to 1859 are full of the hopes and fears to which the various delays and law proceedings gave rise; regret at the delay and the consequent deprivation as one or other of the knights, who had watched the case in anxious anticipation of an increase of income, passed away without receiving any benefit; and of indignation at the slow progress, dilatoriness and law

quibbles resorted to in order to postpone the hearing.
(See Appendix XI.)

Sanguine expectations of obtaining redress, anticipations of an increase of from two to three hundred
a year to the one shilling a day allowed, dwindled as
the years passed and their cause was deferred from
term to term; and hope dying hard, they were thank-
ful to accept the sixty pounds a year derived from
the lapsed canonry finally allotted to them.

The sum varied according to the proceeds or revenue
derived from the "new canonry," as it was called by
the knights. In 1863, the amount they received only
reached the sum of thirty pounds fourteen shillings.

In a letter dated January 19th, 1853, he says: "The
knights' case before the Chancellor does not appear
to make much progress. We are just told that the
Dean and Canons are about to demur to the jurisdic-
tion of that Court. Should the demurrer be allowed,
I am told our case will be the stronger. But will it
be the sooner terminated? Time will tell, but it may
be a long time. Procrastination is to these fat divines
rich living; while to the lean old soldiers it is short
commons. However, with the fins of the Dogger
Bank codfish,* and the wings of the Windsor Park
pheasants,† my larder can furnish more than one

---

* Sent FitzGibbon from Ramsgate by Major Plenderleath, a
brother of his old friend and brother officer of the 49th.

† A brace of pheasants sent annually as a New Year's gift to each
Military Knight by H. R. Highness the Prince Consort.

sporting dinner. Thanks to the sinners rather than the saints—the cormorants."

On December 5th, 1856, he writes: "I send you a copy of a note from our solicitor, that you may see the progress making in our suit against the Dean and Canons here. I begin now to indulge hope a little; but even if not successful, I will not be disappointed. Your father, who knows so much of 'the glorious uncertainty of the law,' will approve of the resolution. But if my income be increased, and I live to be out of debt, I fear I shall not then know how to 'demean myself' in circumstances so entirely new to me."

The copy sent is but the usual lawyer's letter, reporting proceedings, and there being "every prospect of success attending our efforts."

This hopeful prospect was, however, not realized, and the disappointment felt by his clients was proportionately great. Sir John Doyle died without receiving any benefit from the lapsed canonry finally granted them, and FitzGibbon enjoyed it only for one year and a half. Small though the addition was, the knights owed it, certainly to some extent, to FitzGibbon's energy, perseverance and determination to do his best to succeed.

Other friends who were most instrumental in aiding him to force the case upon the attention of the authorities, were Colonel North, of Wroxham Abbey; Sir Francis Doyle and General Read, M.P. for Windsor. Charles Grenfel, also M.P. for Windsor, was also one of the most active supporters of the claim, and FitzGibbon was able to repay him in kind. When the representation of Windsor was being hotly contested by Mr. Grenfel and Lord Charles Wellesley in 1859, Fitz-Gibbon brought up the knights in a body to vote, and turned the poll in favor of the man who advocated his cause.

This was almost the last flash of the old energy and enterprise. The malady, a sort of epileptic or apoplectic seizure, which eventually caused his death, showed its first symptoms shortly after, and though he recovered from the first attack, he never regained the old strength. His grand constitution, a life of steady abstemiousness and healthy exercise, his steady perseverance and sanguine temperament, enabled him to rally after each successive attack with surprising vitality.

The knights' case ended, there was no longer any incentive to exertion, but he kept up a lively correspondence, his handwriting and diction showing few signs of decaying powers. When reading the papers now and then, the old fire flashed out in protest against injustice or pusillanimous fears.

The following letter, written after reading the report of a debate in the House of Commons, on the question of the rumored threatened invasion by the French, is an instance :

"*August,* 1860.

"SIR,—I have just read the communication addressed to you, signed " H," and published in the *Star* of this morning. I am in the eightieth year of my age, and too feeble to express at much length in writing the feelings excited in my mind by the perusal of that paper. But I cannot refrain from expressing myself as follows :

" I entered the army as a private soldier in the year 1798, and was placed on half pay as a captain on the reduction of the army in 1816. I have met the French repeatedly in action among the sand-hills of Holland in 1799, and other enemies of England in other countries for several years afterwards.

" I have ever looked with contempt upon batteries and breastworks in almost every position. I look upon fighting face to face as the true mode of trial for the British soldier. Batteries and other works of defence I have thought rather diminished the soldier's bravery.

" I consider it impossible for the French to land half a million of men in England, perhaps even half that number could not be brought over at one time. Have we not five millions capable of bearing arms ? Could we not in a few days bring together half a million of these to meet the French ? Would not our men be filled with indignation against any enemy who dared to insult us by such invasion ?

" I know that the French soldier advances to meet the British bayonet with more hesitation, I will not say trepidation, than he would advance to meet any other enemy. The British soldier rejoices in his bayonet. It does not require much skill or manœuvring to bring an enemy at once to close quarters. We have only to rush upon an opposing line and decide the issue at once by a hand-to-hand encounter. No two lines have ever yet crossed bayonets in battle. I was often assured that it was done at the battle of Maida, but I did not believe it. Long after that battle, Sir James Kempt, who commanded our battalion making that charge, declared in my presence that the bayonets did not cross. The French, while advancing, hesitated, and at last halted, turned round and ran away; but they delayed too long in doing so; the British rushed in, and laid upwards of three hundred of them on their faces with the bayonet. Very many years after, I repeated this to Commodore Sandham of the navy, who said to me: 'I am glad you mentioned this matter to me, for I was that morning a lieutenant in one of the ships which landed our force in the Bay of St. Euphemia, and witnessed the action from our decks. After the battle was over the men were re-embarked, together with many wounded French soldiers, and it was curious to see the wounded in the sick bay the following morning—all the French on their faces, being stabbed in the back; while all the British lay on their backs, being shot in front by the volley which the French fired as they advanced to the charge.'

" Would that I could cry aloud in the ear of every Briton, calling upon him to hold in contempt all defensive works. An enemy must land upon an open beach. We must know of his coming many days before he can possibly come. We may, therefore, be to some extent prepared. Even though we be not at hand to meet him, telegraph and rail-cars can soon bring us upon him; and then if we do not kill and capture his army, we deserve to be conquered and enslaved. But of the issue I have no doubt.

" I do not now hesitate to declare that no army from France will ever invade England. For it is manifest to me that no nation of 20,000,000 people can ever be overcome by any force which can possibly be brought from abroad. I am ashamed of the debates in the House of Commons upon the question of the projected defences. They fill me with indignation. Is it that those members are chiefly of the feeble aristocracy, the plutocracy and dandyocracy, that they seek to defend our country by means of spade and pick-axe, rather than by strong hands, stout hearts and British bayonets?

" It requires but little previous drill to qualify our yeomanry to fight the battle of·the bayonet, and therefore I rejoice at the organization of our volunteers. Of these we may organize a number quite equal to the destruction of any invading force. Upon these our old men, our women and children, may look with confidence, with pride and affection, and they will never be disappointed.

" I pray of you to publish this, which may be called a rash effusion, but I write it with the fullest conviction.

" Your obedient servant,

" AN OLD SOLDIER, WHO DESPISES ALL FEAR

" OF INVASION."

FitzGibbon clung more closely to the fireside as the end approached, and seldom quitted the precincts of the Castle. He was always glad to see and chat with his old friends from Dublin, London and Canada, and many visited him. The old love for Canada returned with redoubled force; the burden of all the latest letters is to be once more among the old scenes, and to be to his grandchildren what his grandfather had been to him. So strong was this longing that his medical attendant was consulted on the possibility of his being able to endure the voyage. But it was not to be. The soldier who had fought for Canada was not to find a grave within her borders.

During one of his many visits to the Castle, his nephew, Gerald FitzGibbon, induced him to have a photograph taken to send to the grandchildren he wished so much to see. It was sent with a loving message and apology for what he considered an "unsoldierly beard," but his hand had grown "too infirm to trust it with a razor." It is from this photograph that the frontispiece is taken.

He died at Windsor, on December 10th, 1863, and was laid to rest in the catacombs of St. George's, beside those he had loved and honored most among his fellow-knights.

Thus ended the life of one whose enthusiastic temperament and excitability led him often to run counter to the world's opinion, or the more coldly calculating worldly wisdom of his superiors, but whose fearless integrity and honest singleness of purpose carried him to the goal he sought; one whose sole aim in life was to be an honest man, a simple soldier, to do his duty to his country, good to his neighbor, and walk humbly with his God.

CHAPTER XIII.

I T is not so very many years since, even in good society, it was no uncommon thing to hear preference expressed for " regulars " in contradistinction to the " militia." While British regiments were quartered in Upper Canada they took precedence of the militia here as elsewhere. But it was among the ignorant only that this precedence was given in private, with an insolence which showed a disregard for the feelings, and ingratitude for the services of the men who had fought so well in defence of their homes, and whose knowledge of the country, as well as of the foe, had contributed much to the success and glory of the army.

A letter appeared in the Niagara *Spectator* of December 3rd, 1818, which was calculated to do considerable harm at the time. In it, apparently, the writer made assertions which accused the officers of His Majesty's regulars of decrying the services and standing of the militia, with whom they had fought side by side during an eventful war, and statements which would persuade the readers of the paper that appeals to the Commander-in-Chief for either compensation for losses suffered during the war, or redress of wrongs inflicted upon the settlers by the ruthless marauders who, if not of them, at any rate accompanied the invading armies, were disregarded and treated with indifference.

Among the Archives of the Militia Department at Ottawa there are a number of such petitions with the reply received — some of them docketed by FitzGibbon's hand, possibly as Assistant Adjutant-General—of which FitzGibbon speaks in the letter appended herewith. I have not, however, been able to find the particular one referred to. These papers are unedited, and but partly assorted; the files, too, incomplete, owing, no doubt, to the vicissitudes attendant upon fire and frequent moving. Fitz-Gibbon's letter was published in the Montreal *Herald* of December 26th, 1818, and probably appeared in other papers of the period. It is dated:

"YORK, *Dec.* 8th, 1818.

"*To the Militia of Upper Canada:*

"GENTLEMEN,—I cannot, in justice to my brother officers, and with due regard to the respect which I bear you, permit to pass uncontradicted the gross falsehoods written by Mr. Gourlay and published in the Niagara *Spectator* of the 3rd inst.

"There were few officers in Canada during the late war who were not known to me, and I have ever heard them speak of you with respect, and frequently in the fervor of admiration.

"I do therefore step forward to repeal this impudent calumny, and to oppose to your honest indignation, the man who would seek to destroy the cordial good-will which has hitherto subsisted between us, and which, under the blessing of divine Providence, contributed so much to the glorious successes during the late contest with our neighbors.

" I cannot upon this occasion forbear exposing the falsehoods of Mr. Gourlay's representations on the subject of the Petitions of which he speaks. It is within my knowledge that the answer of His Royal Highness the Prince Regent to the address of the Commons House of Assembly of March last was transmitted to that House during the last session, and that the Prayer of the Petition in favor of Angelique Pilotte was promptly and most graciously answered by His Royal Highness.

" These facts have casually come to my knowledge, and I think it very reasonable to suppose that the others have been equally attended to.

" I have the honor to be, gentlemen,

" JAMES FITZGIBBON." *

When the first edition of this book had gone to press, the question of a suitable design for the cover arose. After looking through a number of conventional patterns without success, the idea of a sketch of the "Veteran's" swords was suggested. FitzGibbon had given his service sword to his son James when he was gazetted to Her Majesty's 24th Regiment, in 1844, and the only swords now in possession of the family are the straight cross-hilted one he wore as a Military Knight of Windsor, and the dress sword given him by Sir Augustus d'Este (see page 242). The following is a copy of the letter which accompanied it, and which I am able to include in the present edition:

---

* For letter on Canadian Militia, see Appendix XII.

"*August*, 24th, 1839.

"DEAR AND MUCH ESTEEMED SIR,—By the vote of your fellow-citizens, and by the testimony of the most reverend and of the highest authorities in Upper Canada under the Governor, it has been made manifest that you were favored by Providence in having and availing yourself of the opportunity of saving your Province from the incalculable evils which must have been consequent upon the falling of Toronto (to say the least) into the temporary power of licentious rebels; in the sequel it will be seen how far and in what manner, from the Crown itself to the ranks of educated intelligence amongst your fellow-provincials, such an important service has been appreciated, acknowledged and rewarded; in an humble individual like myself it calls forth all the respect and admiration which those in private station who love their country delight to offer in return for public benefit.

"The service which it has been your great good fortune to render to your Province having been of a military nature, perhaps a token of the sentiments mentioned in the previous paragraph, and with which I am so livelily affected towards yourself, should be of the same character?   May I therefore venture to request that you will favor me and do me the honor of accepting the accompanying sword, and may I indulge the hope that the circumstance of having worn it myself will not unfavorably affect the feeling with which you will accept of it.

"Renewing assurances of my esteem, permit me, my dear sir, to subscribe myself,

"Yours most sincerely,

"AUGUSTUS D'ESTE.

"No. 1 Connaught Square, London.

"To LIEUT-COL. FITZGIBBON, of Toronto."

The publication of the " Life and Correspondence of Major-General Sir Isaac Brock, K.C.B.," by his nephew, Ferdinand Brock Tupper, in 1845, led to a long and interesting correspondence between the author and " the old 49th man."

" I have received your letter of the 15th ultimo," FitzGibbon writes from Montreal on June 19th, 1845, " the perusal of which has revived in my memory many of the most interesting circumstances of my early life.

" Mr. Maingy's box has not yet been received here, but as soon after the perusal of your book as I can write them, I will send you such particulars of the mutiny at Niagara,* as will give you a very full knowledge of that unfortunate event in the history of the 49th. I accompanied Sir Isaac Brock from York (now Toronto) to Niagara, when he crossed over Lake Ontario, and had seized and imprisoned the chief mutineers. All the examinations were had in my presence, or, I should rather say, I was permitted to be present, for I was then but the sergeant-major of the regiment. I was sent to Quebec with the prisoners, and witnessed all the proceedings before the court-martial which tried them, and all the particulars which were elicited became known to me.

" Of the passing events and occurrences of my early life I have no early written record. Within the last twenty years I have committed to paper some particulars still remembered by me, others yet remembered I have not recorded. But in compliance with your request I will send you all I think at all deserving your notice, which from my present impression you will find, I fear, little interesting, The perusal of

---

* See Page 54.

your book may revive some events forgotten by me,
and perhaps in other respects guide me in making my
notes.

" I write this short note merely to acknowledge the
receipt of yours, and to give you an assurance of my
great desire to be at all instrumental, even in the
humblest degree, in adding to the fame of my earliest
and best benefactor. And if there was another man
for whom I felt an almost equal degree of regard and
gratitude, that man was John Savery Brock. I am
indulging the hope of one day seeing his widow and
children in Guernsey. But I can say no more now.

" I am just arrived from Upper Canada, and have
resumed my duties as Clerk of the Honorable the
Legislative Council of Canada. I will endeavor soon
to retire from them because of age and consequent
debility.

" That I may do honor to the General's memory, I
have ever striven to serve my country well, and the
Almighty has blessed my poor efforts more than in
early life I had ever anticipated."

The recollections subsequently sent to Mr. Tupper
added much to the value of the second edition of the
work.

On other matters there are many interesting items.
On November 26th he writes:

" Lord Metcalfe left us this morning for Boston on
his return. God grant he may reach England alive.
We never can expect such a man again. I am this
moment returned from Government House, whither
I was summoned to witness the swearing in of Earl
Cathcart. I have a few minutes only to give you

rapidly a few answers to your queries before the mail closes. Lieutenant Johnson was taken prisoner—not wounded. I was taken a few minutes before him,* and was in prison with him until January following.

"The Jesuits' garden,† for many years after 1807, was used as a parade to my knowledge. At present, I believe, it is so used, but I know not positively. I will acquaint you by next mail. Lieut. Johnson was not exchanged in the ordinary way. By the convention entered into between the Duke of York and Marshal Brunn, it was agreed to restore all the prisoners taken on both sides, and so we were released.

. . . .

"In noting the services of the 49th in Canada, would not the capture of Colonel Bœrstler's detachment at the Beaver Dams in June, 1813, by my detachment of forty-nine men—for that was the precise number, including myself—be an appropriate item?

"Perhaps modesty ought to keep me from putting this question; but, selfishness and vanity apart, I think it properly belongs to the credit of Sir Isaac Brock. When I brought in those five hundred prisoners and delivered them up to General Vincent, I then thought I would have given the world's wealth to have General Brock there alive to say to him, 'Here, sir, is the first instalment of my debt of gratitude to you for all you have done for me. In words I have never thanked you, because words could never express my gratitude for such generous protection as you have hitherto unceasingly extended to me.'

"You will find a brief account of it in a little periodical publication published many years ago in

---

* Egmont-op-Zee (see page 29).   † Quebec.

London, called, I believe, the 'Soldier's Companion.'"*

The account given of the mutiny at Fort George called forth some angry protests from friends of Sir Roger Hale Sheaffe, and led to a bitter controversy in the press. The following letter will throw a side-light upon that page of our history:

"MONTREAL, *December* 27th, 1845.

"MY DEAR SIR,—The first information I had of your book was communicated to me by a letter from Lt.-Col. Loring from Toronto, enclosing one to him from Sir R. H. Sheaffe. I extract the following from Sir R.'s letter:

"'But another worthy of notice must have been less notorious, to which FitzGibbon can testify, that those prisoners who were ordered to rejoin their regiment (whom I accompanied) told him that there was no officer under whom they would rather serve than myself—which he told me on our way up the river.'

"Inasmuch as I never accompanied Sir R. up the river, I could not have had any conversation with him there. The proceedings of the court-martial were conveyed by me from Quebec to York, having left Quebec—where Col. Sheaffe then was—on the 6th of January, 1804, and I delivered the packet to Col. Green, Military Secretary to Lt.-General Hunter, in York, I believe, on the 24th of the same month, having travelled through snow for nearly six hundred miles, drawn by the same horse, and through long tracts of unsettled forest.

"Immediately after this I rejoined the Regimental Headquarters at Fort George—Col. Brock having removed thither from York during the preceding

---

* See **page** 78.

autumn. Col. Sheaffe returned to Upper Canada
from Quebec the following summer, I being at Fort
George while he was ascending the river. I suppose
he must have mistaken me for some other non-
commissioned officer who then accompanied him. In
another place he writes: 'Make it known to Fitz-
Gibbon, from whom I should like to receive a
certificate of what was told him by the prisoners
and of Rock's declaration.' Now, of this declaration
I never heard or learned anything until I saw Sir R.'s
letter to Lt.-Col. Loring, and therefore my letter to
Lt.-Col. Loring, which Sir R. now has, declares my
ignorance of those circumstances. Of Rock's declaration I was not likely to know anything, having been
at Fort George when the mutineers were shot at
Quebec on the 2nd of March, 1804.

" When I wrote the account of the mutiny I took
for granted that Sir Roger would at once be satisfied
that I was the writer, and as I desired very much to
spare his feelings, I gave my best consideration to
your request, and I decided that I must give the
statement such as I wrote it, or decline doing so
altogether; for to omit the expressions of the elder
Fitzpatrick to Major Wulff's servant would be keeping out of view the real source of the discovery of
the conspiracy. Beyond that statement I studiously
guarded myself against giving any other facts to
prove that the mutiny was chiefly (I will not say
altogether) caused by Sir R.'s irritating and insulting
language, even to officers as well as to all others, at
parade and drill. I would not place at your disposal
statements to prove all this. I left the controversy
between you and Sir R.'s defenders, giving the one
expression only of Fitzpatrick, which, if not given,
would have left very incomplete the account I
gave you of the mutiny; and from that account, as

published by you, you very forgivingly omitted Sir R.'s name, which in my account was given.

"I have not the least desire to conceal from any one that I am the writer of that statement, nor do I desire to conceal any statement I have made should circumstances arise which, in your judgment, may reasonably call for further publication. *On my own account* I have no desire for concealment.

"But to all I have written or may yet write, showing forth the conduct of Sir Roger as a regimental commanding officer, I would add that I have heard in those days irritating and insulting language used to officers and men of other regiments at parade and drill, by at least six other commanders of regiments, which in these days would not be tolerated for one week.

"Were I to repeat now to Sir Roger the substance of the conversations I had with him in Quebec while the mutineers were on their defence, when they made many charges against him in extenuation of their own guilty conduct, to none of which will I here further allude, he would more justly appreciate any subsequent admissions they may have made when under sentence, as to his conduct as their commanding officer. He questioned me in detail from day to day during the trials as to these charges (for my name being on the list of witnesses I could be present in court only when called on to give evidence), and I told him very fully why they then attacked him, and I could plainly see that ever after he became less and less irritating and insulting to those under his command. But years elapsed before he could acquire that degree of self-control which ought to characterize every officer and gentleman, and were I near him now I could bring to his recollection some mortifying rebuffs which were given him from time to time afterwards by some under his command for his unjustifiable language and manner toward them. But he at length became a good commander of a regiment, for he was at heart kind, benevolent and religious; but these sentiments were, in his earlier days of command, nearly if not entirely over-ruled by his extreme ideas of military authority and power, and by his over-weening opinion of his own military talent for drill, and his own unequalled zeal in the public service. In proof of this I could give many facts.

"I hope and trust your controversy will have been brought to an end before this letter reaches you, and that the indiscreet friends of Sir Roger will have ceased to attack you. Should they not, I would venture to suggest to you to ask for an interview with any one of those friends, or any one deputed by them, and show them this letter, and for their information I here declare that I can give numerous facts which, if published in these days of improved military manners, would be most painful to Sir Roger and disparaging to his reputation.

"I have carefully looked over what I have now written, and I beg leave to add that I have not employed my pen at all as a partizan in the controversy between you and Sir Roger. How far you might have prepared your book without those references or allusions to Sir Roger I have not enquired, nor do I think myself competent to judge. You asked me for a statement, and I gave it. Considering all the circumstances of the case I still think myself justifiable in writing the one I gave. I am of opinion that truth is not always to be withheld because its expression may wound the minds of public men whose public conduct, when truly stated, may subject them to public animadversion or censure. Let me beg of you, however, not to make any further use of what I have written unless you may feel yourself under a strong necessity for doing so; at least during the short time which Sir Roger must yet have to live.

"I remain, my dear Sir, most sincerely yours,

"JAMES FITZGIBBON."

In the postscript of this letter reference is made to an article written in answer to a question asked by one of his sons, and in a subsequent letter he thanks Mr. Tupper, through whose hand he concludes "Queenston" had appeared in the *Naval and Military Gazette*.

Later, another "defender of the 41st Regiment" attacked Tupper. His answer, which appeared in the New York *Albion*, FitzGibbon carried to the editor of the Montreal *Courier* for insertion in that paper (it appeared on May 14th, 1846). FitzGibbon adds:

"The writer of the attack upon you is Mr. Richardson, commonly called Major Richardson, he having, it is said, held that rank in the Spanish Legion under General Evans. He is at present in this city (Montreal). He has written some novels, of which that called "Wacousta" is one. He conducted a newspaper in Canada for some time, which broke down some two or three years ago."

The correspondence with Mr. Tupper continued with little intermission after FitzGibbon returned to England. Though he never paid this often planned-for and talked-of visit to Guernsey, Mr. Tupper and his daughter visited him after his appointment as Military Knight at Windsor.

Scattered throughout these letters are references to many of the men whom he had served with, or under, while in Canada, to the routine of his life, his desire to return to Canada, and to his ever unflagging interest in the questions which might affect or influence the welfare of the "Provinces." In that written on January 28th, 1848, is a brief opinion of one of his former commanders :

" General Vincent died here on Friday last, aged about 82. He was at all times a feeble man, both in mind and body, and to me the wonder has been that he lived so long. His death places the 69th at the disposal of the Commander-in-Chief. His funeral will be attended by two of the old 49th men, namely, Major Bleamire and me. Possibly Lieut.-Colonel Plenderleath and Major Brock may attend also."

After the issue of the second edition of the " Life and Correspondence of Sir Isaac Brock," several of his brother officers, in acknowledging the receipt of a copy, mention FitzGibbon—among them Capt. Brackenbury,* who writes in September, 1848 :

" In a cursory glance over the contents of the work (which I have begun to devour), I am delighted to find that you have placed our common friend, Fitz-Gibbon, in such bold relief. He is richly entitled to the distinction, and it may be of service to him in his present position—at all events his old age will be cheered in thus finding himself in such honorable juxtaposition with his heroic and almost idolized patron."

---

* See page 56.

And again—

"My quondam associate and gallant friend, Fitz-Gibbon, has spoken and written of my services toward himself in too flattering terms. About three months since (having accidentally discovered that I was in the land of the living), he wrote me one of the most beautiful, feeling and graphic letters I ever perused."

Evidently this friendly recollection was repeated to FitzGibbon, or mention made of it by his old friend Mr. Tupper, to draw forth the following reply. As it contains a reference to an item of military red tape which must often have influenced the soldiers' fortunes, I quote it in full:

"Your account of Captain Brackenbury is most gratifying to me. I entirely concur with you in thinking that his exchange to the 17th Light Dragoons was an unfortunate move. It was brought about without his knowledge, and of course without his consent. Lieut. O'Bierne, of the latter regiment, was placed on the staff of General Drummond in 1808 or 1809,* and it became necessary to transfer him to a regiment on that station else he would have to be placed on half pay. The friends of Lieutenant Bartley, of the 49th, were applied to, and offered the exchange, which they declined. Then Brackenbury's friends were applied to, and they accepted the offer. One morning on the Champs de Mars, in Montreal, Colonel Sheaffe came upon the parade and very formally saluted 'Lieutenant Brackenbury, of His Majesty's 17th Light Dragoons.' 'Why, Colonel, do you amuse yourself at my expense this morning?' 'It amuses

---

* 1809 is the date given by Brackenbury.

me not, because what I say is too true, and that we must lose you, which we all regret.' And so we lost Brackenbury. That Lieutenant Bartley, then junior to Brackenbury, and altogether unequal to him in every respect, arose to the command of the regiment, and led it in several actions in China, and was created a K.C.B. Poor fellow; he died on board a steamboat after leaving Alexandria on his return home from India."

In a postscript to a letter with which is enclosed one from Dr. Winder, Librarian to the Legislative Assembly, but late of the 49th, that Mr. Tupper might read what Dr. Winder says of his book, is the following:

" My friend Winder is too severe upon the Americans. In any event I have no fear for the North American provinces; they are stronger to defend than Americans are to attack. The latter are a feeble people to make war *beyond their own frontier.* They cannot find idle and vagabond individuals enough in their country to compose an army of one hundred thousand men, and their militia will not leave their own shores to invade ours. Witness their conduct during the battle of Queenston. Their troops were at best a disobedient and disorderly set of men, and the provinces could drive back an army of the above number. Their success in Mexico has not altered my former opinion of them; it was owing chiefly to the weak resistance of a miserable race well known to the invaders."

The above is characteristic.

Query: Would his opinion be altered any more by the nation's recent success in Cuba?

The letter, as written at the request of Lord Seaton (Sir John Colborne), referred to in the Preface, will be found in the appendix to this edition. It was evidently this to which Miss Strickland refers in her letter on pages 263-4.

The receipt of copies of the Niagara *Mail*, of May, 1853, sent FitzGibbon by an unknown friend, and the perusal of an able article in its columns, induced him to write to the editor. He had also received copies of the *Mail* of October and December, 1852, in which the account of the laying of the foundation-stone of the new monument to " the memory of my first commander and earliest and best patron, the lamented leader of our gallant soldiers, devoted militia men and Indian warriors at Queenston on October 13th, 1812."

" The paper just received gives me infinite pleasure by its account of your growing prosperity. Upon several occasions since my return from Canada I have been called an enthusiast and a visionary because of the opinions I often expressed in London of Canada's future progress in wealth, prosperity and social happiness, and now I see my highest hopes more than realized. Your situation is peculiarly favorable, your entire rear being forever covered by your northern climate, which climate is a blessing to your people because your winters *make men of you*, such men as you never could be were your summer perpetual. Even with your present population, I consider the British provinces now fully adequate to their own defence without any assistance from the parent State."

Mr. Kirby's reply pleased FitzGibbon so much that he made an effort to have parts of it inserted in one of the London papers. In this he failed, but was more successful later.

" On receiving the *Mail* (Niagara) of the 5th July, the day before last," he writes on August 11th, " I enclosed it to the secretary of one of our principal statesmen, and this morning received a note from him :

(Copy)   ' *August* 10th.

" ' SIR,—I beg to acknowledge your note and enclosure of yesterday, which I hope to have the opportunity of placing before ———— at the first moment of his leisure.'

" Immediately after I went to the reading-room, and there saw in the *Morning Chronicle* of this morning the whole of your editorial commentary on the speeches of Lords Ellenborough and Brougham, at full length as copied ' from the Niagara *Mail*, 5th July.' This is some satisfaction to me after the disappointment of my first efforts."

After asking the editor to put his name on the regular subscription list of his paper, FitzGibbon goes on to make a statement which in these days of recognition of the value of cheap postal rates with the Mother Country is significant.

" I receive a good many papers from Canada weekly, and for some time sent them through the post-office to my friends in these kingdoms, but lately they have been charged 8*d*. each, so that I cease to send them.

I addressed a letter to the Postmaster-General requesting to be allowed to circulate the Canadian papers, putting upon them each a penny stamp. In answer, it was said 'that it was not thought expedient to adopt my suggestion.' Could not the press in Canada join in a crusade against the authorities in St. Martins-le-Grand ? That is, besiege them by a succession of missives of a very polite and pungent character. I think they would comply."

In July, 1855, after apologizing for delay in replying to a letter from Mr. Kirby, he adds:

" Every day during this time (a month) have I wrestled with Dr. Young's thief of time until in desperation I put the question, ' Shall I write now, or ever after keep silence ? ' and I have mustered firmness enough to seize my pen, exclaiming ' By G—d, I will write.' I remember Uncle Toby's oath to Corporal Trim, and hope that this my offence will not be recorded against me.*

" On the 14th December last I wrote to the Secretary of the Admiralty suggesting to their lordships that now, while building so many gun and mortar boats for the Black Sea and the Baltic, they might quickly and unostentatiously have a number of them so constructed as to be passed through our canals into the Upper Lakes, so that on any emergency a fleet of them could, in less than one month, be sent from

---

* NOTE.—I have quoted this in order to contradict the assertion made that FitzGibbon was in the habit of using strong expletives —assertions that have no foundation in truth, other than such instances of a quotation as above. He had seen the evil effects of swearing too often to indulge in it habitually.

England into those lakes before the Americans could build one vessel of war in any harbor on the lakes, and our vessels could then and thereafter forever prevent their building one, their dock yards being all within range of our guns and mortars.

" In about a month I received a note from the Secretary acknowledging my communication, and conveying their lordships thanks for it.

" On receiving this answer, I wrote to my friend the Hon. John Young, one of the members for Montreal (who had sent me his pamphlet proposing the enlargement of the Welland Canal for further mercantile accommodation), mentioning my correspondence with the Admiralty, and suggesting to him to have in view those gun and mortar boats, and to confer with the Admiralty, so that the increase in the size of the locks should be made to correspond with instructions from them as to the size of the boats. I have not since heard from Mr. Young. But now that the recent danger of war is passed (as I am confident it is) we should look far into the future, and quietly, without any display, make ample enlargement in our Canadian canals to let pass such boats as are now built, for thereby shall we be best able to repel all hostile aggression upon Upper Canada, at least.

" Let us well defend that section, and it will ever be our best bulwark against all future aggression.

" I am glad to see the good feelings now so cordially cultivated by the people residing on both sides of your extended frontier. May those feelings be continually increased more and more.

" I have long been convinced that the improvement and happiness of each of those communities will be better secured and more increased by keeping them apart than by any union or annexation whatever.

" By exercising two different modes of government

the field of experience will be greatly extended. Each party, or rather each government, may be warned by the errors of its neighbor, or encouraged to follow a good example wherever happily exhibited.

"The power of each will often be a salutary check upon the ambition, presumption or cupidity of the other. No sooner is the power of any nation become predominant than it becomes aggressive, and the usual result is war, with all its crimes, miseries and horrors. Better for the United States people that the provinces should become powerful, and thereby be a check upon the aggressive spirit of the men who from time to time administer their government, than that those men should be permitted to make war so that they and their followers and partizans may enrich and aggrandise themselves at the expense of their own country, and by the plunder and ruin of their neighbors.

"Never heretofore has the world seen two nations so qualified to set a good example to all other nations as Great Britain and the United States; and it appears to me that nothing but the pride, ambition and cupidity of statesmen on either side can produce a war between them. But if the peoples severally will exercise due forethought, prescience, and discretion, they will firmly resist all measures tending to war between them. Hitherto the peoples of the nations were never sufficiently intelligent and co-operative as to exercise due control over those who governed them. Hence now the danger is great that they will not take the wisest course to constrain those governments to act wisely. It is high time, however, that they should arouse themselves to assume that part which legitimately belongs to a people who are qualified to obey good government, and to control and regulate an erring one."

In these letters FitzGibbon dwells on many questions of interest to Canada. The animosity between the two bodies, Roman Catholics and Orangemen; the rapidly increasing taxation in England as tending to drive many men of moderate means to seek exemption from it in Canada, and the advantage to that country of including men of education and refinement with means among the emigrants to its unsettled but fertile localities; the importance of strengthening the relations with the Mother Land by mutual understanding and consideration; of Canada having a just appreciation of her value and of winning respect from her nearest neighbor by being ever in a position to repel invasion and to hold her own in any question of importance to both. He also asks for and refers to many friends on the Niagara frontier—among them an old " 49th " man.

" Your paper of the 28th July, 1858, I received fourteen days after date (!), being the second time it has come in that short space, and each time by the Quebec packet. I see in it recorded the death of an old brother officer of mine in the '49th '—Mr. Garrett. I placed him at the head of one of the three advance companies on the morning of our attack on Montgomery's, on 7th December, 1837."

. . . .

A letter from Mr. Kirby, referring to the recent enrolment of the 100th Royal Canadian Rifles, prompts the following :

" After much consideration I have enclosed your letter to the private secretary of the Commander-in-

Chief, the Duke of Cambridge, having first taken a copy of it and sent to Colonel the Baron de Rotten-berg. I think you will not be displeased at my thus making use of your letter. It is well written, and its tone and tenor are very honorable to you. Whatever impressions have been made heretofore in the minds of the Duke and the Colonel must be improved by its perusal."

The following extract from a letter written by another "49th man," to whom FitzGibbon had also sent a copy of Mr. Kirby's letter, is interesting in connection with FitzGibbon's endeavor to interest the Commander-in-Chief in the Canadian regiment.

"Mr. Kirby's letter respecting the One Hundredth regiment is much to the purpose, and written in a good spirit. I think it has had some effect, for I see the Duke of Cambridge has been at Shorncliffe and reviewed the corps, which is a step in the right direction. To crown all, and completely to make up for past seeming neglect, the Queen should now present their colors with a few gracious words such as she knows how to speak, and then all would be right."

Later, FitzGibbon adds, after the presentation of the colors to this regiment by H.R.H. the Prince of Wales (January 13th, 1859) :

"The Prince of Wales' Canadian Regiment has been most favorably brought into public notice. I hope that the good conduct of the regiment will hereafter become an example to be held up to the army at large, and have a salutary effect upon the other regiments; and who can tell how far other colonies may not contribute in like manner to the nation's power and defence? Couple this idea with the building of some half-dozen more leviathans as men of war, and see how all would be indissolubly linked together in prosperity and power."

The publication of Mr. Kirby's historical poem, 'The U. E. Loyalist," won much interest from Fitz-Gibbon. He endeavored to arrange for an English publisher, but without success. He ordered several copies to send to the old friends who had known Canada in 1812-14.

On the 18th of October he writes:

" Knowing so many of the defenders of the Niagara frontier during the war of 1812-13 and '14, I felt a strong desire to write to you during the month of September, and give you anecdotes of individuals whose zeal, devotion and personal bravery I witnessed. But I could not make the attempt, fearing that I could not now do them adequate justice. Having been on detached service in the army, my party afforded a rallying point for individual militiamen to present themselves whenever a collision of any kind was effected. Especially lads under twenty years of age came, with a cheerfulness and eagerness which delighted my own men and gave them a bravery of spirit which gratified me exceedingly to witness."

Winding up his letter with the words, " This is all I can achieve at the present"—a reference to the oft reiterated regret at failing strength and shaking hands—FitzGibbon adds the characteristic wish, "and you will please me by having my name always printed with a capital G."

FitzGibbon was the friendly medium through whom copies of Mr. Kirby's books were conveyed to the Queen and the Prince of Wales. On March 31st, 1860, he reports other correspondence with Colonel Phipps, Her Majesty's Secretary.

"On the morning of the 27th inst., I received your letter of the 6th inst., the perusal of which so pleased me that I felt convinced the perusal of it by Colonel Phipps would be very pleasing to him also. I therefore at once sent it to him by post, with a note from myself, of which the following is a copy:

"'DEAR SIR,—I have this day received from Niagara the accompanying letter. I think the perusal of it will give you satisfaction. I have served in military and civil capacities in both the Canadas during forty-five years, and I entirely concur in what Mr. Kirby writes of the Canadian people. His description of them will, I am sure, be pleasing to you, therefore I send this letter to you, at the same time not thinking that private communications like this are ever brought under the notice of Her Majesty. I hope you will not tax your time by acknowledging the receipt of Mr. Kirby's letter, or even by returning it to me.

'I am, etc., etc.

'To Col. the Hon'ble Charles Phipps,
          Buckingham Palace.'

"Yesterday I received a note which I did not expect, accompanied by your letter. I send you the note herewith rather than a copy of it. Your letter was in his possession for two days, and I think it likely he laid it before Her Majesty and the Prince of Wales, for I may say it was beautifully written and could not fail to please them, now that the Prince has decided to visit Canada."

On the 29th of September he writes:

" I hope the Prince will get to Queenston, where it would rejoice me to be to join with my old Lincoln fellow campaigners, the Kirbys (if any remain), the Merritts, the Chisholms, and the many others whom I would gladly name. How much would I gladly write on those old times could I but do so."

This was, however, the last letter of the correspondence which has been entrusted to me. I cannot but regret that one written after the Prince's return to Windsor is not among them, that thus we might have further corroborative evidence of his interest in securing to Mrs. Secord the honors, so justly her due, for her loyal efforts on June 23rd, 1813.* I refer to this more particularly as in a pamphlet recently published, the author, to prove his contention that Mrs. Secord did not walk the distance of nearly twenty miles to warn FitzGibbon on that memorable day, mutilated the certificate given her by Fitz-Gibbon, which he professed to quote from three recognized authorities, by erasing the word twenty and substituting the word " twelve." Such action is unworthy the pen of one claiming the name of historian.

---

* See pages 81-84.

Although FitzGibbon was in many skirmishes and engagements with the enemy, both in Holland and Canada, and ever sought the front ranks against the foe, I found among the matter from which the first edition of "A Veteran of 1812" was compiled no record of his ever having been wounded.

Since the issue of the book, however, the following story has been given me by one who had it from my grandfather's lips:—

One day while on detached duty, in June, 1813, I was alone in the bush, my principal object being to keep a vigilant watch on the enemy and prevent all communication between the two Forts, Erie and George. I and a certain number of my men acted as advance scouts. It was a close, warm day. I had walked several miles noiselessly, as was my habit, and as was necessary to avoid discovery. I stood a moment leaning against a tree. Although the sun was high there was deep shadow all about me, and the silence of mid-day in the Canadian woods. Presently I became conscious of someone near me. I turned, and as I saw the figure of a man some yards from me, he fired. The ball struck me, and with a deadening sense of numbness I staggered—it was but a second. My assailant turned and fled. Scarcely realizing my action, I pursued him over tangled underbrush and through the maze of tree trunks. Something caught his foot, he stumbled and fell. A moment and my hand was on his collar. He had dropped his piece in his fall, and with it in my other hand I threatened to brain him with the stock. Winder* had heard the shot, and now came up. Between us the man was taken to camp, and after obtaining all the information of the enemy we could from him, we let him go. Later I heard he reported that no bullet would kill me, for the ball had certainly struck me.

My friend Winder wished me to lie up and apply for leave, for I was so bruised and stiff as to find difficulty in moving about for a day or two. I would not, however, as had I done so another man would have been put in my place, and I therefore lose the opportunity of doing good service. Why had the ball not killed me? Winder and I went to the spot where the shot was fired, and found that the ball had first penetrated the stem of a young sapling. This, with the thickness of my tunic, and my action in turning, had probably saved my life. This was the only wound I ever received.

I have used the first person to tell the story as nearly as possible in FitzGibbon's own words. During the riot in Toronto, on July 12th, 1834 (see page 176), FitzGibbon speaks of his efforts to quell it, and being ably assisted by several of the magistrates. Referring to this an old resident of Toronto told me that he well remembered the day.

" Colonel FitzGibbon was a fine, strong, big man. He went into the crowd with a quiet smile on his

---

* Lieut. Winder, 49th.

face, gave his orders with determination, and where-
ever he was disobeyed or caught men fighting, he just
took them by the collar and put them into the jail
hard by. I saw him and Colonel Higginson put as
many as thirty of the worst rioters inside the jail
doors that day, and they weren't a bit flurried,
neither."

The kind act of Her Majesty, referred to on page
272, was a grant of a small pension to FitzGibbon's
only daughter, that in case of his death she might be
provided for. She lived but a short time to enjoy it,
but it procured for her many invalid comforts and
luxuries otherwise unattainable. It also enabled Fitz-
Gibbon to take her to Dublin, where she died and was
buried beside her kin in the old churchyard at Irish-
town. A great grey slab to the left of the main
entrance door marks the spot.

FitzGibbon was a strong advocate of the value of
physical drill to a soldier, and the present day regime
would delight him.

When quartered in Quebec, he saw how the men on
guard suffered from the cold. Knowing that action
alone would keep the blood circulating, and that the
monotonous pacing to and fro was not sufficient, he
invented a system of physical drill that might be
practised even in the sentry box. A large man himself, the need of exercise was imperative, and, taught
by experience, he endeavored to thus benefit others.
During his last visit to Dublin he stayed with his
brother in Merrion Square. The square being reserved

for the residents, he would take his sword, let himself in, and seeking the most secluded spot, practise the sword exercise for an hour, not always without an admiring audience of boys. One morning, the weather being unusually bad, his brother bade him take his exercise indoors "if he must have it." Piling the chairs on the library table that he might have sufficient space, FitzGibbon obeyed, while the lawyer heedless of the swinging sound of the old soldier's sword play, speedily became absorbed in the intricacies of a case then before his court.

A crash! He turned to see a heavy but thin-legged chair, one of its legitimate supports neatly severed, lying prone on the ground, while the swordsman paused aghast at the result of a more than usually energetic lunge. Is it a wonder that the startled owner bade him "go practise his — gymnastics on the street"?

The mutilated chair was extant for many years, and its story the delight of FitzGibbon's great-nieces and nephews, who reproached his biographer for omitting it.

In some of his latest letters to his nephews, Fitz-Gibbon speaks of having invented a series of exercises which he could practise in bed, "for being now so feeble I cannot rise very early. These serve to keep the blood circulating freely, and conduce greatly to my physical health."

In one of FitzGibbon's letters to his Guernsey friend, Mr. Ferdinand Brock Tupper, he so epitomizes his own character, that I cannot do better than close this chapter with the quotation. *Apropos* of the lamentable lack of energetic men and minds at a period of national importance, he writes:

"The dread of responsibility appears to me to be the most prevailing evil of the day. Surely it were better to fail in nobly daring to achieve great objects than thus meanly to shrink from difficult duties."

APPENDICES.

APPENDIX I.

WHEN the policy of the French Directory, 1798, turned their ambition to still further conquest and aggression, Holland was the first victim of the Republican ambition. They had revolutionized that ancient commonwealth, expelled the Stadtholder, and compelled its rulers to enter into a costly and ruinous war to support the interests of France, and though their engagements had been performed with fidelity, they determined to subject them to a convulsion of the same nature as that which had been terminated in France by the 18th Fructidor.

The Dutch, having had an opportunity of contrasting the old régime with the new, were now ripe for a return to the former. The French Directory saw this leaning to old institutions with disquietude. They recalled their minister from the Hague, and replaced him by a man of known democratic principles, with instructions to overthrow the ancient Federal Constitution, overturn the aristocracy and vest the Government in a directory of democratic principles entirely devoted to the interests of France.

Obedience to these instructions soon robbed the inhabitants of Holland of all their ancient liberties. Antagonism to the directors became so pronounced as to rouse the fears of France lest it should undermine their influence in Holland. To prevent this, General Daendels was ordered to take military possession of the government.

While Napoleon's operations and desperate conflicts had been going on in the south of Europe, England had roused herself from the state of inactivity in which she had been held through her own want of confidence in her military powers, and an expedition was prepared more in proportion to her station in the war as one of the allied powers than any she had hitherto projected.

Holland was selected both as being the country nearest British shores in the hand of the enemy, and as the one where the most vigorous opposition might be expected from the inhabitants.

The treaty between Russia and England of June 22nd, 1798, stipulated that the latter should provide 25,000 men for the descent on Holland. To re-establish the Stadtholder, and terminate the revolutionary tyranny under which that opulent country groaned; to form the nucleus of an army which might threaten the northern provinces of France, and restore the barrier which had been so insanely destroyed by the Emperor Joseph; to effect a diversion in favor of the great armies then fighting on the Rhine, and destroy the ascendancy of the Republicans in the Maritime Provinces and naval arsenals of the Dutch, were the objects proposed in this expedition. The preparations were such as to extort the admiration of French historians. The harbors of England resounded with the noise and excitement of the embarkation. The first division sailed on the 13th of August, but, delayed by contrary winds, only anchored off the Helder, North Holland, on the 27th; disembarked under Sir Ralph Abercrombie, and were met by General Daendels at the head of 12,000 men, opposed to 2,500. A well-directed fire from the ships carried disorder into the ranks of the Republicans, and drove them back to the sand-hills, from which they were expelled by the British by six in the evening. The Dutch evacuated the Fort at the Helder during the night, and the British occupied it the following day.

The Russian troops not arriving, the English commander was obliged to remain on the defensive, which gave the Republicans time to collect their forces, 25,000 in all, of which 7,000 were French, under General Brune, who had assumed the command-in-chief. He determined to attack the British, and on September 10th, all the columns were in motion.

Vandamme, who commanded the right, was directed to move along the Langdyke, and make himself master of Ernnsginberg; Damonceau, with the centre, was to march by Schorldam upon Krabbenham, and there force the key of the position; while the left was charged with the difficult task of chasing the British from the Sand-dyke, and penetrating by Kampto Petten. Restricted to the dykes and causeways intersecting in different directions a low, swampy ground, the engagement consisted of detached conflicts at isolated points, rather than any general movement; and, like the struggle between Napoleon and the Austrians in the marshes of Arcola, was to be determined chiefly by the intrepidity of the heads of columns. Repulsed at all points, the French resumed their position at Alkmaar. On September the 12th and 13th, the Russians, 17,000 strong, and 700 British arrived, and the Duke of York assumed the command. On the 19th, the Russian advance was defeated, and though the Duke of York advanced to their support, the Allies were obliged to retire to their fortified line and evacuate Schorl. In this battle the Republicans lost 3,000 in killed, wounded and prisoners; the British, 500 killed and wounded, and as many prisoners; the Russians, 3,500, besides twenty-six pieces of cannon and seven standards.

The Duke of York, being reinforced by a fresh brigade of Russians and some English detachments, again assumed the offensive, but the heavy rains prevented an attack until October 2nd. Alkmaar was abandoned by the Republicans.

Despite this success, the prospect was not encouraging to the British commander. The enemy's force was daily increasing, while no reinforcements were coming to him. The heavy rains which set in with unusual violence made the roads impassable for artillery. The expected movements of the Batavian troops in favor of the House of Orange had not taken place, the climate was affecting the health of the British troops, and it was evident that, unless some important place could be captured, it would be impossible to remain in North Holland.

Haarlem was decided upon as the most likely to furnish the necessary supplies. To this end an attack was made on the French on the narrow isthmus between Beverick and the Zuyder Zee. The battle was well contested, the loss being nearly equal on both sides, and though the honors remained with the Allies, they were obliged to retreat and fall back upon the intrenchments at Zype. On the 7th, they retired to the position they had occupied before Bergen, and the Republicans, on the 8th, resumed their position in front of Alkmaar.

An armistice was signed on October 17th, the principal terms being that the Allies should evacuate Holland by the end of November; that 8,000 prisoners, whether French or Dutch, should be restored, and that the works of the Helder should be given up entire, with all their artillery.

Before December 1st, all three conditions were fulfilled, the British troops had regained the shores of England, and the Russians were quartered in Jersey and Guernsey. (Condensed from "Alison's Europe.")

APPENDIX II.

EXTRACT from the Returns of the 49th, during the six months from the 13th November to 31st May, 1811:

Private Patrick Lallagan.
26th Jan., 1811.

Deficient of frill, part of his regimental necessaries.
Sentenced 100; inflicted —

13th Feby.

Deficient of a razor, part of his regimental necessaries, and for producing at an inspection of his necessaries a razor belonging to Private James Rooney, thereby attempting to deceive the inspecting officer.
Sentenced 200; inflicted 100.
Also to be put under stoppages of 1/ per week until the razor is replaced.

Edward Marraly.
15th Nov., 1810.

For being deficient of a shirt, part of regimental necessaries.
Sentenced 200; inflicted 75.

John Turner.
4th April.

For having in his possession some pease for which he cannot honestly account, and for making an improper use of the barrack bedding.
Sentenced 400; inflicted 250.

Corporal Francis Doran.
28th March.

An accusation made by some married men of his having defrauded their wives of part of the bread issued for them, between the 25th of Feb. and 24th March, is sentenced to 100 lashes, which, however, appear not to have been inflicted, but a weekly stoppage of 1/6 until the quantity of bread, valued at 2/7 currency, was recovered, was deemed sufficient.

There are numerous entries of "Drunk before dinner although confined to barracks."

Sentenced 150; 100 inflicted.

"Drunk before morning parade although confined to barracks." Sentenced 200; 150 inflicted.

"Quitting the barracks without leave after tattoo." Sentenced 300; 295 inflicted.

[Is it anything to be wondered at that the men deserted?]

APPENDIX III.

THE lot of land referred to on page 59 was situated in the Township of Tecumseh, in the Home District, and Province of Upper Canada.

APPENDIX IV.

IN September, 1812, the Americans learned that a number of bateaux were coming up the river, laden with supplies, the party being under the command of Adjutant FitzGibbon. A gunboat and also a Durham boat were fitted out at Ogdensburg, and despatched to intercept and capture the British expedition and stores.

Leaving Ogdensburg late at night, the enemy landed on Toussaint Island, near where the bateaux lay. The only family on the island was seized, with the exception of a man, who, being a staunch defender of the British flag, made his escape, and by swimming reached the Canadian shore. The alarm given, the militia rallied, and when the Yankees made the attack they met with such a hot reception that they abandoned the Durham boat, which drifted down the river and fell into the hands of the Canadians. About sunrise the gunboat came to anchor, and was immediately fired upon. At the second discharge five of the eighteen on board were wounded, but before a third volley could be delivered, the remainder brought a cannon to bear on the Canadian boats, which were compelled to move out of range, being provided only with small arms. The Americans then beat a hasty retreat for Ogdensburg. ("History of Leeds and Grenville," p. 34.)

APPENDIX V.

MONTREAL *Gazette*, Tuesday, July 6th, 1813: "Intelligence of the last week from the seat of war in Canada is not of a sanguinary nature; but, however, it is not the less interesting, and we have much pleasure in communicating to the public the particulars of a campaign, not of a general with his thousands or his hundreds, but of a lieutenant with his tens only. The manner in which a bloodless victory was obtained by a force so comparatively and almost incredibly small, with that of the enemy, the cool determination and the happy presence of mind evinced by this highly meritorious officer, in conducting the operations incident to the critical situation in which he was placed, with his little band of heroes, and the brilliant result which crowned these exertions, will, while they make known to the world the name of Captain FitzGibbon, reflect new lustre, if possible, on the well-earned reputation of the gallant 49th Regiment, and class this event with the most extraordinary occurrences of the present accursed war.

"We shall at present make no further comment, but refer our readers to the following details of Mr. FitzGibbon's operations, as communicated to us by a friend who had the particulars from the best authority:

" ' Immediately after the gallant affair of our advance on the 6th ultimo, Lieut. FitzGibbon made application to General Vincent to be employed separately with a small party of the 49th Regiment, and in such a manner as he might think most expedient. The offer was accepted, and this little band has since been constantly ranging between the two armies. Many events would naturally occur on such a service which would be interesting, but are necessarily prescribed in our limits of details, and we will confine ourselves to two very extraordinary occurrences. About the 20th ultimo, Lieut. FitzGibbon went in pursuit of forty-six vagabonds, volunteer cavalry, brought over by a Dr. Chapin from Buffalo, and who had been for some time plundering the inhabitants round Fort Erie and Chippewa ; he came near to them at Lundy's Lane, about a mile below the Falls, but discovered that they had been joined by 150 infantry. As his force was but forty-four muskets, he did not think it advisable to attack, and therefore his party was kept concealed. He, however, rode into the village at the ending of the Lane, dressed in grey, to reconnoitre, but could not perceive the enemy. Mrs. Kirby, who knew him, ran out, and begged him to ride off, for that some of the enemy's troops were in a house at a short distance. He saw a horse at a door, and supposing that there were none but his rider in the house, he dismounted and approached it, when an infantry soldier advanced and presented his piece at him. He made a spring at him, seized his musket, and desired him to surrender, but the American resisted and held fast. At this instant a rifleman jumped from the door with his rifle presented at FitzGibbon's shoulder, who was so near to him that he seized the rifle below the muzzle and pulled it under his arm, keeping its muzzle before him and that of the other musket behind him. In this situation, Lieut. FitzGibbon called upon two men who were looking on, to assist him in disarming the two Americans, but they would not interfere. Poor Mrs. Kirby, apparently distracted, used all her influence, but in vain. The rifleman, finding he could not disengage his piece, drew FitzGibbon's own sword out of its scabbard with his left hand, with the intention of striking at him, when another woman, a Mrs. Defield, seized the uplifted arm, and wrested the sword from his grasp. At this moment an elderly man named Johnston came up and forced the American from his hold of the rifle, and Lieut. FitzGibbon immediately laid the other soldier prostrate. A young boy of thirteen years, a son of Dr. Fleming, was very useful in the struggle, which lasted some minutes. Lieut. FitzGibbon, thus relieved, lost not a moment in carrying off his two prisoners and the horse, as the enemy's force were within two hundred yards of him, searching a house round a turn in the road.

" ' At seven o'clock on the morning of the 24th ult., Lieut. F. received a report that the enemy was advancing from St. David's, with about a thousand men and four pieces of cannon, to attack the stone house in which he was quartered at Beaver Dam. About an hour afterwards he heard the report of cannon and musketry. He rode off to reconnoitre, and found the enemy engaged with a party of Indians, who hung upon his flanks and rear, and galled him severely.

" ' Lieut. F. despatched an officer for his men, and by the time of their arrival the enemy had taken up a position on an eminence at some distance from the woods in front. He estimated the enemy's strength at 600 men and two field-pieces—a 12 and a 6-pounder. To make the appearance of cutting off his retreat, Lieut. F. passed at the charge-step across the front to gain the other flank under a quick fire from his guns, which however did not the slightest injury. He took post behind some woods, and saw the Indians were making very little of the enemy, and it would have been madness in him, with forty-four muskets, to dash at them across open fields, where every man he had could be so easily perceived.

" ' Many of the Indians were at this time taking themselves off, and he began to think of his own retreat. He had a hope, however, that Colonel De Haren would soon join him ; but fearing the enemy would drive him off, or make good his retreat, he determined to play the old soldier, and summon the enemy to surrender. He tied up his handkerchief and advanced, with his bugles sounding "Cease firing." A flag was sent to him by a Captain McDonald of the Artillery. Lieut. F. stated that he was sent by Colonel De Haren to demand their surrender, and to offer them protection from the Indians, adding that a number had just joined from the North-West who could not be controlled, and he wished to prevent the effusion at Fort George, which he always resisted, because the position and means of the enemy enabled him to reinforce with far greater facility than the American army could."

APPENDIX VI.

HINTS TO A SON ON RECEIVING HIS FIRST COMMISSION IN A REGIMENT SERVING IN THE CANADAS.

BY AN OLD WOODSMAN.

THE troops should be drilled in the woods, most frequently by companies, and occasionally in greater numbers. Without much practice they cannot have much confidence in themselves or in one another, and must, through ignorance, greatly expose themselves to the enemy's fire.

In 1814, the 6th and 82nd Regiments joined Sir George Drummond's division of the army before Fort Erie, and in the first affair with the enemy in the woods they lost many more men than any other corps present, because they knew not how to cover themselves. For several days afterwards the men of these regiments were mixed with the files of the Glengarry Light Infantry, a provincial corps, until they acquired some skill and experience in the woods.

I will state here thus early that I consider the rifle in the woods, as well as in the open ground, a contemptible weapon. I do not hesitate to say, "Let all my enemies be armed with rifles." With the musket and bayonet, British troops have only to advance instantly after the first fire, and they may hunt the enemy through the woods without pause or rest.

The rifle I consider of peculiar value only when used in places inaccessible; but in the woods, where the men must run, either after their enemy or from him, the blood must circulate freely, the men must become excited, and then there is an end to perfect steadiness in taking aim, and the least inaccuracy reduces the rifle in this respect to the level of the musket, while it is in all other respects far inferior to it.

The soldier should fire to the right of the tree ; thus a very small section of his head and right arm and shoulder is exposed. I have known an officer to tap his servant on the shoulder, and exclaim, "Fire from the other side of the tree, you blockhead," but the words were hardly spoken before the servant was shot dead.

The soldier, when advancing, should not go straight forward, but at an angle to some tree to the right or left of the one he quits ; because it is much easier for his enemy to hit him coming directly towards him than if he runs at a considerable angle. So also in retreating, he should run to the right or left, having in each case previously fixed his eye upon the tree to which he intends to run ; and if he can fire to advantage before he quits the tree that covers him, so much the better, as the smoke may conceal his retreat, and his enemy will not know where next to find him until he fires again.

An enemy is most readily discovered in the woods by looking for him as low down as possible beneath the branches of the trees. The reverse of this would, however, be the fact where much underwood grew, or in a copse. The moving of a branch or young tree will often show the place of an enemy.

The greatest attention and care are required from every man to preserve his distance from his neighbor, and to keep in the general line as much as circumstances will permit. It is impossible to do so exactly, but much practice will give both experience and confidence, and with the active aid of experienced officers and sergeants the forest may be scoured in fine style by well-practised men with musket and bayonet, acting against riflemen, or against any description of American troops, inexperienced as they all, officers as well as men, must be for many years after the commencement of a war.

A company should be practised to close to the centre or any other point, and to dash through the enemy's line, and then wheel by subdivisions to the right or left, and rush along upon the flanks and rear of his position. Rout and confusion of the enemy may be confidently expected as the result of such an onset, which should be executed with the greatest possible rapidity.

After much practice, rapidity of evolution cannot be too strongly recommended. It gives to the attacking party the highest degree of blood. The captain went back to his commanding officer, Lieut.-Col. Bœrstler, and soon after returned saying that Colonel B. did not consider himself defeated, and could not surrender. Lieut. F. proposed that Colonel Bœrstler should send an officer to see Colonel De Haren's force, when he would be better able to judge of the necessity. He soon returned with a proposal that Colonel B. should himself be shown the British, and if he found the force such as to justify his surrender, he would do so. To this, Lieut. F. said he would return to Colonel De Haren with Colonel B.'s proposal.

The real intention of showing the enemy our small force never existed, but appearances must be kept up. Upon his return Lieut. F. found that a Captain Hall with twelve Dragoons had just arrived. He told him what had passed, and asked him to assume the rank of Colonel for the occasion. Lieut. F. then returned and stated that Colonel Hall, being now the senior officer on the spot, did not think it regular to let the enemy see his force, but that it was perfectly ample to compel the surrender. From motives of humanity, five minutes would be allowed for acquiescence, and if refused hostilities would recommence at the expiration of this period. Colonel B. agreed to surrender on condition that the officers should retain their horses, arms and baggage, and that the militia and volunteers (among whom were Dr. Chapin and his marauders) should be permitted to return to the States on parole.

" ' When the extent of our force is considered, it is no wonder that these conditions were immediately acceded to. Lieut. F. at this moment most opportunely met with Colonel Clarke, of Chippewa, who came galloping up, and who proceeded to assist him in disarming the enemy, as Colonel Hall could not appear, and his only officer (an ensign) must remain with his men.

" ' Colonel De Haren immediately afterwards appeared with the flank companies of the 104th Regiment, and the whole affair was soon settled, thus putting into our possession twenty-six officers, one 12-pounder and one 6-pounder, two caissons and two wagons, and above five hundred prisoners, including about twenty Dragoons. Had not Colonel De Haren arrived at that moment, this large number of the enemy would have yielded to forty-three soldiers of the 49th, for all the arrangements were made previous to the arrival of that officer. The Indians behaved well ; they killed and wounded during their skirmishing about fifty of the enemy. We are informed that at the moment of the surrender many of the Indians had gone off—the number engaged did not exceed eighty. Thus terminated a bloodless victory on our part. If promotion and reward await the officer selected to be the bearer of despatches announcing an enemy's defeat, we cannot doubt but that the hero of this achievement will receive that favor from his sovereign to which his services have established so just a claim, and who, we believe, has no other patronage but his own distinguished merit.'"

In another column in the same issue of the *Gazette* is the following:

"On Saturday last arrived in this city four officers and one hundred and nineteen non-commissioned officers and privates, forming part of the American prisoners captured on the 24th ult. by the gallant Lieut. FitzGibbon and his small party of the 49th Regiment, in the advance of our army under General Vincent. They embarked yesterday evening on board the steamboat for Quebec, under the guard of Capt. Renvoisez, of the 3rd Battalion of the incorporated militia. The remainder arrived this morning in bateaux."

FROM the Report of the Court-martial held to enquire into the cause of Bœrstler's surrender, held at Baltimore, 17th February, 1815:

"The detachment was ordered to lay at Queenston on the night of the 23rd, and to march early the next morning. It did so, laying upon its arms and in silence without lights, and having taken precautions to avoid surprise and preventing the country people from carrying intelligence to the enemy.

"Before eight and nine o'clock, morning of 24th, at a place called 'Beaver Dams,' a mile and a half in advance of DeCou's. De Cou's stone house seventeen and a half miles from Fort George *via* Queenston, and sixteen *via* St. Catharines.

"That the surrender was justified by existing circumstances, and that the misfortune of the day is not to be ascribed to Lieut.-Col. Bœrstler or the detachment under his command."

From Major-General Lewis' deposition:

"He had been frequently pressed to send a detachment to the vicinity of the Beaver Dams during the latter days of his command of animation and confidence, while it creates surprise and panic among inexperienced defenders.

The Indians, when retreating and coming to a ravine, do not at once cross the ravine and defend from the brow of the side or hill looking over the ravine to the pursuing enemy; they suddenly throw themselves down immediately behind the bank they first come to, and thence fire on their pursuers, who must then be entirely exposed, while the Indian exposes his head only, and when pressed and compelled to abandon his position, he fires and retires, covered by the smoke and the bank, so that his pursuers cannot tell the course of his retreat, whether to the right or the left, or directly to the rear, which last the Indian may now do with comparative safety, being for a short time hid by the bank from the view of his pursuer, until he, the pursuer, arrives at the brow of the bank, by which time the Indian has, most probably, taken post in a new position, where he can only be discovered by his next fire.

If an Indian be pursued from post to post, and obliged at length to fly for his life, and if his pursuers still press upon him until he becomes exhausted, he then looks for some thick cover wherein to hide himself, and there takes shelter. Should the pursuers come near to his place of concealment and be likely to discover him, then, as a last resource, he closes his eyes, not because he will not look at the upraised tomahawk, but because it is possible that the glistening of his eye may betray him, when, but for it, he may remain undiscovered.

I recommend that an intelligent Indian be attached to each regiment for a sufficient time to teach all his lessons—of which these now stated are a few—to the officers and sergeants.

Before the termination of the late American war, which ended in 1815, I had a scheme in contemplation of which the following is an outline:

I intended to have asked for leave to raise a corps of three hundred men, the officers and men to be chosen or approved by me only; to be clothed in grey, not green (grey, being the nearest to the color of the bark of the forest trees, is least discernible); the caps to be of the same cloth as the dress; the jackets and caps to have loops sewn on them of the same colored tape, and so placed as when filled with small sprigs of foliage or even single leaves, that the whole body from the waist upwards would have the appearance of a bush. Men so disguised and well trained, and well posted in the woods, could not be discovered until they would fire upon an advancing enemy. This fire must be carefully withheld until an enemy comes so near that almost every shot will tell. Under the cover of the smoke, after firing, the rank in front might rapidly retire any given number of paces behind the rank already posted in the rear, and which rank in rear could not be discovered until the enemy was again fired upon.

Now, I hold that there is a certain quantum of fire against which no troops will stand, and a second discharge so destructive as I suppose this fire must be would certainly drive back an enemy ; but if disorder only, or even mere hesitation, were seen among the enemy, and an instant sound of "advance" were given, and a prompt dash made, the flight of an enemy must inevitably follow.

Under such circumstances, I repeat it, I hold the rifle in great contempt ; and I would most sedulously inculcate and impress this opinion on the minds of my own men. I would make them rejoice in their own musket and bayonet, and laugh in derision at the far-praised American rifleman, and all his boasted skill in shooting squirrels and wild turkeys.

The greatest pains should be taken by officers and sergeants, to acquire a thorough knowledge of their every duty down to the very minutest particular, and every proper opportunity should be seized to let the men see that this knowledge was possessed in a high degree by them. The men rejoice in following such, knowing and feeling how much their own success, and even safety, depends upon a proper exercise of skill, discretion and cool courage by their leaders. The soldier, once convinced of his leader's good qualities, promptly obeys him, because he feels that his own safety is best secured by his doing so. I have sometimes spoken in the following words to the young officers around me : "That officer is not perfectly qualified to command who could not make a soldier run his head into an enemy's great gun, upon being commanded by him to do so." Such an order firmly given by a good and a beloved officer to his well-trained soldiers, would be, I have no doubt, heroically obeyed. Such officers only can make soldiers achieve brilliant actions. One of the most efficient means of winning the highest degree of the soldier's good-will and confidence is by carefully keeping him out of every unnecessary danger, and often going yourself to reconnoitre, rather than to send another to do so. A partisan officer gains another great advantage by going himself: he sees with his own eyes, and can therefore best decide what should next be done, or he can report far more accurately to his general or other officer commanding, than from any statement made by another to himself.

I applied for and obtained leave to select fifty men from the regiment to which I belonged, and was employed in advance of the centre division of the army on the Niagara frontier in 1813. Having three sergeants, I divided the party into three sections. For the purpose of facilitating our movements in the vicinity of the enemy in the woods at night, and perhaps even to enable me to pass through his line of posts unobserved, I purchased three cow-bells of different sizes and tones, and placed one in charge of each sergeant. By the tinkling of one or more of these bells I proposed to deceive an enemy by leading him to believe that cows only were near him (cows in the forest usually have bells hung round their necks), whereas the bugle, whistle or word of command might expose us. Thus, too, by previously concerted sounds the several sections could be kept together, and enabled to move in any direction in connection with each other at night through the woods. This was not reduced to practice, but I nevertheless hold it to be practicable, and may be useful.

At one time I ascertained that the enemy's cavalry horses were picketed on the Niagara common in front of Fort George. I proposed during the night to take twenty of the most active of my fifty chosen men, and rush through the outer pickets and run directly to the horses and stab as many as possible; and, lastly, each man to spring upon a horse and gallop out by the road to Queenston. The enemy's picket on that road could not suppose that we were enemies until we had already passed through them, and beyond the range of their fire. Before I could carry this plan into effect, I was suddenly ordered off in another direction, and the opportunity was lost. Desperate, perhaps foolish, as this attempt may appear, yet I had very sanguine hopes of success. The locality was perfectly known to us. We had an inexperienced enemy before us, who could not readily be brought back into good order from panic and confusion, and especially at night; and I had men who could appreciate the work they had to do, and who were taught to rejoice in being able to accomplish what other men would not think of even attempting. I was not insensible to the feeling of reluctance which arose out of the consideration of destroying the horses; and I mention this to avail myself of the opportunity it affords of recommending to you, and through you to your men, the cultivation and exercise of humanity as one of the noblest attributes in the character of a soldier.

One day, while in the vicinity of Fort George, which the enemy occupied with 6,000 men, a thunder-storm came on, with torrents of rain. It fell in sheets, so that neither a gun nor a musket could be fired a second time. Had our division of the army, then ten miles distant, been near, it could have marched in and swept the whole of the American position at the point of the bayonet, for the works were then accessible at almost every point. The enemy would not then have dreamt of being attacked during the storm; they would have been taken by surprise, while our men, rejoicing in their advantage, would rapidly have carried all before them. For many weeks the division did not approach the enemy nearer than three miles, and at such a distance no prompt advantage could be taken of any error on his part, or of any fortuitous circumstance, and these should always be looked for with most untiring watchfulness.

Therefore, if possible, always keep within striking distance of your enemy, especially if he be inexperienced. If he press too severely upon you, retire; if he halt, do you halt also; if he retire, follow him; if he blunder, smite him. He cannot surround you if you take due precaution.

Knowing that the enemy had extensive barracks and stores at Black Rock, I marched my party by night to where the village of Waterloo now stands, near Fort Erie, and concealed them in barns during daylight. While next day examining the enemy's number and condition with my glass, and carefully concealed, for they did not yet expect us back to the frontier, the officer commanding our advance, with his Staff-Adjutant and a Colonel of Militia, quite unexpected by me, walked up in full view of the Americans, and, over trenches and brooks supported by it, and also over fallen trees and other obstacles. After much practice with it, I thought most favorably of it in many points of view. One dark and rainy night an alarm was given, and the troops were marched to their respective alarm posts. It occurred to me to carry this pike with me to help in the darkness, and I did so. Almost every man in my company fell down at least once, some of them many times, while we were marching ; with the aid of the pike I went along with confidence and safety. After much reflection, I considered it a weapon of great value for particular purposes. For example, a small body of men, say fifty, well selected, well trained, well led, with patrols or counter-signs, or other signals carefully chosen, and particularly adapted to the occasion, might rush through an enemy's outposts and into his camp—I do not mean an entrenched or fortified camp, but one taken up for the night only—and traverse it in every direction, killing and routing all before them. The enemy would soon be in utter confusion, especially if composed of inexperienced troops. Their fire would be quite at random, and probably be more destructive to one another, while it lasted, than to the attackers. It should be most strongly impressed upon the minds of your men that fire at night does amazingly little execution. The experience of the night affair at Stony Creek, in June, 1813, planned by, and executed under, the direction of Sir John Harvey, would have been of great value to me had the war continued and opportunities been afforded me of making night attacks. I think fighting at night has never been practised to one-tenth of the extent to which it is possible to carry it. Charging with the bayonet or pike by day, and with the pike only by night, may be carried, as I firmly believe, to an extent which has not yet been imagined, or very rarely imagined. Here is, I think, a splendid field to practise in. Become an adjutant if you can ; drill your own men in your own way ; devise new expedients whereby you may teach men easily and rapidly ; know them well, and let them know you well, and if you arrive at the command of a regiment so trained by yourself, and an opportunity offer for trying your men, you may add a new chapter to the art of war. Remember my opinion, often expressed in your hearing, that no two corps have ever yet crossed bayonets in battle. Rush upon your enemy and he will surely fly. Let your men never be permitted to doubt this great truth, for such I am confident it is.

Should you obtain the command of a company, I recommend you to set apart a place in the company's arm-chest for two or more pikes, broad swords, small swords (foils, I mean), sticks and baskets, boxing-gloves, cricket-bats, quoits. Obtain leave from your commanding officer to keep your company off duty one day in a week, or even one in a month. March them in fatigue dress to a neighboring field or play-ground. Let them run races, jump, leap, wrestle, use the pike, sword, stick, cricket-bat, quoits, as each may desire or you direct. Swimming should also be practised. Manage by some means to have a stock purse from which to give prizes to the victors in each exercise or play. All this I consider compatible with maintaining the most perfect authority over your men, and, if well conducted and managed, will increase their respectful regard for you. Be kind and condescending, but never, no, not once, be flippant or familiar with them. Suppose a regiment so practised : how quickly could you select the best qualified men for any special service. Imagine the confidence these men would have in themselves and in each other. Surely, in service such men could often be turned to good account.

Much of what I have stated in these sketches may be thought too fanciful, and perhaps frivolous, or even ridiculous ; but from, the portion of experience which has fallen to my share, I have formed the opinion that an officer, non-commissioned officer, or even soldier, is valuable in proportion to the amount of and number of his expedients, his resources and his foresight, and, above all, in his knowledge of the comparative qualities of those whom he commands (if he is a commander) and those to whom he is opposed. I have been in the habit of imagining that there is in the possession of two opposing armies a certain quantum of courage and confidence, usually unequally divided and always liable to fluctuation. It is for a commander to so play his game that he shall from day to day and from one affair to another win from his adversary's scales more or less of these qualities, and transfer the gain to his own scales ; and no expedient, however trifling, which may raise him in his own men's estimation, or may lead them to suppose themselves superior much to my regret, as the success of my intended project must, I thought, mainly depend upon keeping them entirely in ignorance of our having come back to the frontier. This commander then told me that he had proposed to the general officer commanding, General De Rottenburg, to attack Black Rock, and asked for three hundred men, but the General would give only two hundred, and he asked me if I thought the place could be taken, and the barracks and stores destroyed by so small a force. I had already, the evening before, ordered four bateaux to be brought down from their place of concealment up the Chippewa creek, and I expected to have them the following night, and in them I had determined to attack Black Rock with my party, at that time only forty-four rank and file, and I answered his question by telling him so. He laughed, and said, "Oh, then, I need ask you no more questions; but go and bring the two hundred men." He ordered me not to attack during his absence, but to wait for him, and he came up the following day. He consented that my party should lead the advance, and cover the retreat on coming away, should we be attacked. At two the following morning we moved off. My men, being select and good boatmen, soon gained the opposite shore, but, owing to the strength of the current and the boats being filled with men, further down than we intended. I then saw that the other boats would be carried still further down, and must be at least half an hour later in landing than my men. Yet my orders were to advance immediately on landing. I did so, and in twenty minutes we drove the enemy out, one hundred and fifty militiamen, who fled to Buffalo, and we were in full possession of all before the main body came up. Everything was then burned except eight large boats, which we filled with military stores and provisions and brought away.

After this affair, the American army being still in Fort George and the town of Niagara, I had reason to believe that the American Fort, Niagara, was garrisoned by a few men only, and these chiefly wounded men and convalescents. I had ascertained, too, that the American boats were kept on their own side of the river, and it was said that the American general had them kept there lest his men, on being attacked by us, should fly to them, and make off to their own side. In this state of things it occurred to me that it was possible to surprise that fort, and that the capture of it would lead to the inevitable surrender of the American army on our side. With this view, I carefully examined the state of the water a short distance below the Falls of Niagara, and felt satisfied that a boat might cross in safety, which, I believe, was never before imagined by anyone. I then sketched a plan to the following effect : I proposed to increase my party to eighty men ; to have Lieutenant Armstrong and twenty men of the artillery attached to me ; to have a boat built quickly, and during the night to transport the men across to the other side with three days' provisions in their haver-sacks ; to hide them in the woods during the whole of the following day ; after dark to march quickly through Lewiston—then only a few houses—to Fort Niagara, and immediately assault and carry it ; then, by firing a given number of guns, or by some other signal, to have boats start from the Four Mile Creek on Lake Ontario, on our side, with 200 or 300 men already embarked, and pulled speedily across the mouth of the Niagara River, and landed to reinforce my party in the Fort ; at daylight to attack the Americans in front from the woods, and our men from Fort Niagara to cannonade them in rear with their own guns, and thus their destruction or surrender must, as I then thought, and have since been convinced, be inevitable.

Having completed this sketch, I showed it to one of the most experienced captains in the regiment, who, on reading it, among other things, said : "I warn you now, that if you propose this scheme to the general, it will be the ruin of you. It will at once be said that your success already this summer has turned your brain, and you will be no more trusted." Wanting sufficient confidence in myself, and having had little experience, I declined moving further in it, and I have since had the mortification of seeing that the then dreaded part of the river has since become a common ferry ; for upon the supposed impossibility of crossing it by boat was founded my friend's chief objection. In truth, the whole scheme was not only practicable, but of comparatively easy achievement.

An American boarding-pike came into my possession on the Niagara frontier, in 1813. I often carried it with me in the woods, and practised with it in every possible way—in thrusting at trees with it without letting it out of my grasp, in darting it from me at trees at every distance within the range of my strength, in leaping

in skill and tact to their enemies, ought to be considered beneath
his notice.

While suggesting so many things to be taught, I would caution
you not to tease or fret your men by too much drilling or teaching.
Much of what is here mentioned might be taught with little trouble
to the soldier by choosing the fittest moment for giving the lesson;
and then, too, it will make the deepest impression.

One item more of my practice I must not withhold from you,
namely, that I always carried a prayer-book in my pocket, and on
Sundays read to the men the service, or part of it, and the psalms
of the day ; and on the day following an affair with the enemy I
read part of the service and such thanksgiving and psalms particularly selected for the occasion as I thought most appropriate. And
I can assure you the men were the more orderly, the more brave,
and in every respect the better for this practice; and it added more
to my authority and influence over them than any other conduct or
treatment of mine had ever done.

Be assured that the soldier, before his enemy especially, is by no
means insensible to his duty to his God, and to his great need of
repentance and pardon through a merciful Redeemer. The devout
and earnest offering up of prayer in his presence affects him deeply,
and makes him grateful to his officer for thus leading him, as it
were, into the presence of his Saviour to sue for salvation, when he
knows not what a day or even an hour may bring forth.

APPENDIX VII.

EXTRACT from despatch to Lord Glenelg, Colonial Secretary, taken
from Sir Francis Bond Head's " Narrative," etc. :

" *Despatch No. 132.*
                              "TORONTO, 19th *December*, 1837.

" MY LORD, —I have the honour to inform your Lordship that on
Monday, 4th inst., this city was, in a moment of profound peace,
suddenly invaded by a band of armed rebels, amounting, according
to report, to 3,000 men (but in actual fact to about 500), and com-

manded by Mr. M'Kenzie, the editor of a republican newspaper; Mr. Van Egmont, an officer who had served under Napoleon ; Mr. Gibson, a land surveyor ; Mr. Lount, a blacksmith ; Mr. Loyd, and some other notorious characters.

"Having, as I informed your Lordship in my despatch, No. 119, dated 3rd ultimo, purposely effected the withdrawal of her Majesty's troops from this province, and having delivered over to the civil authorities the whole of the arms and accoutrements I possessed, I of course found myself without any defence whatever, excepting that which the loyalty and fidelity of the Province might think proper to afford me. The crisis, important as it was, was one I had long earnestly anticipated, and accordingly I no sooner received the intelligence that the rebels were within four miles of the city than, abandoning the Government House, I at once proceeded to the City Hall, in which about 4,000 stand of arms and accoutrements had been deposited.

"One of the first individuals I met there, with a musket on his shoulder, was the Chief Justice of the Province, and in a few minutes I found myself surrounded by a band of brave men, who were of course unorganized, and, generally speaking, unarmed.

"As the foregoing statement is an unqualified admission on my part that I was completely surprised by the rebels, I think it proper to remind, rather than to explain to your Lordship, the course of policy I have been pursuing.

"In my despatch, No. 124, dated 18th ultimo, I respectfully stated to your Lordship, as my opinion, that a civil war must henceforward everywhere be a moral one, and that in this hemisphere in particular, victory must eventually declare itself in favour of moral and not of physical preponderance.

"Entertaining these sentiments, I observed with satisfaction that Mr. M'Kenzie was pursuing a lawless course of conduct which I felt it would be impolitic for me to arrest.

"For a long time he had endeavoured to force me to buoy him up by a Government prosecution, but he sunk in proportion as I neglected him, until, becoming desperate, he was eventually driven to reckless behaviour, which I felt confident would very soon create its own punishment.

"The traitorous arrangements he made were of that minute

nature that it would have been difficult, even if I had desired it, to have suppressed them. For instance, he began by establishing Union lists (in number not exceeding forty) of persons desirous of political reform, and who, by an appointed secretary, were recommended to communicate regularly with himself, for the purpose of establishing a meeting of delegates.

"As soon as, by most wicked representations, he had succeeded in seducing a number of well-meaning people to join these squads, his next step was to prevail upon a few of them to attend their meetings armed, for the alleged purpose of firing at a mark.

"While these meetings were in continuance, Mr. M'Kenzie, by means of his paper, became more and more seditious, and in proportion as these meetings excited more and more alarm, I was strongly and repeatedly called upon by the peaceable portion of the community forcibly to suppress both the one and the other. I considered it better, however, under all circumstances to await the outbreak, which I was confident would be impotent, inversely as it was previously opposed; in short, I considered that, if an attack by the rebels was inevitable, the more I encouraged them to consider me defenceless the better.

"Mr. M'Kenzie, under these favourable circumstances, having been freely permitted by me to make every preparation in his power, a concentration of his deluded adherents, and an attack upon the city of Toronto, was secretly settled to take place on the night of the 19th instant. However, in consequence of a militia general order which I issued, it was deemed advisable that these arrangements should be hastened, and accordingly, Mr. M'Kenzie's deluded victims, travelling through the forests by cross roads, found themselves assembled, at about four o'clock in the evening of Monday, the 4th instant, as rebels, at Montgomery's Tavern, which is on the Young Street macadamized road, about four miles from the city.

"As soon as they had attained that position, Mr. M'Kenzie and a few others, with pistols in their hands, arrested every person on the road, in order to prevent information reaching the town. Colonel Moody, a distinguished veteran officer, accompanied by three gentlemen on horseback, on passing Montgomery's Tavern, was fired at by the rebels, and I deeply regret to say that the colonel, wounded in two places, was taken prisoner into the tavern, where in three hours he died, leaving a widow and family unprovided for.

"As soon as this gallant, meritorious officer, who had honourably fought in this province, fell, I am informed that Mr. M'Kenzie exultingly observed to his followers, '*That, as blood had now been spilled, they were in for it, and had nothing left but to advance.*'

"Accordingly, at about ten o'clock at night, they did advance, and I was in bed and asleep when Mr. Alderman Powell awakened me to state that, in riding out of the city towards Montgomery's Tavern, he had been arrested by Mr. M'Kenzie and another principal leader; that the former had snapped a pistol at his breast, that his (Mr. Powell's) pistol also snapped, but that he fired a second, which, causing the death of Mr. M'Kenzie's companion, had enabled him to escape.

"On arriving at the City Hall I appointed Mr. Justice Jones, Mr. Henry Sherwood, Captain Strachan, and Mr. John Robinson, my aid-de-camps.

"I then ordered the arms to be unpacked, and, manning all the windows of the building, as well as those of opposite houses which flanked it, we awaited the rebels, who, as I have stated, did not consider it advisable to advance. Beside these arrangements, I despatched a message to the Speaker of the House of Assembly, Colonel the Honourable Allan M'Nab, of the Gore District, and to the Colonels of the Militia regiments in the Midland and Newcastle districts; an advanced piquet of thirty volunteers, commanded by my aid-de-camp, Mr. Justice Jones, was placed within a short distance of the rebels.

"By the following morning (Tuesday) we mustered about 300 men, and in the course of the day the number increased to about 500; in the night, an advanced piquet commanded by Mr. Sheriff Jarvis, was attacked within the precincts of the city by the rebels, who were driven back, one of their party being killed and several wounded.

"On Wednesday morning we were sufficiently strong to have ventured on an attack, but, being sensible of the strength of our position, being also aware how much depended upon the contest in which we were about to be engaged, and feeling the greatest possible reluctance at the idea of entering upon a civil war, I despatched two gentlemen to the rebel leaders to tell them that, before any conflict should take place, I parently called upon them, as their Governor, to avoid the effusion of human blood.

"In the meanwhile, however, Mr. M'Kenzie had committed every description of enormity; he had robbed the mail with his own hands, had set fire to Dr. Horne's house—had plundered many inoffensive individuals of their money—had stolen several horses, had made a number of respectable people prisoners; and having thus succeeded in embarking his misguided adherents in guilt, he replied to my admonition by a message, that he would only consent that his demands should be settled by a national convention, and he insolently added that he would wait till two o'clock for my answer, which in one word was, "*Never.*"

In the course of Wednesday the Speaker of the House of Assembly, Colonel the Honourable Allan M'Nab, arrived from the Gore District at the head of about sixty men, whom he had assembled at half an hour's notice, and, other brave men flocking in to me from various directions, I was enabled by strong piquets to prevent Mr. M'Kenzie from carrying into effect his diabolocal intention to burn the city of Toronto, in order to plunder the banks; and, having effected this object, I determined that on the following day I would make the attack.

"Accordingly, on Thursday morning I assembled our forces, under the direction of the Adjutant-General of Militia, Colonel FitzGibbon, clerk of the Assembly.

"The principal body was headed by the Speaker, Colonel Allan M'Nab, the right wing being commanded by Colonel Samuel Jarvis, the left by Colonel William Chisholm, assisted by the Honourable Mr. Justice M'Lean, late Speaker of the House of Assembly; the two guns by Major Carfrae of the Militia Artillery.

"The command of the Militia left in the city remained under Mr. Justice Macaulay, and the protection of the city with Mr. Gurnett, the Mayor.

"I might also have most advantageously availed myself in the field of the military services of Colonel Foster, the commander of the forces in Upper Canada, of Captain Baddeley of the corps of

Royal Engineers, and of a detachment of eight artillerymen, who form the only regular force in this province, but, having deliberately determined that the important contest in which I was about to be engaged should be decided solely by the Upper Canada Militia, or, in other words, by the free inhabitants of this noble province, I was resolved that no consideration whatever, should induce me to avail myself of any other assistance than that upon which, as the representative of our Gracious Sovereign, I had firmly and implicitly relied.

"At twelve o'clock the Militia force marched out of the town, with an enthusiasm it would be impossible to describe, and in about an hour we came in sight of the rebels, who occupied an elevated position near Gallows Hill, in front of Montgomery's Tavern, which had been long the rendezvous of M'Kenzie's men. They were principally armed with rifles, and for a short time, favoured by buildings, they endeavoured to maintain their ground; however, the brave and loyal militia of Upper Canada, steadily advancing with a determination which was irresistible, drove them from their position, completely routed Mr. M'Kenzie, who, in a state of the greatest agitation ran away, and in a few minutes Montgomery's Tavern, which was first entered by Mr. Justice Jones, was burnt to the ground.

"Being on the spot merely as a Civil Governor, and in no way in command of the troops, I was happy to have an opportunity of demonstrating to the rebels the mildness and beneficence of her Majesty's Government, and well knowing that the laws of the country would have ample opportunity of making examples of the guilty, I deemed it adviseable to save the prisoners who were taken, and to extend to most of these misguided men the royal mercy, by ordering their immediate release. These measures having been effected and the rebels having been deprived of their flag (on which was inscribed in large letters,

"'BIDWELL, AND THE GLORIOUS MINORITY
1837, AND A GOOD BEGINNING'),

the Militia advanced in pursuit of the rebels about four miles till they reached the house of one of the principal ringleaders, Mr.

Gibson, which residence it would have been impossible to have saved, and it was consequently burned to the ground." *

* " By my especial order."

In the original despatch as first published and circulated in Canada, there was no foot-note attached to this paragraph. In the second edition, as stated in the account given by FitzGibbon, whose letter to Lord Glenelg had provoked that nobleman to make Sir Francis practically acknowledge the falseness of his first statement, the foot-note is appended.

I have copied the despatch verbatim, spelling, grammar, and punctuation, exactly as I find it in a copy of the " Narrative," second edition, now in the possession of the Rev. Canon Bull, Rector of Lundy's Lane (Drummondville).

I need add but one more extract from this specious production, relative to the actual outbreak of rebellion and Sir Francis Head's devious policy :

"Mr. M'Kenzie and his party, finding that at every point they were defeated in a moral attack which they had made upon the British constitution, next determined to excite their deluded adherents to have recourse to physical strength. Being as ready to meet them on that ground as I had been ready to meet them in a moral struggle, I gave them every possible advantage. I in no way availed myself of the immense resources of the British empire ; on the contrary, I purposely dismissed from this province the whole of our troops. I allowed Mr. M'Kenzie to *write* what he choose, *say* what he chose, and *do* what he chose ; and without taking any notice of his traitorous proceedings I waited, with folded arms, until he had collected his rebel forces, and had actually commenced his attack." [The italics are his.]

" I then, as a solitary individual, called upon the militia of Upper Canada to defend me, and the result has been as I have stated, viz., that the people of Upper Canada, came to me when I called them ; that they completely defeated Mr. M'Kenzie's adherents, and drove him and his rebel ringleaders from the land.

(" When her Majesty's Government published this despatch they omitted the following paragraphs and words printed in italics) :

" These are historical facts which it is impossible to deny; and the plain inference is, that the inhabitants of Upper Canada, as I have often publicly declared, detest democracy, and revere the noble monarchical institutions of the British Empire."

I need quote no more, the concluding paragraphs of this remarkable despatch being but an attack upon the Under Secretary for the Colonies, and also in italics. It is difficult, however, to refrain from adding an extract from another of the valiant Governor's despatches, dated Toronto, Jan. 26th, 1838, and numbered II., as bearing upon the above:

"Events have since proved that the judgement I had formed of the dangerous effects of conciliation was not incorrect. Treason, which had long slumbered in this province having been fanned by conciliation suddenly burst into a flame. The details of the late rebellion, as contained in my Despatch dated December 19th (No 132) have already explained to your Lordship that on the 7th of December last the brave militia of Upper Canada drove the rebels from their position at Gallows Hill; that their place of rendezvous, Montgomery's Tavern, immediately fell into their possession, and that, on a small party reaching it, they found, brought out, and unfurled in triumph before their comrades, the traitors' flag, upon which was inscribed in large letters,

"'BIDWELL AND THE GLORIOUS MINORITY;
1837, AND A GOOD BEGINNING.'

My Lord, if that flag had, as was expected by its followers, triumphantly entered Toronto, I have no hesitation in saying it would have waved over the corpse of every loyal subject in the city; indeed, we have received evidence that a general massacre of the Queen's loyal subjects would have been attempted."

Might we not without prejudice endorse the remark attributed to Judge Ridout by Sir Francis, who devotes several pages of the volume to abuse of that gentleman for having "violated all political decency by publicly declaring that I, the Lieutenant-Governor of Upper Canada, deserved to be tarred and feathered," and that he, Judge Ridout, "would lend a hand to do so."

APPENDIX VIII.

Copy of FitzGibbon's letter to Lord Glenelg, written after the publication of Sir Francis Bond Head's despatch:

"Toronto, Upper Canada,
"*August* 10th, 1838.

"My Lord,—In the month of April last I received in a Dublin newspaper an extract of a despatch to your Lordship from Sir Francis Head, dated the 19th of December last. Some of the statements in that extract were at variance with facts, and were likely to injure my character with Her Majesty's Government, instead of doing me that justice which was due to me from His Excellency, and which was and is well known here to be undoubtedly my due. I therefore addressed a letter to your Lordship, dated the 17th of April, and having appended to it a statement of the events which occurred in this city under my own observation, previous to the 13th of December last. I placed both in the hands of Sir George Arthur, with a letter to His Excellency, dated 5th of May, requesting that they might be transmitted to your Lordship.

"The reasons which led me to proceed thus far were stated in the letter to your Lordship; but on the 11th of May, I was induced by representations made to me to apply to His Excellency not to transmit the said documents, but to return them to me, and His Excellency was pleased to comply with this request, and they were returned to me accordingly.

"Now, however, in reading in a newspaper 'An explanatory memorandum, addressed by Sir Francis Head to Lord Glenelg, dated 21st of May last,' I feel I cannot, in justice to myself, remain any longer passive while Sir Francis Head reiterates statements, not only to Her Majesty's colonial minister, but subsequently in a document wherein I am particularly named, and which has been transmitted to the House of Commons; in which statements I cannot concur, and upon which I may hereafter be called upon to give evidence.

"In this letter I will confine myself to three of these statements, namely :

"1st. The statement made relative to the burning of the rebel Gibson's house, made in the despatch of the 19th of December last, is not correct; for Sir Francis himself ordered me to have it burned, and when I was about to remonstrate against the order, he said: 'Stop; hear me—let Gibson's house be burned forthwith, and let the militia be kept here until it be burned;' and then, without a moment's delay, he galloped away from me. In obedience to this order, I took a party of men with me to Gibson's house, three miles beyond where we then were, and nine from this city, and had it burned.

"2nd. The paragraph in the despatch, where it is stated that 'In the course of Tuesday the Speaker of the House of Assembly arrived and,' etc., is only so far correct as that 'eleven o'clock at night' may be said to be 'in the course of Tuesday.' For the Speaker did not arrive at the City Hall until about eleven o'clock on Tuesday night.

"Some hours before his arrival, about six p.m., being then dark, seeing me about to send a picket up Yonge Street (the great northern road so called), he positively forbade me to send a man out. I said I could not endure to see the city left open to the ruffians who threatened it; to which he answered: 'We cannot defend the city, we have not men enough; let us defend our posts;' and further added: 'It is my positive order that you do not leave this building yourself.' I replied: 'I pray of your Excellency not to lay those imperative orders upon me, for I ought to be in many places, and I ought to be allowed to exercise a discretionary power where you are not near to give me orders;' to which he replied: 'If you go through the city as you have heretofore done, you will be taken prisoner;' and seizing me by the arm with both his hands, he exclaimed, 'If we lose you, what shall we do?' Nevertheless I soon after left the hall, and took the sheriff, W. B. Jarvis, Esquire, with a picket, up Yonge Street, above a mile distant from the City Hall, and there posted and gave specific instructions for the conduct of his picket, after which I returned to the City Hall, and deeming it most candid to do so, reported to His Excellency what I had done; and he rebuked me for it, not harshly certainly, but he expressed his disapprobation of what I had done. In about an hour afterwards this very picket repulsed the rebels with some loss, and saved the town, for they were then coming for the express purpose of setting it on fire. It was probably more than an hour after they (the rebels) were so repulsed that the Speaker arrived at the City Hall with a reinforcement of about sixty men from Hamilton.

"3rd. In the 'Explanatory Memorandum,' in his answer to the second question, Sir Francis Head states, in the second paragraph, 'However, notwithstanding the attitude which I publicly deemed it politic to assume, I privately made all the arrangements in my power to be ready to move whenever the proper moment should arrive.' Upon this statement I beg leave to observe that for some weeks before the 5th of December I had, occasionally, opportunities of conversing with His Excellency on the state of the Province, and he uniformly resisted (with one exception only, see note at end) every suggestion of mine for defence. So far did he carry his resistance to my advice that he refused to appoint twenty officers to fill vacancies in one of the city regiments which I then commanded, and which was an ordinary duty to be at any time performed, and without which appointments the regiment could not be rendered efficient for any service. Upon that occasion His Excellency said : 'I will make no alteration during the winter, having no apprehension whatever of any movement on the part of Mr. Mackenzie or his adherents.'

"The details which I could give on this subject are many and remarkable, even down to so late as Saturday evening previous to the outbreak, which took place on Monday. It was only on Monday morning that I was appointed to act as Adjutant-General of Militia, nor until then did I expect or know that His Excellency intended to appoint me. I had during the preceding summer told him that I would not accept the office, and this I felt constrained to tell His Excellency, because having then been sent for by him, and questioned on the state of the Adjutant-General's department, I gave him a most unfavorable account of it, whereupon His Excellency asked me why I had not before made the state of the department known to him ; to which I replied, 'Had I done so, your Excellency might have supposed that I desired to have the Adjutant-General dismissed and myself appointed in his stead. But now that I have made this statement to your Excellency, I never will accept the office.'

"On Monday morning, the 4th of December, when Sir Francis Head sent for me, I found His Excellency with a Militia General Order in his hand appointing me Acting Adjutant-General of Militia; and on my entering the room, he said, 'You have already said you did not desire to be Adjutant-General of Militia, nevertheless I have appointed you, trusting that you will not withhold your services from me in the present state of public affairs,' and I consented.

"And here I will briefly state, by way of recapitulation, that Sir Francis Head uniformly resisted every advice to guard against approaching dangers; and that had his course been pursued by all others, Toronto would inevitably have been taken by the rebels, with the arms, banks and all else in the city. Thousands of other rebels would soon have joined them, and thousands of base Americans would have overrun the Province, at least so much of it as lies westward of Toronto. The consequences would have been most disastrous, and much of the evils which might have thus been inflicted on the innocent and loyal would have been irreparable, and the cost of recovering the Province would have been immense, the injury to the nation incalculable.

"On the other hand, I affirm that were it not for the warnings I gave, and the precautions I took, and the personal efforts made by me, this city would have been taken by the rebels on Monday night, that the saving of the city on Tuesday night was owing to my having placed the sheriff's picket on Yonge Street, which I did contrary to the positive orders of Sir Francis Head; and yet for the sending out of which picket he takes the merit to himself in the despatch of the 19th of December last. The accuracy of these facts and opinions I have no doubt I can prove before any impartial tribunal.

"Of the facts not hereinbefore stated, I beg leave to offer the following in corroboration: A volunteer corps under my command offered to do duty over the Government House after the departure of the troops, and His Excellency declined the offer. A number of the citizens met in the City Hall in the evenings and mounted guard during the night over the arms lodged therein. The week before the insurrection, His Excellency ordered me to go to the City Hall in the evening of the day on which he spoke to me and dismiss those guards, leaving only two constables to sleep in the buildings, and I did so dismiss them. His Excellency on that occasion said to me, 'But that I do not like undoing what I have already done, I would have the arms removed from the City Hall and placed in the Government House under the care of my domestics, so confident am I that no danger need be apprehended.' And on Saturday, when I said to His Excellency, 'In short, sir, when I came here this morning I expected you would permit me to go into the city and take every half-pay officer and discharged soldier I could find and place them this very day in the fort,' His Excellency exclaimed, 'What would the people of England think if they saw us thus arm?' and, in continuation, he added, 'Besides, the militia in the city would feel themselves insulted if they were thus passed over and the military called upon.' To which I could not help replying, 'Pardon me, sir, if I say that I think they would rejoice to have the military as a nucleus to rally round.' At this time there were present the Chief Justice, Mr. Justice Jones, the Executive Councillors, Messrs. Allan and Sullivan, the Attorney and Solicitor-General and the Speaker of the House of Assembly.

"More might be here stated in support and elucidation of the foregoing, but I purposely make this statement as brief as I can consistently with showing your Lordship that it is incumbent on me to express my dissent from much that has been stated by Sir Francis Head in the document above quoted from, inasmuch as it is there made to appear that I had concurred in His Excellency's proceedings.

"Although I feel myself deeply, perhaps irreparably, wronged and injured by Sir Francis Head, yet I disavow any desire or wish to bring reproach or blame upon him; and I declare that I would not write this letter to your Lordship did I think I could, under such extraordinary circumstances, without dishonor to myself and perhaps injury to Her Majesty's Government, withhold the knowledge I possess of those transactions, and the more especially as Sir Francis has introduced my name as if I had concurred in his opinions and approved of his proceedings.

"To the paragraph in this 'Memorandum' in which my name appears, and to the two preceding paragraphs, I beg leave most respectfully to refer your Lordship.

"On perusing carefully what I have written, it gives me pain to see to what an extent this brief recital disagrees with the statement of Sir Francis Head, yet in no instance can I in justice to myself, with due regard to truth, abate or mitigate the force of any one of the statements herein made by me.

"I have the honor to be, etc., etc., etc.,

"JAMES FITZGIBBON."

[The note referred to on page 339 I have not thought it necessary to repeat, as it has already been given in substance in Chapter IX.]

APPENDIX IX.

AFTER the meeting of the last session of the last Parliament of Upper Canada, the following address was voted by the Assembly to the Governor-General, the Right Honorable Charles Poulett Thomson:

"MAY IT PLEASE YOUR EXCELLENCY,—We, Her Majesty's dutiful and loyal subjects, the Commons of Upper Canada, in Provincial Parliament assembled, humbly pray that your Excellency will be pleased to inform this House if the royal assent has been given to the bill passed last session, entitled 'An Act to enable Her Majesty to make a grant of land to James FitzGibbon, Esquire'?

"(Signed)   ALLAN N. MACNAB, *Speaker*.

"Commons House of Assembly,

"Eighth day of January, 1840."

"CHARLES POULETT THOMSON—In answer to the address from the House of Assembly, of the 8th instant, the Governor-General desires to inform them that, after a full consideration of the subject, Her Majesty's Government have come to the conclusion that they could not advise Her Majesty to confirm the bill passed by the Provincial Legislature during the last session, but reserved for Her Majesty's confirmation, to enable Her Majesty to make a grant of land to James FitzGibbon, Esquire.

"Her Majesty's Government, sensible of the long and valuable services of Mr. FitzGibbon, came to this decision with much reluctance; but they felt that the confirmation of such an act would be inconsistent with the principles laid down for the disposal of the waste lands of the Crown in the British colonies, and confirmed in that province by an Act of the Legislature, and that it would establish a very inconvenient precedent.

"If, however, the Legislature of Upper Canada should desire to mark their sense of Mr. FitzGibbon's service by a pecuniary grant, the Governor-General would have much satisfaction in recommending such a grant for Her Majesty's approval."

APPENDIX X.

EXTRACT.—"The Committee have taken the Memorial of Colonel FitzGibbon into their anxious consideration. They feel sensibly the difficulties and embarrassments under which Colonel FitzGibbon has labored in consequence of the delays which have arisen in satisfying his acknowledged claims on the public; and have carefully examined into the history of his case, in order to place their view of it fully before your Excellency.

"There can be no doubt that had the intention of the Legislature of Upper Canada been carried into effect at the time it was first expressed, Colonel FitzGibbon would, while obtaining no more than what the gratitude of that province felt due to him, have also gained the means of preventing those embarrassments which have since so cruelly pressed upon him. Her Majesty's Government, however, felt objections which the provincial authorities were unable to remove, to the remuneration of Colonel FitzGibbon by a grant of land, though they expressed their readiness to concur in a pecuniary grant for the same purpose.

"This, however, the then state of the finances of Upper Canada does not appear to have permitted, and the consequence was a part of that delay by which Colonel FitzGibbon appears to have so deeply suffered.

"The claims of the Memorialist have not, however, in the opinion of the Committee, been at all weakened by the postponed satisfaction of them. Repeatedly recognized, and never (so far as the Council are aware), doubted or questioned by any one, the very circumstances that they have hitherto been ineffectually urged, tends to give them increased weight, and will in the opinion of the Committee justify the most favorable recommendation and support which their duty will permit them to offer and afford.

"It is on this account that the Committee have arrived at this opinion, that an amount of land scrip, corresponding in nominal value with the five thousand acres of land which the Legislature of Upper Canada, in 1838, thought Colonel FitzGibbon entitled to, would not be an equal compensation to that which it was at first proposed to grant. On the contrary, besides the injurious consequences of delay, the course would, in effect, deprive Colonel Fitz-Gibbon of nearly one-half in point of value of the remuneration originally proposed.

"The Committee, therefore, respectfully advise your Excellency to recommend Colonel FitzGibbon's case to favorable consideration at the next session of the Legislature, for a grant of such sum of money as shall be considered a fair equivalent for the land originally proposed to be given to him.

"With regard to the application for an advance, the Committee have felt deep regret that they have not found it proper for them to advise that it should be complied with. However strong their opinion of the justice of Colonel FitzGibbon's claim, or the probability of its being favorably entertained by the Legislature, they are not prepared to advise your Excellency to make an advance of public moneys in anticipation of the decision of the Parliament on the subject."

APPENDIX XI.

"LOWER WARD, WINDSOR CASTLE,
"*March*, 1859.

"We, the undersigned Military Knights of the Chapel of St. George within the Castle of Windsor, beg leave to call your attention to our case.

" As you may have heard, in the year 1855 our case was brought before Parliament, which resulted in directions being given by Lord Palmerston to the Attorney-General to file an information on our behalf. Our case is, shortly, this : The Charity was founded by King Edward III., who declared that the Knights would be 'forever comfortably maintained' out of the funds of St. George's Chapel. In the reign of King Edward IV., the Dean and Canons procured an Act of Parliament, without the knowledge of the Knights. and upon representations which were untrue, whereby the Chapel was freed from the maintenance of the Knights ; but it was stated in the Act that the Knights had been otherwise provided for. This statement was also untrue, and no provision was made directly for the Knights until the reign of King Henry VIII.

" King Henry VIII., in a letter which he addressed to the Dean and Canons, informed them that he would settle lands on the college for our maintenance ; and by his last will he directed lands to be made over by the Crown to the college of the value of £600 per annum for our maintenance ; and his successor, King Edward VI., accordingly made over lands of that value, and the Dean and Canons, on their part, covenanted to apply the same as the Crown should direct.

" These documents form the foundation of the present Charity, the rights of which we are seeking to establish.

" The account of the rents arising from the lands so settled on the college was kept quite distinct by the Dean and Canons during the reigns of Edward VI., Queen Mary, and part of the reign of Elizabeth, and the same were wholly applied for the benefit of the Knights, excepting thereout the necessary repairs of the land, and a small sum to the Dean and Canons for preaching sermons in the chapel.

" The whole of the documents show that the lands were settled upon the college for us and for our benefit, and that no such lands would ever have been settled except to make a provision and to provide a retreat for military men. When we first employed our present solicitors, Messrs. Turnley & Luscombe, they enquired if any declaration of the trust subsequent to the deeds of Edward VI. had been executed, and we informed them of a book deposited in the Chapter House at Westminster, said to have been executed by

Queen Elizabeth; but upon those gentlemen attending at the Chapter House to inspect this document, which throughout had been set up as an original, they ascertained that it was not an original. They discovered that this document was not signed, sealed, nor authenticated in any way, but merely consisted of several leaves of parchment folded together and fastened within covers, and that several of the most important parts appeared altered and new leaves interpolated after the book had been originally made up. Our solicitors instituted most rigid enquiries, in which they were assisted by an eminent antiquary, in order to ascertain whether any document similar to the one in the Chapter House at Westminster had ever been executed, but the result of the enquiry clearly proved that such document had never been executed by Queen Elizabeth, or any other sovereign.

"If Queen Elizabeth had executed a Declaration of Trust, the original ought to have been in the possession of the Dean and Canons, but they, by their answer, entirely repudiated the existence of any such document, as also the authenticity of the document in the Chapter House at Westminster.

"If this document had been genuine and free from interpolations, our solicitors informed us that they believed, as the law then stood, we should have no chance of success, but feeling thoroughly satisfied that the same was not genuine, and that in the absence of it we had a perfect case, they begged the solicitors of the Attorney-General to cause it to be struck out of the Information; but, after a long correspondence, our solicitors' requests were disregarded, and the book was continued in the information as a genuine document, against our wish and in opposition to the repudiation of the Dean and Canons themselves.

"Prior to the case going into court, a consultation took place between the Attorney-General and our counsel, and the result of such consultation led us to believe that the Attorney-General would frame his case as though the book was not genuine; but, on the hearing, to our surprise, the book was put forth as a genuine document, and it was upon the interpolated parts of it, before referred to, that the learned judge gave a decision unfavorable to us. Upon all the documents in the case, with the exception of this book, the Master of the Rolls was entirely in our favor, as his judgment shows, but he assumed, the Attorney-General having adopted the book, that it had been duly executed by Queen Elizabeth, and upon the footing of it decided against us.

"After the decision of the Master of the Rolls, we had notice that the Crown would not appeal, but upon representing the facts above referred to, to Mr. Reynolds, of the Treasury, and begging that an appeal might be presented, leaving out the book, the Crown finally decided to appeal. We were, however, astonished to observe that on the appeal this very book was again set up, and our efforts to get it struck out have proved of no avail. We are therefore anxious that a case should be prepared, and the most eminent counsel appear on the appeal on our behalf to urge the rights of this important and, we may say, national institution, on behalf of the army, as in the event of the appeal being decided against us, the benevolent object of this institution will be forever lost.

"We should state that the present income of the Charity is now upwards of £15,000 per annum, yet we are only paid 1s. per day, the same as in the time of Queen Elizabeth, when the income was but £600 per annum. You will therefore at once perceive that it is impossible for us to furnish the necessary funds for the preparation of our case, counsel's fees, and other expenses on the appeal, which will be very considerable. We therefore take the liberty of troubling you with the above statement, and if you will kindly assist us in our efforts to assert the rights of this ancient national institution, we shall feel extremely obliged.

" We have the honor to be

" _____ _____ "

APPENDIX XII.

THE following letter needs no introduction. It speaks for itself
in the practical knowledge of the subject. The men who are so
willing to serve in our "national army" to-day, and the government who support it because it is the will of the people, will read
with interest an expression of opinion, and the *pros* and *cons* of
a militia in 1855—a period now sufficiently distant to be regarded
as history.

"THE CANADIAN MILITIA.

"LOWER WARD, WINDSOR CASTLE,
"*January 24th,* 1855.
" *To the Editor of the ' Niagara Mail.'*

"SIR,—The following extract I take from a Toronto newspaper
of the last month, just received by me :

"'Against this it was urged by Mr. Brown and Mr. Mackenzie,
and other members of the Assembly, that the whole militia system
was a sort of farce ; and that it served but to fill the *Gazette* with
advertisements and to tickle the vanity of young fools, and some
old ones too, at seeing their names in print, besides keeping up
expensive offices.'

"Having been Assistant Adjutant-General in Upper Canada for
many years, I gave my best attention to its militia. The two most
frequent objections made to the existence of an organized militia
were : first, the loss of time caused to the farmers in summer and
harvest-time by attending on training days ; and second, its utter
uselessness or inefficiency because it was not drilled and kept
always fit to take the field.

"The first question I put to myself was, 'Ought we or ought
we not to have a militia ?'

"The years I served in the militia were from 1816 to 1827, and
then I was convinced that it would be most unsafe to be without
an organized militia, even though we then had our chief cities and
military posts garrisoned by British regular troops.

"But had I thought otherwise during those years, yet the

rebellion in 1837, and the inroads made over our border in 1838 by robbers and ruffians from the neighboring States, must have proved the absolute necessity of having our people so organized as to be available for self-defence with the least possible loss of time—say in three or four days, or in a week at the least.

" Let us now suppose our people not organized in any way, and that an emergency suddenly arose for calling them forth to defend their country, their property and their families—how long would it take to form those of any one county into companies and regiments of infantry, with colonels, majors, captains, and sub-alterns, and staff; and also to form companies of artillery and troops of cavalry, with all their officers? How could all these officers be speedily selected, recommended for their several commissions and appointed to their several posts? Lieutenants of counties might, no doubt, be appointed, or even be kept always in existence to perform that duty on the occurrence of an emergency.

" Then every officer from the colonel to the ensign would have to be nominated and approved, all at once, and afterwards all the non-commissioned officers. Under such circumstances I would ask any reflecting man to consider what an amount of jealousy and ill-will would be created by such numerous appointments so hurriedly made, even if the person recommended were ever so impartially selected—which they would not be, for many would think themselves more eligible than those so appointed over them ; and how long would it take to bring such discordant materials into harmony as to ensure from the juniors to the seniors that amount of willing obedience and cordial support so indispensable to success in the labors of military training and in all other military duties ; and how long would it then take to bring them into the field in any tolerable state of organization, to say nothing of discipline?

" I take for granted that the reflecting men among the militia of Canada will never desire to be found, in an hour of danger, in such circumstances as these thus rapidly sketched. My own view of the militia is, that regiments of infantry, companies of artillery and troops of cavalry should continue to be formed as they are now. That their commander should be authorized to call out their several corps once in each year, or twice at the most. These parades I would not consider as for drill or training, but that the officers should see their men, and the men their officers; that each might know his place in the company, and the companies their place in the regiment.

"More than this could not well be done at a single day's meeting; but such a meeting would afford an opportunity of exchanging neighborly and kindly greetings among all, and many would probably avail themselves of the occasion to dine together. A day so spent would not be mis-spent. Far otherwise; it would call into lively exercise the kindly feelings of patriotic men, assembled together in the noble character of their country's defenders, and as the mutual guardian of their own firesides and families. Every man of generous mind and manly spirit would cheerfully attend such meeting and then return to his home a more pleased and happy man.

"In the present mode of appointing officers to the militia, jealousy or envy can only be created on the appointment of each to the first commission; and if any reasonable impartiality be observed by commanders of regiments, seldom will cause of dissatisfaction be given, and then only in the one instance at a time.

"The regiments of militia of Canada can now, in any case of emergency, be assembled at their places of regimental rendezvous in the course of four, five or six days, according to the extent of the limits, and this would suffice for any domestic emergency which could arise. As for war, its approach must be known many months before it could appear in the shape of invasion, and in anticipation of it only should recourse be had to extensive drilling. Then would drilling be cheerfully attended to and the exercises eagerly and rapidly learned, as I witnessed in Montreal, in 1812, and as happened in Upper Canada at the same time.

"During peace the only drill I would recommend for the militia would be for volunteers, officers or men, in the regiments, troops of cavalry or companies of artillery, by such teachers among themselves as had retired from the regular army, of whom many are always to be found scattered in the Province. To all such, being purely volunteers, drill would be matter of amusement, as well as improvement, and in the event of war occurring these volunteers, so taught, would aid in training their comrades.

"Again I ask, can any reasoning man think of dispensing with the militia after the experience of 1837 and '38 ? The Province is now much richer than it was then. It is rapidly increasing in riches. Have riches ever been safe in this world without protection? If the British Provinces of North America were so rich as to excite the cupidity of ruffians and plunderers, both domestic and foreign, to make war upon the country in those days, how much more tempting must your continually and rapidly increasing riches be hereafter ? Therefore do I earnestly counsel the people of Canada to cherish a militia system, notwithstanding the expense, which however is inconsiderable, improving such system as time and experience may hereafter suggest.

" Let them be assured that their safety from foreign aggression must ever be in proportion to their means of self-defence and their power to punish all aggression. Without the possession of such power, and a true manifestation of it before the eyes of all men, and a manly exercise of it when required, the people of Canada would soon cease to be respected by their neighbors, and would soon cease to respect themselves, and would ultimately become objects of contempt, insult and aggression to the hordes of lawless men in the United States, so well known as sympathizers or filibusters.

" Against all such, and against all foreign aggression, the people of the British Provinces, if duly prepared, are even now abundantly capable of self-defence. Let them cherish the remembrance of the campaigns of 1812, '13 and '14, the history of which their sons and successors must ever be proud of ; and the example then set it must ever be their pride to follow, until their country becomes the envy of other nations, as unconquerable, contented and happy.

" I venture to give this advice through your journal to my old friends on the Niagara frontier, confident that they will appreciate my feelings and my motives. And from the *Mail* I venture to hope that other journals in Canada will copy it for the consideration of their readers.

" Praying for the continued prosperity of the North American Provinces,

" I remain, sir,
" Your obedient servant,

" JAMES FITZGIBBON."

APPENDIX XIII.

"Being in London, in 1849, I was requested by a statesman* to give him some of my opinions on the state of the Canadas. Whereupon I committed to writing the following 'observations,' and delivered them to him in manuscript.

"Soon after, it occurred to me to have them printed, for private circulation, and accordingly I had three hundred copies struck off.

"Now, in November, 1855, I am again in London, and because of the many angry articles in the newspapers on our present relations with the United States of America, I print, for private circulation, three hundred copies more.

"And, by way of appendix, I add a copy of a letter which I addressed to the editor of the London *Spectator*, in February, 1848.

"MEMORANDUM of Opinions entertained and expressed in Canadian Affairs, in the year 1838, by an Officer long resident in Canada, and which he transmitted from Toronto, in writing, to the Lords of the Admiralty, and to three eminent statesmen in England, in June of that year.

"Do not unite the two Canadas under one Legislature, as you will thereby punish the loyalists in Upper Canada for the misdeeds of the disaffected in Lower Canada. I am convinced that, if so united, those of French descent in Lower Canada will unite with the present opposition in Upper Canada and rule their adversaries with vindictive harshness.

"The House of Assembly in Lower Canada voluntarily and contumaciously abdicated its functions and its privileges. Let that Province be, in consequence, governed by a governor and council, for five or ten years, until it appears that a representative government can again be prudently restored to it. This governor and council can, no doubt, govern that Province better than it has yet been governed ; and thus a practical proof may be given of the superiority of such government for a province while yet too immature for self-government. Leave Upper Canada to itself. Cherish

---

* Lord Seaton.

it and it will become daily more and more an efficient bulwark against aggression.

"If, however, union be decided upon, let it be the union of all the provinces, whereby the British race will be so predominant as to leave no hope to the other race of acquiring or gaining any ascendancy ; and, consequently, no proceedings to that effect will be seriously thought of by that race.

"In making this statement I have no idea of treating the Canadians of French descent, after such union, as not fully entitled to equal privileges and advantages of every description as their other fellow-subjects in Lower Canada. From my long acquaintance with their social virtues and amiable qualities, I respect and love them.

"Let the union of all the provinces be Federal, or other, as the Imperial Parliament may decide.

"The United States have but four ports or harbors peculiarly eligible for naval purposes, namely, Boston, New York, the Chesapeake, and Pensacola. With such a seaboard, and without a numerous sea-going people, the United States cannot become a great naval power. Their commercial marine employs about one hundred thousand seamen, ten thousand only of whom are native Americans. But add to them the Bay of Fundy, with the harbors therein ; Halifax, the noblest naval station in America ; the islands in the Gulf and in the River St. Lawrence, and the shores of that river on the south side up to Quebec, then down the north shore to Labrador ; the island of Newfoundland, with the fisheries in the neighboring seas and on their extensive coasts ; the boundless coal-fields of New Brunswick and Cape Breton, with the inexhaustible forests of timber in all the provinces, and at one blow you quadruple the naval means of the United States, and by the same blow you cut off the right arm of England's naval power.

"Let it be further considered that the canals now in course of construction will lead to the building of ships upon the lakes in Upper Canada, the hulls of which may be floated down to Quebec, and there be rigged and equipped for sea, and may then be loaded with provisions for the use of the navy, or for other home consumption, whereby a saving of public money might be made. The time will come when all the ships wanted by England, either for commerce or war, may hereafter be built on these lakes and floated down to the ocean. And if the canals now in the course of construction be not large enough, they may be increased in size to any required extent, and the vast future increase of trade will pay for all such increase ; for the waters of the St. Lawrence never rise more than three feet above their lowest level, the lakes above neutralizing or regulating such rise by their vast surfaces; the increase of the canals may therefore be made at the least possible cost. The Mississippi can never be canaled at all, because its waters sometimes rise sixty feet above its lowest level, having no lake to check or regulate its periodical overflowings.

"Therefore 'let not these provinces be lost or given away.'

"Thus far I wrote to England in 1838. To which I add, now in July, 1849, the following statement of facts and opinions :

"In the summer of 1848, this last summer, the hulls of two American steamboats, built at Sackett's Harbor, on Lake Ontario, and intended for service on the Pacific Ocean, were floated down the St. Lawrence to Montreal. During a few days' stay at that city, their officers had dinners given to them by the officers of the garrison and by the citizens. Thus was achieved in part what, in 1838, I had stated to the Lords of the Admiralty would, I had no doubt, be accomplished at no distant day. And only a few days ago I read in a newspaper in London an account of two more steam vessels being floated down this present summer.

Let the British Government and people consider what might not improbably follow the possession of all those advantages to the American people. With Russia in possession of the Baltic and the Black Sea on one side, and all North America in possession of the people of the United States on the other, and both allied for the purpose of driving Great Britain from the ocean, how long could England supply herself with timber, hemp, and all the other materials required for sustaining her ships of war and her mercantile marine? Let it not be forgotten that such a coalition between that Despotism and that Republic has once already been contemplated, namely, in 1812.

"Need I again repeat the memorable words of his late Majesty, William the Fourth, 'Let not these provinces be lost or given away.'

APPENDICES.

"As to the military power of the United States, the time is, I consider, far distant when it can become formidable, *beyond their own frontiers*, to any country well defended. Their people are too comfortable to go for soldiers, and to submit to military discipline and be shot at for a soldier's pay. Hence their chief difficulty in raising a numerous army; and their militia have hitherto refused to serve beyond their own frontier. The armies of the United States must, for ages to come, be chiefly made up of heterogenous masses of foreigners. When in Congress, in 1812, the question of declaring war against Great Britain was debated, Mr. Pickering, of Massachusetts, asked how the United States could injure England? General Porter said he could take Upper Canada with a corporal and six men to carry a flag; believing that the majority of its inhabitants were ready to join the United States. Such was then the general belief in those States, and such it was also in 1837. Yet when the days of trial came, the majority promptly gave the lie to General Porter and his confident and credulous countrymen. Yet now again is the same belief more loudly proclaimed than ever. And now again I do confidently declare my unwavering belief that the majority of Canada will as promptly as ever belie that slander, if they be not now unjustly or unkindly treated by the Imperial Government in the present anomalous crisis. Other members of the Congress said, 'Let us invade the Canadas with fifty thousand men at Amherstburg, fifty thousand men at Niagara, and fifty thousand at Montreal!' I was then in Canada, and well knew, as I then said to my friends, that the United States Government could not raise fifty thousand; and in point of fact their whole regular army, during that war, never amounted at any one time to twenty-five thousand. Their armies invaded Upper and Lower Canada in the consecutive summers of 1812, 1813 and 1814, and at the close of each campaign they did not possess an inch of either Province. While our army captured their chief fortress, Fort Niagara, at the end of the second campaign, and kept it until peace was concluded, in February, 1815, when it was restored.

"As to the American armies, I do not hesitate to characterize them as very refractory, not even excepting their officers. And the more numerous they be, the more unmanageable, I am confident, they must become. Many proofs of insubordination were given in evidence before the Court Martial which tried and condemned General Hull for his surrender of Fort Detroit to General Brock in 1812. One instance of this I give from those proceedings, as published in the United States.

"While General Hull's army were marching through the forest, on their route to Detroit, in July, 1812, they halted one day, as usual, about three o'clock. Soon after the General's tent was pitched, he heard an unusual noise in the camp, and sent one of his aides-de-camp to inquire the cause and report it to him. This officer soon returned and said, 'It is nothing, General, only a company of Ohio volunteers riding their captain upon a rail!'—a species of indignity tantamount to tarring and feathering.

" This fact, with other similar ones, the General brought before the court to show how little he could expect to achieve with an army so constituted as that which he commanded.

" Two other facts, to the same effect, I now give here from information received by me from two American officers while in conversation with them in Canada.

"On my arrival at Fort George, Niagara, with a detachment under my command, from Kingston, in January, 1813, I found there a captain of the American army, lately taken prisoner on that frontier. Having once been myself a prisoner of war in France, in 1799, I felt a consequent sympathy for this officer, and therefore called upon him. I repeated my visits daily for some time, and our acquaintance became a rather intimate one. One day he said, 'I left my native State in the south, some three months ago, to make war upon you British in this Province. I then entertained very unfavorable opinions of British officers. I believed them to be a proud, haughty, tyrannical class of men. In a few days after joining our army at Buffalo, I was sent in command of the advanced detachment to attack your batteries, and succeeded in capturing one of them. But General Smyth not having promptly supported me, I and my detachment were taken prisoners.

" ' Soon after my arrival in this fort, the officers of the regiment here invited me to become an honorary member of their mess, and I accepted the invitation. But instead of their being proud and haughty, I find them frank and kind, and very attentive to me. I look through my windows over your barrack square, and I see that

those officers treat their men with more condescension and kindness than we can treat ours. Were we to deal with our men as I
see you deal with yours, we should lose all authority over them.
We feel ourselves compelled to keep them at a distance—in short, to
rule them with a rod of iron.'

"The second conversation I had was with Thomas Jefferson
Sutherland, the *soi-disant* general commanding the assembled body
of sympathizers collected in Detroit, in 1838, to invade Canada.
In attempting to reconnoitre our borders, he came over on the ice
with his aide-de-camp, when his path was crossed by Colonel
Prince, of Sandwich, who was driving by in his sleigh. The
Colonel shrewdly suspecting what their object must be, pulled up,
and, jumping out with his rifle, in an instant made them both
prisoners and drove them to Sandwich. They were soon after sent
to Toronto, where the general was tried by a militia court-martial,
of which I was the acting judge advocate. After the trial the
proceedings of the court were sent to England for the decision of
the Imperial Government, and the prisoner was transferred from
the garrison to the district gaol in the city, for safe keeping, until
further orders.

" Entertaining for him a rather different kind of sympathy than
he and his myrmidons had lately proclaimed for our Canadian
people, I visited him occasionally, and gave him a few volumes to
be perused by him on his passage to Van Diemen's Land, whither
I doubted not he would soon be transported. Thus I became on
somewhat intimate terms with this American also.

"One day he addressed me to the following effect : ' By my late
proceedings I have acquired a kind of experience which I little
expected on joining my sympathizing countrymen, and for which I
am likely to pay far too dear a price. I am now convinced that
the people of the United States are, as soldiers, very unmanageable, even from the highest to the lowest of them. I one day
detached from Detroit my second in command, General Theller,
with a schooner, full of men, to take possession of Point Pélé
Island, below Amherstburg, and there to wait until I should join
him with the remainder of our force. On passing Amherstburg,
however, he thought it had a very defenceless appearance, and he
suddenly decided on attacking it in the hope of taking the feather

out of my cap, as the saying has it, and thereby raising himself at once to eminence. He made the attack, but failed, being with his men and schooner captured by your people. And thus was my then plan entirely frustrated. In short, our people are very unfit materials for soldiers.'

"Much to this effect has already become public by what has appeared in the newspapers of the recent doings in Mexico; and much more, no doubt, existed, but which may never become public. Neither does the success which attended the American army in Mexico at all change my opinions of the inefficiency of that army. The hope of finding riches in that country, no doubt, induced many to join that army, and the well-known feeble character of the Mexicans gave more confidence and energy to the Americans than they could display before an army of undoubted skill and well-known individual strength and bravery.

"From the experience I have had during the late war in Canada, and from all that I have heard and read, I have no doubt but that the present population of the North American Provinces, cordially united, and supported by troops now (1849) in those provinces, would promptly defeat and drive back into their own territory an invading American army of one hundred thousand men.

"Let the Imperial Government now unite those provinces, and then be just and indulgent to their people, and neither separation by the desire of the provincials nor conquest by the United States, need be apprehended.

"So united, and held by affection to the parent State, as I am fully convinced a large majority of the provincials ardently desire to be, their neighbors may invade the provinces, but assuredly with no better result than attended their armies in 1812, 1813 and 1814.

" *To the Editor of the London ' Spectator ' :*

"Sir,—In your paper of Saturday, under the head of ' Important News from Canada,' I have read your comments thereon. Although unwilling to write on politics, I yet cannot refrain from addressing to you some opinions and observations on that Province and its politics.

"And I begin by declaring that I have no fear nor apprehension of the North American Provinces ever becoming part and parcel of the United States of America; nor do I believe that for generations to come the people of those provinces will desire to be separated from Great Britain, if they ever do desire such separation. Neither have I any fear that the party now having the majority in the Canadian Assembly will adopt a single measure with a view to dissever, or even to weaken the connexion with the parent State. I am personally acquainted with almost all the leaders of that party, and there are among them some of the most loyal men in the Province. But Mr. Papineau is not, I believe, and I am confident will not be one of the persons chosen to form the new Executive Council of the Province. I am of opinion that he will not even take a seat in the Assembly for either of the two constituencies which have returned him, because of some grave differences of political opinions which he and the majority severally hold. Neither do I believe, as has been insinuated, that Lord Elgin has hitherto done anything to discourage that majority from placing confidence in his Excellency. Their strength is now great enough to enable them to carry through the Assembly every measure for the good of the Province which they may propose, and I have such confidence in their disposition and their judgment that I do not fear they will offer any other. To this I will add that I am not a supporter of this party, and never have been; and I would be better pleased if the other party had such a majority as these now have. But as I have no doubt of our connexion with the parent State being safe in the keeping of either party, I am not displeased with the late change. In one point of view I am rather pleased with it, because I am confident that with the power which the present majority have they will, during the present Parliament, prove that it is not separation they desire, but fair play in working out the true principles of responsible government, which are now much better understood in Canada than they were when the breach was made between Lord Metcalfe and his Executive Council.

"Should these my opinions be well founded, time will soon show that this party is as loyal as their rivals; and then the British people will cease to look upon us in Canada as disloyal, or even discontented; and they will cease to offend or insult us by the continued expression, through the press, of their doubts, their fears and suspicions of our loyalty. The reality of this loyalty will soon, I am confident, be placed above suspicion; and our affections for our relatives and connexions at home, and our good-will to our fellow-subjects at large, may be freely and mutually cultivated, although we be separated from each other by the broad Atlantic.

"Neither have I many fears, after the long experience of the past, that the Colonial Ministers in England will err much hereafter in dealing with us. They can now have no other motive or desire than to advance us in prosperity; which prosperity, however, being now chiefly dependent upon our own care and management, should we fail to secure it, we must blame our own representatives, and not Earl Grey or his successors here in England.

"I have resided in Canada, and in every city in it, east and west, for more than forty-five years, and few men have had such good opportunities of knowing its people as I have had; and few can feel a more ardent wish for their prosperity and happiness than I do; and I look to the future for all the British Provinces with the most cheering and confiding hope.

"I am, sir, your obedient servant,

"JAMES FITZGIBBON,
"*Late Colonel of the 1st Regt. of Toronto Militia.*

"LONDON, Monday, *February* 21st, 1848."

NOTES.

———

IT has been suggested to me that the question of what became of the five acres of land mentioned in Chapter X. as still retained by FitzGibbon, may be asked, as I have not referred in any way to its being sold or otherwise disposed of.

FitzGibbon's many friends, both in Canada and in England, having faith in his integrity and confidence in the ultimate sanction of the Government being obtained to the grant of land or its equivalent, lent him money, either personally or by endorsing notes for him, in order to relieve him from the annoyance of small debts, duns from the actual butcher and baker of daily life. Upon the failure of the grant, the remnant of his property, with the exception of a small lot, was sold to help to repay these generous loans. This lot was claimed by his heirs, and sold to the city corporation. Part of it extended across the roadway of Brock Street, south-east of Queen Street.

———

From an autograph letter of FitzGibbon's, now in the possession of Dr. Coleman, of Belleville, Ontario, I learn that some of the dragoons who appeared so opportunely under Captain Hall at Beaver Dam, were men from a corps raised by Colonel Coleman soon after the outbreak of the war. The letter is an instance of FitzGibbon recommending one who had just claims upon the Government, for a position which might serve as a reward for services rendered to his country.

Personal and Press Comments

ON THE FIRST EDITION OF

A VETERAN OF 1812.

~~~~~~~~

"A brief but stirring biography."—*London Times.*

"An interesting and valuable biography."—*Montreal Witness.*

"Enjoyable reading from cover to cover. . . . Rich in movement and color."—*Quebec Chronicle.*

Your book is not only a loving tribute to a patriotic soldier, but a very interesting history also of Canada at an important period."—*Extract from letter from Lady Tupper, 97 Cromwell Road, London.*

"I shall read it with great interest, for I look upon Col. FitzGibbon as one of our most famous Canadian heroes, and every Canadian should remember his name with respect and gratitude."—*Col. Geo. T. Denison.*

"Fathers can put into the hand of a son few books that teach more striking lessons of loyalty to allegiance, fidelity to trust, and fearless devotion to duty than the life of Colonel FitzGibbon."—*Peterboro' Examiner.*

"So meritorious that we may express the hope that the writer will continue and enlarge her researches, and produce a general history of that period, possessed of the same charm as her biography."—*Toronto Globe.*

"It not only sketches in sufficient detail the events in the life of the subject, but it leaves the reader with a good impression of the personality of the man and a good general background of the times in which he lived and the events in which he bore a part."—*Buffalo Illustrated Express.*

"The whole career of FitzGibbon is worthy of record for the lesson it conveys. We know no better narrative to incite youth to act honestly and unselfishly, and to exercise that difficult duty of abnegation or self-control than the career which is traced in these pages."—*Montreal Gazette.*

"The book deserves to be widely read. We would recommend it to parents for home reading, as well as to Sunday Schools and public libraries. It will take its place as one of the most important and most readable of the contributions yet made to our Canadian biographic and historic literature. An inspiring example of patriotism."—*Christian Guardian.*

"We have made with extreme pleasure the acquaintance of 'A Veteran of 1812.' The lady who has written the book omits to state her relationship to the subject; whatever it be, she has related the career of James FitzGibbon very well, and done justice to a man who deserved it. Exceedingly interesting, . . well told and deserves to be read,"—*Athenæum, London, England.*

"Miss FitzGibbon has succeeded in writing a thoroughly connected and interesting account of a man whose personality was sufficiently pronounced, and whose courage, integrity and singleness of purpose were strong enough to leave an impression on his time. . . . The work contains many illustrations, and is one of deep interest to all students of Canadian history."—*Journal Royal Colonial Institute, London, England.*

"I wish you were here to realize the delight my little mother (Mrs. Seymour, *née* Powell, aged 93) is experiencing from 'The Veteran.' Your grandfather's likeness charmed her ; she thinks it so good, and as she reads it seems like renewing her youth. I suspect I will not be the only one to thank you very heartily and sincerely for all your hard work, for it must have been laborious, even though a labor of love."—*Extract from letter from Miss Seymour, Ottawa, Ont.*

"I was in the middle of Wolseley's 'Marlborough' when the 'Veteran' arrived, and I set to work at him at once, and never left off till I had got to the last line of your errata. . . . I congratulate you on your performance. It is excellent, well sustained throughout ; gives a real and characteristic idea of the old man, and gives a pleasant notion of the writer, too, as an unaffected, inartificial, sincere and not altogether book-making biographer."—*Extract from Letter from Hon. Gerald FitzGibbon, Lord Justice of the Court of Appeal, Ireland.*

"I have greatly enjoyed reading your new and bright volume entitled, 'A Veteran of 1812.' Although the name of Lieut. FitzGibbon, of 1813, your grandfather, is a household name among the old families of this historic district, we yet needed such pages as yours to know his true greatness among his kindred and for his country. . . . Your book is *in memoriam* indeed, and is, better still, more instructive, more durable than *granite column.* I am therefore glad that it is now given to the public of Canada, and especially of this Province. Its pages are full of splendid lessons to our people of every class and age."—*Extract from Letter from Rev. Canon Bull.*

"I have read 'A Veteran of 1812' through from cover to cover, including the appendices. As a Canadian I thank you for this valuable accession to Canadian literature. It fills a gap that required the filling up by someone who would take the trouble to closely investigate the events of the time. I well remember the events of 1837 so far as Toronto was concerned, and can say that you have described them with much accuracy, and, I may add, in a felicitous manner. . . . To your grandfather, in my opinion, belongs the credit of having saved Toronto—others were willing to profit by Colonel FitzGibbon's exertions."—*Extract from Letter from D. B. Read, Esq., Q.C., author of " Life of Sir Isaac Brock, K.B."*

"Such fearless, simple-hearted men as Colonel FitzGibbon, the hero of this plain, unvarnished tale, saved Canada in her hour of peril. Canada was too entirely handed over to the time-serving politician to do them fitting honor in their lifetime ; and it is consoling to know that a more grateful generation of Canadians has arisen to keep alive the memory of those who fought for Canada's right to live under British institutions when there was serious fighting to be done. The authoress of the present volume does not disclose her relationship to her hero, but she has compiled this biographical narrative with loving zeal, and everyone who cares for Canada's past will thank her."—*Canadian Gazette, London, England.*

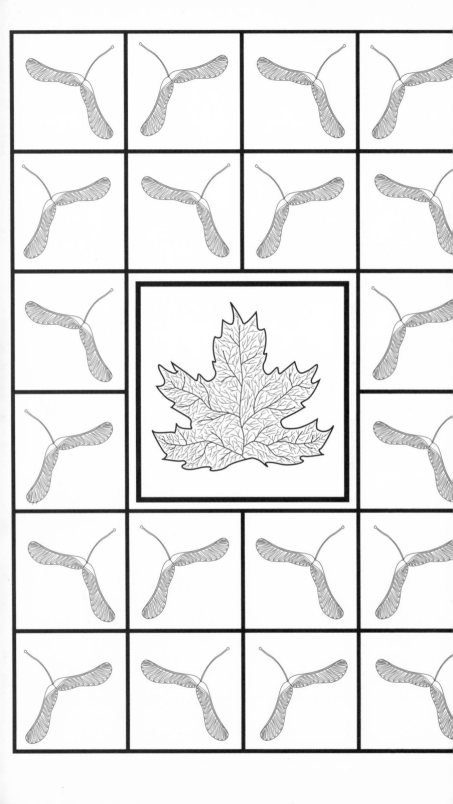